SUPE
AND
PHILOSOPHY

The Blackwell Philosophy and Pop Culture Series
Series Editor: William Irwin

A spoonful of sugar helps the medicine go down, and a healthy helping of popular culture clears the cobwebs from Kant. Philosophy has had a public relations problem for a few centuries now. This series aims to change that, showing that philosophy is relevant to your life—and not just for answering the big questions like "To be or not to be?" but for answering the little questions: "To watch or not to watch *South Park*?" Thinking deeply about TV, movies, and music doesn't make you a "complete idiot." In fact it might make you a philosopher, someone who believes the unexamined life is not worth living and the unexamined cartoon is not worth watching.

SUPERMAN
AND
PHILOSOPHY

WHAT WOULD THE
MAN OF STEEL DO?

Edited by Mark D. White

A John Wiley & Sons, Inc., Publication

This edition first published 2013
© 2013 John Wiley & Sons, Inc.

Wiley-Blackwell is an imprint of John Wiley & Sons, formed by the merger of Wiley's
global Scientific, Technical and Medical business with Blackwell Publishing.

Registered Office
John Wiley & Sons, Ltd, The Atrium, Southern Gate, Chichester, West Sussex,
PO19 8SQ, UK

Editorial Offices
350 Main Street, Malden, MA 02148-5020, USA
9600 Garsington Road, Oxford, OX4 2DQ, UK
The Atrium, Southern Gate, Chichester, West Sussex, PO19 8SQ, UK

For details of our global editorial offices, for customer services, and for information about
how to apply for permission to reuse the copyright material in this book please see our
website at www.wiley.com/wiley-blackwell.

The right of Mark D. White to be identified as the author of the editorial material in
this work has been asserted in accordance with the UK Copyright, Designs and
Patents Act 1988.

Library of Congress Cataloging-in-Publication Data

Superman and philosophy : what would the Man of Steel do? / edited by Mark D. White.
    pages   cm. – (The Blackwell philosophy and popCulture series)
  Includes bibliographical references and index.
  ISBN 978-1-118-01809-5 (pbk. : alk. paper)
  1. Superman (Fictitious character) 2. Philosophy in literature. 3. Comic books, strips,
etc–Moral and ethical aspects. I. White, Mark D., 1971–
    PN6728.S9S866 2013
    741.5′9–dc23
                                                            2012050375
A catalogue record for this book is available from the British Library.

Cover image: © PeskyMonkey/istockphoto
Cover design by www.simonlevyassociates.co.uk

Set in 10.5/13pt Sabon by SPi Publisher Services, Pondicherry, India

Printed by Courier/Westford

1 2013

Contents

Introduction
It's a Bird, It's a Plane …
It's Philosophy!

Superman may not have been the first superhero, but ever since his introduction in *Action Comics* #1 in 1938, he has been the model for every superhero to follow. For the past 75 years, Superman has thrilled millions with his adventures in comic books, movies, and television shows. His legacy transcends national, cultural, and generational borders, mainly because he strikes so many universal themes. He's a strange visitor from another planet who longs to be human. He's a mild-mannered farm boy from Kansas who wins the heart of a cosmopolitan reporter from the big city. He's the idealistic big blue boy scout who befriends a cynical dark knight detective. Finally, he's the ultimate hero who serves as an inspiration for the rest of the world's costumed protectors—and a few of its best philosophers.

Many people struggle to identify with Superman, regarding him as too perfect, too noble, too good. These qualities just make him an ideal, though, not something to reject but something to aspire to. When we scratch the surface, we find Superman is not that simple. In fact, he raises a lot of intriguing philosophical questions. If Superman is that good, why does he so often resort to violence? Why does he lie to protect his secret identity, and how does he reconcile this with a reporter's devotion to the truth? Could Lex Luthor be right in telling us Superman is the real threat to humanity? Is Superman the realization of Nietzsche's *Übermensch*—and is that a good or bad thing? Just how important is the big red "S," the cape, and the spit-curl to

Superman and Philosophy: What Would the Man of Steel Do?, First Edition. Edited by Mark D. White.
© 2013 John Wiley & Sons, Inc. Published 2013 by John Wiley & Sons, Inc.

who Superman is? And is there a good reason why Lois can't tell that Clark Kent is really Superman?

Superman and Philosophy addresses all these questions and more. It doesn't matter whether you're a casual Superman fan or if you've read all the comics, seen all the movies, and watched all the live-action TV shows and cartoons. The 20 chapters in this book will answer some questions you've always had, make you think about Superman in ways you never realized were possible, and teach you a little philosophy along the way. So tell the Chief you're taking the day off, find your own Fortress of Solitude, and start reading. Up, up, and away!

I would like to thank Bill Irwin, the real Superman behind the Blackwell Philosophy and Pop Culture series, for giving me the honor of editing this landmark volume. (I really didn't need to see him in the costume, though. The Supergirl costume, I mean.) I also thank Connie Santisteban and Jeff Dean at Wiley-Blackwell for supporting this book from start to finish. Special thanks go out to my contributors, who have a job at my large metropolitan newspaper whenever they want. Finally, all my thanks to the wonderful creators who have made Superman such a symbol of heroism for the last 75 years, especially the two who started it all, Jerry Siegel and Joe Shuster.

Part One

THE BIG BLUE BOY SCOUT

ETHICS, JUDGMENT, AND REASON

Chapter 1

Moral Judgment
The Power That Makes Superman Human

Mark D. White

"Do whatever you think is best. I trust you."

Lois Lane to Superman[1]

Superman has incredible powers and, luckily for us, he chooses to use them for good. But good intentions are not enough to actually *do* good with his powers—he must know *what* to do with them as well. Most of the time this is simple: see bank robber, catch bank robber. Hear Jimmy Olsen's signal watch, get him out of trouble. Find out Doomsday is threatening Metropolis, fight Doomsday (even to the death).

But not all choices are so clear-cut. Often there will be two or more disasters Superman needs to prevent. His enemies put him in such situations—"What will you do now, Superman: save the bus full of schoolchildren or your precious Lois?"—because that's one of the few ways the writers of Superman can challenge him (aside from using kryptonite or magic). Sometimes he can find a way to save both the kids and Ms. Lane—after all, he is Superman—but other times he must make a choice. In such cases, all the superpowers in the world don't matter, and it all comes down to *judgment*, the ability to make tough choices in difficult situations. The need for judgment is what brings all superheroes down to Earth, and what ultimately makes them relatable to their fans despite their fantastic abilities.

Superman and Philosophy: What Would the Man of Steel Do?, First Edition. Edited by Mark D. White.
© 2013 John Wiley & Sons, Inc. Published 2013 by John Wiley & Sons, Inc.

The Trinity of Moral Philosophy

Moral philosophy (or *ethics*) is the area of philosophy dealing with what we should do, what kind of people we should be, and what kind of lives we should live. There are three basic schools of ethics: utilitarianism, deontology, and virtue ethics. *Utilitarianism* says that we should do those things that maximize the "good" in the world, whether that good is understood to be happiness, well-being, or some other valuable part of life. *Deontology* emphasizes the morality of actions themselves without relying exclusively on their consequences, and is often put in terms of the "right" instead of the "good."[2] Finally, *virtue ethics* changes the focus from actions to actors, describing the characteristics of a good or virtuous person and then taking what such a person would do as the basis for virtuous action. A simple Web search for "what would Superman do?" reveals the popularity of the virtue ethics approach![3]

To some extent, each of these three schools of ethics can be understood as laying out simple rules or formulas for making moral decisions. Utilitarianism demands that you consider the benefit and harm to all people affected (and as far into the future as you can anticipate) of each potential action, and then choose the option with the most total benefit compared to harm. Deontology would have you assess each potential action according to a moral standard, often in the form of rules or duties, and then choose the option with the highest moral "status" according to that standard. Virtue ethics is the farthest removed from rules or formulas. Nonetheless, it asks us to imagine what someone we imagine as virtuous would do in a similar situation and then do likewise.

For example, suppose Jimmy Olsen is considering telling a young woman that he's a full-fledged reporter (instead of a photographer) for the *Daily Planet* in hopes of impressing her and getting a date. If he were a utilitarian, he would assess the consequences of his deception: maybe he'd get a date, but he'd either have to keep up his ruse while he was with her (and involve his friends and colleagues in it), or else his dream girl would find out and stick his camera somewhere even Superman couldn't find it. It could work out, if he's very lucky, but likely not. If he were a deontologist, the issue would be much simpler: lying is usually considered to be wrong, especially if it's done for personal gain. Or he could be a virtue ethicist and ask what his

Big Blue buddy would do—but he could never imagine Superman lying to a woman to get a date. ("He wouldn't have to," Jimmy may grumble.) Despite their differences in approach and focus, the three schools of ethics often agree on the "big" moral issues, such as murder, theft—and lying, even if only to get a date. Even for Jimmy. (Sorry, Jimmy.)

But Like Superpowers, Ethics Only Gets You So Far

If only we could deal with all of our moral questions as easily as we did with Jimmy and his love life. Let's take a more complicated example: Lois is investigating corruption in the Metropolis mayor's office, but in order to get the last piece of information that will make the story complete and bring down the guilty parties, she has to blackmail one of her sources. Lois knows full well that blackmail is illegal—she's reported on it many times—but at the same time she believes that this story will strike a major blow to corruption and make Metropolis a better place to live for all its citizens.[4] While Jimmy was thinking of doing something normally regarded as bad or wrong merely to get a date, Lois has what most would consider a good reason to commit blackmail. So she has to decide: is it OK to use blackmail in her situation?

In this case, our three schools of ethics are less helpful because there are good reasons on both sides of the argument. Ethical theories are very good at nailing down reasons to do or not do something, but not so good at comparing reasons for one action to reasons for another. Utilitarianism would seem to offer the best way out. But it is incredibly difficult to calculate and compare the good and bad consequences of breaking the story and committing blackmail. Deontology avoids the messy business of valuing consequences and having to put everything into numbers, and instead focuses on the right and wrong in the situation. But deontology still leaves us with the difficult issue of whether to commit the wrong (blackmail) in order to further the good (fight corruption). Finally, virtue ethics would have us ask what the good person would do, but we have to assume good people would also struggle with these issues. Certainly, exposing wrongdoing and obeying the law are both virtuous actions, but which one is more important?

What all three ethical schools are missing—at least in their simplest forms—is a theory of *judgment*. Philosopher Immanuel Kant (1724–1804), a deontologist famous for his categorical imperative that generates moral duties, believed that judgment was necessary for putting those duties to work in real-life situations. Abstract duties and rules require "a power of judgment sharpened by experience, partly in order to distinguish in what cases they are applicable, and partly to gain for them access to the human will as well as influence for putting them into practice."[5] But while Kant's categorical imperative provides formulas that determine whether a general plan of action (or *maxim*) is permissible or forbidden, it doesn't tell us what to do when duties or obligations conflict, such as in Lois's case. In fact, there is no rule or formula that can help her make this decision; if there were, that rule would someday come in conflict with another, requiring another rule, and so on. As Kant wrote:

> although the understanding is certainly capable of being instructed and equipped through rules, the power of judgment is a special talent that cannot be taught but only practiced. Thus this is also what is specific to so-called mother-wit, the lack of which cannot be made good by any school.[6]

If Lois were a Kantian deontologist, she would recognize a duty to expose wrongdoing as well as a duty to obey the law, two duties that conflict in her current predicament. According to Kant, there is no higher-order rule or duty to tell her which is more important, because that depends on the situation—so she must use her judgment, her "moral compass," to determine the right answer.

Although Kant was a deontologist, this idea of judgment can be applied to the other two ethical theories as well. Like deontologists, virtue ethicists need to balance different virtues that may conflict, with no recourse to a higher "meta-virtue" that can solve the problem. Utilitarians seem to have it easy, since their "balancing" consists of comparing goods and bads on a common scale of utility or happiness. But they can't possibly anticipate and calculate all of the consequences of their actions, so they need to decide which are most important—and this takes judgment. Specifically, contemporary philosopher Barbara Herman writes that judgment of this kind provides "moral salience," which a person needs "to pick out these elements of his circumstances or of his proposed actions that require moral attention."[7]

If Lois were a utilitarian, she would presumably focus on the big things: the benefits to the citizens of Metropolis of exposing government corruption and the risks of someone discovering her blackmail. She may also consider the effects on the person she would blackmail, but may judge his well-being to be less important, given his role in the corruption scandal. She may also consider the effects on her friends and family if she were convicted of blackmail, but may dismiss these concerns because she believes these people would support her. Given the impossible task demanded of utilitarians, she has to focus on the most salient moral consequences—but at the risk of forgetting something that may have changed her mind.

Tragic Dilemma in Your Pocket (Universe)

Despite his superpowers, Superman still confronts ethical dilemmas and still needs to use judgment to solve them. For him, however, the stakes are usually much higher than those the average person deals with. The weight of Superman's choices is often like that of world leaders' choices, potentially affecting millions of lives and the future of nations.

One of Superman's darkest hours came during an adventure in an alternate "pocket" universe in which he encountered three Kryptonians—including that universe's version of General Zod—who escaped imprisonment in the Phantom Zone and killed the entire population of that universe's Earth.[8] After defeating them using gold kryptonite, which robbed them of their powers (but didn't affect Superman because he was from a different universe), Superman had to decide what to do with them. He felt they had to be punished for killing five billion people, but the Phantom Zone projector was destroyed, so they couldn't be returned there. He could simply leave them on the scorched Earth of the pocket universe, but the criminals promised to find their way to Superman's universe once their powers returned—stronger than Superman's—and then destroy him and his Earth.

In the end, Superman proclaimed to them, "What I must now do is harder than anything I have ever done before. But as the last representative of law and justice on this world, it falls to me to act as judge, jury ... and executioner."[9] He opened a canister containing green kryptonite (from their universe), and the three criminals pled for their lives as it killed them. Superman shed a solemn tear and then returned to his own universe, clearly distressed by what he had done: "I know that from now on things can never truly be the same again."[10]

Superman faced an impossible decision: either kill the three Kryptonian criminals or risk them invading his own universe and threatening to destroy another Earth. Philosophers call this a *tragic dilemma*, a choice situation "from which it is impossible to emerge with clean hands."[11] There is no way out of this dilemma for Superman; whatever decision he makes will be morally horrible in some way. Nonetheless, he must make a choice, because even flying away would be a choice to let the Kryptonians live to destroy his own world. And even after he made a choice, the choice he judged to be best (or least bad), he still felt remorse and regret—not for the choice he made, but for the fact that the circumstances forced him to make a choice at all.

Soon after his return, Superman suffered an episode of split personality, adopting the alter ego of a vengeful, terrorizing hero named Gangbuster. After discovering his breakdown and the harm it had caused, he went into exile from Earth due to his tremendous guilt— another exercise of judgment balancing his duties to humanity and his responsibility to protect it from his instability.[12] After some time away he meets a cleric, a priest from Krypton, who uses a Kryptonian relic, the Eradicator, to help Superman get past his guilt so he can return to Earth. Visiting the gravesite of the criminals he killed, Superman explains to the cleric, "I hate what I did that day … but nothing in my power can erase it. I buried them here … but I'll never bury my shame."[13] The cleric realizes the tragic dilemma Superman faced, and assures him, "I have looked into your soul. Yours is the heart of a true hero … If you have sinned, it was in the cause of justice."[14] More important, the cleric helps Superman see that no matter what he did in the past, he can still do good for the people of Earth by returning as their hero—correcting his earlier judgment to go into exile, and restoring Superman to the world that needs him.

I'm Walkin', Yes Indeed

That wasn't the first time Superman doubted himself, and it certainly wasn't the last. Much later, he would suffer two tremendous losses within the space of a year: the death of his father, Jonathan Kent, and the death of 100,000 Kryptonians freed from the Bottle City of Kandor and established on "New Krypton," a planet on the other side of the sun from Earth.[15] To make matters worse, upon returning to Earth after spending a year on New Krypton, Superman was accused of losing touch with humanity. So Superman did what any reflective superhero would do—he decided to take a walk.

In the "Grounded" storyline that lasted over a year (in our time), Superman walked across America, reconnecting with everyday people and their problems, and coming to terms with his own role as Superman and the values of truth, justice, and the American way that he had come to question.[16] Like his exile from Earth, his walk across America forced Superman to confront moral dilemmas that required judgment. In this case, however, the dilemmas were much closer to home, and more familiar to readers, than deciding what to do with three superpowered Kryptonian criminals in a pocket dimension. Furthermore, they served to reaffirm the values that Superman had begun to doubt, thus allowing us to make a connection between judgment and moral character.

For example, in one issue Superman takes a detour from his stroll to fly from Iowa to Kansas to put out a fire at a chemical plant where Lois happens to be conducting an investigation. She tells him about the story she's writing that she hopes will force the plant to upgrade the environmental controls on its equipment and clean up the waste it dumped in a local river. As Superman is about to leave, several plant workers plead with him, explaining that the plant is the main employer in town and that full compliance with environmental regulations will bankrupt the company and put all the employees out of work. The workers plead for their jobs while Lois and the former employee helping her with her article emphasize the environmental costs (and the corruption leading to them). Superman is torn, saying under his breath, "I don't know. It's not all black and white."[17]

The following exchange between Superman and Lois shows the need for judgment in the situation:

SUPERMAN: There might be a right and wrong in the universe, Lois ... but it isn't always easy to tell the difference.
LOIS: Are you serious? Moral ambiguity? From you?! What about the truth? Doesn't the public have a right to know?
SUPERMAN: What good is the truth, Miss Lane, if it just causes suffering?[18]

With all due respect to Lois, Superman's struggle doesn't reflect moral ambiguity. It reflects the fact that in a tragic dilemma like this, in which someone or something is going to be hurt no matter what choice is made, right and wrong aren't obvious—they have to be determined using judgment. In the end, Superman decides in favor of keeping the plant open, despite the harm already done to the environment, and tells the plant employees, "if you promise to do a better job cleaning up after yourselves in the future, you won't have any trouble from me. And I'll be checking in on you to make sure you do."[19] The hard part comes when Superman tells Lois to kill the story that would surely close the plant and put all the employees out of work.

Superman Did *What*?

Let's set aside the issue of Superman *ordering* Lois to do anything—give him a break, he was unbalanced at the time—and focus on their opposing judgments. It's one thing for Superman to form a certain judgment on the situation, but Lois is free to arrive at the opposite conclusion. Being a journalist, she naturally believes that, in the long run, reporting the truth and refusing to bury stories is more important than the short-run harms it may cause, even the loss of hundreds or thousands of jobs.[20] After angrily walking away from Superman after the chemical plant explosion, she writes the article. As she tells Superman when next they meet at the end of the "Grounded" storyline: "Oh, I wrote the article, just like I said I would. I married you, Clark, but I dedicated my life to the truth long before I met you. I'm not going to turn my back on that, even if it does mean losing you."[21]

Lois and Superman both saw the same issues at play—including the value of the truth and the concerns of the workers—but weighed their relative importance differently. As we saw before, there can be no rule or formula to determine which reason for acting is more important; it comes down to judgment. One way to think about judgment is that it reflects a person's basic, core values, which run deeper than any ethical theory, and guide the person in applying them. Lois's judgment was based on who she is, a journalist devoted to the truth, just as

Superman's judgment was based on being humanity's protector and balancing the good of everybody involved. Since Lois and Superman—both good people—have different core values, they judge tragic dilemmas such as the issue of the chemical plant differently.

This understanding of judgment is found in contemporary philosopher Ronald Dworkin's theory of judicial decision-making.[22] When judges face "hard cases"—those not easily settled by a straightforward reading of legal texts and precedents—they must balance the many principles relevant to the case using their judgment, informed by a deep understanding of the legal system. Using his or her judgment, the judge will then arrive at the "right answer," the decision that best maintains the integrity of the legal system and is consistent with written law and past decisions. But every judge may understand these principles, and weigh them against each other, differently from the rest—much as Lois and Superman did regarding the chemical plant.

Lois and Superman each made the decision that maintained their *moral* integrity and was consistent with who they were and the core values they support. Lois would have felt she betrayed her journalistic values had she agreed to kill the story, and Superman would have felt he betrayed his superhero identity had he forced the plant to close. Each of us, when faced with a moral dilemma, must make the choice that reaffirms who we are and who we want to be. Otherwise, we would betray our basic values—essentially, we would betray ourselves.[23]

What Makes Superman Human

Superman's amazing powers give him more options to deal with problems, but they don't help him make better decisions than the rest of us, as the "Grounded" storyline makes clear. Not only did his walk across America help Superman reconnect with normal people, it also helps us connect with him, whether he's strolling through our neighborhood or battling Kryptonian criminals in another dimension. It shows us that, no matter how much his powers distance him from humanity, his need to use judgment to solve moral dilemmas makes him no different from you or me—and serves to ground him no matter where in the universe he may be.

Notes

1. *Superman: Birthright* #11 (August 2004), reprinted in *Superman: Birthright* (2004).
2. Hence, deontologist philosopher W.D. Ross (1877–1971) titled his best-known book *The Right and the Good* (Indianapolis: Hackett, 1930/1988).
3. One counselor even developed a technique using this phrase to help his clients imagine themselves with heroic character traits. See Cory A. Nelson, "What Would Superman Do?", in *Using Superheroes in Counseling and Play Therapy*, ed. Lawrence C. Rubin (New York: Springer, 2007), 49–67.
4. While blackmail is illegal, it is actually surprisingly difficult to explain why it's immoral, since it can be understood as one person offering to keep another person's secret—just for money. On this paradox, see legal scholar Leo Katz's book *Ill-Gotten Gains: Evasion, Blackmail, Fraud, and Kindred Puzzles of the Law* (Chicago: University of Chicago Press, 1996).
5. Immanuel Kant, *Grounding for the Metaphysics of Morals*, trans. James W. Ellington (Indianapolis: Hackett, 1785/1993), 389. (This page number is based on the Prussian Academy edition of Kant's works, and is provided in any reputable version of his work.)
6. Immanuel Kant, *Critique of Pure Reason*, trans. Paul Guyer and Allen W. Wood (Cambridge: Cambridge University Press, 1998), A133/B172. (Most modern editions of this *Critique*, the first of three Kant would write in his "Critical period," are combinations of the 1781 and 1787 editions, signified by A and B, respectively. This quote appeared in both editions, hence the dual page numbering.)
7. Barbara Herman, *The Practice of Moral Judgment* (Cambridge, MA: Harvard University Press, 1993), 77.
8. "The Supergirl Saga," in *Superman*, vol. 2, #21 (September 1988), *Adventures of Superman* #444 (September 1988), and *Superman*, vol. 2, #22 (October 1988).
9. *Superman*, vol. 2, #22.
10. Ibid.
11. For more on tragic dilemmas, see Rosalind Hursthouse, *On Virtue Ethics* (Oxford: Oxford University Press, 1999), chapter 3.
12. See *Superman: Exile* (1998), which reprints *Superman*, vol. 2, #28–30 and #32–33; *Adventures of Superman* #451–456; and *Action Comics*, vol. 1, #643 and Annual 2 (from 1988–1989).

13. *Superman*, vol. 2, #33 (July 1989). (And yes, this is the same Eradicator that became one of the four replacement Supermen after Superman's death; see *The Return of Superman*, 1993.)

14. *Superman*, vol. 2, #33.

15. Ironically, Pa Kent died of a heart attack while Superman was restoring Kandor to normal size in the Arctic (*Action Comics*, vol. 1, #870, December 2008, reprinted in *Superman: Brainiac*, 2009). New Krypton was destroyed, along with all of its inhabitants, in *Superman: War of the Supermen* (2011).

16. "Grounded" began with a prologue in *Superman*, vol. 2, #700 (August 2010), continued in the *Superman* title (with the exception of #712) until the final issue, #714 (October 2011), and was collected in *Superman: Grounded Vol. 1* and *Vol. 2* (2011). The premise is reminiscent of the classic 1970s run in *Green Lantern/Green Arrow* (reprinted in trade paperback in 2012) that saw Green Arrow—man of the people—taking Green Lantern—space cop—on a drive across America in an old pick-up truck to reintroduce Lantern to the problems facing the country. For more on this run, see chapters 8 and 9 in *Green Lantern and Philosophy: No Evil Shall Escape This Book*, ed. Jane Dryden and Mark D. White (Hoboken, NJ: John Wiley & Sons, 2011), 105–135.

17. *Superman*, vol. 2, #707 (March 2011), reprinted in *Superman: Grounded, Vol. 2*.

18. Ibid.

19. Ibid.

20. For more on journalistic ethics, see chapter 3 by Southworth and Tallman in this volume.

21. *Superman*, vol. 2, #714 (October 2011), reprinted in *Superman: Grounded, Vol. 2*.

22. See Ronald Dworkin, *Taking Rights Seriously* (Cambridge, MA: Harvard University Press, 1977).

23. For more on moral judgment and personal integrity, see my book *Kantian Ethics and Economics: Autonomy, Dignity, and Character* (Stanford, CA: Stanford University Press, 2011), particularly chapters 1 and 3. Also, I discuss moral integrity with respect to fictional characters in my chapter "The Sound and the Fury behind 'One More Day,'" in *Spider-Man and Philosophy: The Web of Inquiry*, ed. Jonathan J. Sanford (Hoboken, NJ: John Wiley & Sons, 2012), 231–242.

Chapter 2

Action Comics!
Superman and Practical Reason

Brian Feltham

Imagine the scenario: Superman is locked in combat with General Zod, who is trying to destroy an orphanage filled with young children. Just then, Superman hears that Jimmy Olsen has pressed the emergency button on his signal watch (again). He also hears Lois Lane's screams as she is pushed out of a high window by a dodgy businessman while she is on an investigative mission in Gotham. And if that's not enough, there is a genocidal war getting underway in the Balkans and Superman has just heard someone give the order to open fire. All this is happening right at the same time—what does Superman do? What *should* Superman do?

It's Practically Reasonable

Jeez, it's tough being a superhero. Since his debut in 1938, Superman has been hefting cars, socking villains, catching trains, foiling schemes, and generally saving innocents. Without his superpowers it would have been impossible, and even with them it must have been exhausting. But in the present scenario, Superman's problem is not just a problem of physical effort but one of *practical reasoning*. It is a matter of reasoning about what to do—that's the practical aspect—in contrast with *theoretical reasoning*, which is reasoning about what to

Superman and Philosophy: What Would the Man of Steel Do?, First Edition. Edited by Mark D. White.
© 2013 John Wiley & Sons, Inc. Published 2013 by John Wiley & Sons, Inc.

believe, although the two are often related. (After all, deciding what to do often involves figuring out what is going on!)

Practical reasoning is usually regarded as a part of ethics or *moral philosophy*, but it is not always a moral matter. When Superman gets home from a hard day of punching out Metallo, he might face a choice between cooking pasta or ordering Chinese, or between watching TV or reading a book. These decisions, too, involve a process of practical reasoning. Contemporary moral philosopher Thomas Scanlon says that a reason just is "a consideration that counts in favor" of something.[1] Some reasons count in favor of one thing: it is less effort to order in than cook, less demanding to watch *The Late Late Show* than to read Aristotle. But then there are reasons favoring the other: cooking his own food may save money and he might be eager to finish a chapter that he started this morning.

The choice between watching TV and reading philosophy is rarely a morally loaded matter, but there might still be a right thing to do— not a morally right answer, but a practically rational answer, the one that best accords with the reasons that you have. When moral reasons are in the picture, however, the practically rational choice becomes an issue of moral justification. Moral reasons are a superhero's stock in trade: when you take another person's suffering or disadvantage into account, you are reasoning like a superhero.

Practical reasoning is closely related to another area of philosophy called action theory. The central problem here is working out what counts as an action at all. If Superman backhands General Zod across a playing field, does that count as an action by Superman? Well, if he did it intentionally, then it seems like a clear case; but if his arm twitched or was controlled by Mr. Mxyzptlk, then perhaps not—it may be an event that happened to Superman rather than an action by him. If Superman's arm had simply twitched, it might not be an action at all, and it wouldn't make sense to ask him why he had done that.[2]

Unlike practical reasoning, action theory is usually regarded as a branch of *philosophy of mind*, because intentions, desires, and motivations are in the mind. These two areas of philosophy come together, however, in the form of reasons. Contemporary philosopher Joseph Raz has argued that our actions are most our own when we act for, and are appropriately responsive to, reasons.[3] In such cases, they are least like mere events and we are least like passive observers, and we have some sense of the reason or justification for doing something. A person deliberates, chooses what to do based on the relevant reasons, and does it. Superman is a man of action—which means that he is a man of reason too, or of practical reasoning.

More Powerful Than a Locomotive

Ironically, Superman faces heroic choices in part because he is so powerful. I can't catch a train or carry a plane to safety after its engines have failed, so these never present themselves as options for me. The German philosopher Immanuel Kant (1724–1804) took the view that "ought implies can."[4] By this, he meant that it makes no sense to say that you ought to do something that you are not capable of doing. Not everyone would agree: in ancient Greek thought, for example, it wasn't considered incoherent to say that people ought to do something—in general, to live good lives—even when psychology and circumstances had rendered them incapable of living up to this standard.[5] But many philosophers today take it as a starting point that the ability to do something is necessary to have a reason to do it and, most certainly, before being obligated to do it. This is why freedom of the will is thought to be essential to morality: you can't blame someone for doing evil if they had no free will, that is, no capacity to choose *not* to do it.

But even if "ought implies can" were false, freedom and power remain important to practical reasoning. Catching the jumbo jet doesn't appear on the menu of options that you and I face as we watch the plane plummet toward the ground. This is the sort of disaster we just watch on the news while going about our day. Superman, however, can't stop at watching the news, he has a choice about whether to help or not. Moreover, given his powerful senses, he doesn't experience the bliss of ignorance. He is usually aware when there are lives to be saved, and he nearly always has the power to save them. Most other things that he could do with his time seem relatively unimportant, and for this reason, Superman stays very busy.

There is another reason that Superman might have such strenuous demands placed upon him by morality. It is often thought that our duties to others are constrained by the cost to ourselves. One crucial kind of cost is the risk to our own life and limb. It might be brave to save someone from drowning, but it is only morally obligatory when there is no significant risk of drowning yourself. Superman is, of course, the Man of Steel. Not only can he perform great physical feats, but there is usually very little risk to him in doing so. Of course, the comics often tell stories where he comes up against unusual dangers; but remember that in *The Dark Knight Returns* Superman even managed to survive the explosion of a nuclear bomb.[6] Wouldn't it be great to have (almost) no fear of injury or pain or illness? Yes, but there would also be implications for what we ought to do. Inability and risk place very few limits on the moral duties of the Man of Tomorrow!

We Could Be Heroes …

But perhaps we don't differ as much from Superman as we might think. Unless our personal situation is particularly dire, we all have the capacity to do good for others in need. I bought a DVD recently. I didn't need it—it's a luxury item—and I could have given that money to charity, or to the homeless woman I passed on my way home. Normally I may not have given this any thought but, because I had this chapter to write, I certainly did give it some thought. I could have done many things with the money, but I deliberated and put myself first, purchasing the DVD. I wasn't a hero that day. And similarly, tonight you could watch TV or volunteer in a soup kitchen. You could visit an elderly neighbor to see if he or she is lonely or needs help. You and I can't go toe to toe with General Zod, but perhaps we could volunteer our time somewhere to help others. We all could be heroes, and many of us could be much more heroic than we are.

Given the great power that so many of us normal folks have to do good, why don't we put it to better use? While we might have moral reasons to help others, we also have plenty of reasons to do things for ourselves or those we particularly care about. We have reasons to watch football if we enjoy it, or to hang out with our friends— and the same goes for Superman. Notice how much time he spends saving Lois Lane and his other friends. He doesn't randomly pick someone to save—the fact that Lois is his friend and love is a reason for him to save her in particular. He also takes time out of the superhero business to enjoy something like a normal life. Clark Kent doesn't have much of a social life, but he does spend some time doing things that might seem to fall short of the moral importance of saving lives.[7]

And perhaps there is nothing wrong with making a little time for, and spending a little money on, ourselves. Sure, we don't want to act irrationally and there are reasons pulling in many directions, but these reasons include our own interests along with everyone else's. Of course, we might be inclined to look after ourselves a little too much, and like Superman we should never forget the power that we have to make a difference. The difference each one of us makes might be smaller than that of Superman, but we each make positive differences nevertheless, even in small gestures, like showing a little kindness to the people that we meet. And collectively, of course, we can make a huge difference to the world, an idea that has received increasing attention in recent years. More and more people are asking how much we ordinary folk can do to make the world a better place, and how much morality demands of us.[8]

Superman vs. the Calculator

But how do we pick and choose between our practical options—or, in other words, between our reasons for action? Which reasons count for more and which for less? Which reasons should we act on? There is a common metaphor of "weighing" reasons but this is not wholly adequate. It treats practical reasoning as if we put one reason (Lois's life) into one hand and another reason (Jimmy's life) into the other and see which is heavier. To the extent that the reason is connected with value of some kind—the value of saving a life, for example—we could treat the weight of the reason as being equivalent to the "amount" of the value. But this is just replacing one metaphor with another, as if value comes in quantity, weight, and volume. Does Jimmy count for more because he is heavier, or Lois because she is taller? Of course not, but this doesn't mean that some actions, and some outcomes, aren't better than others, and it doesn't mean that some reasons shouldn't take priority over others.

This talk about which reasons take priority is one way of setting up the fundamental question of moral philosophy: What ought we to do, and how do we decide? There have been many different theories. Kant, for instance, tells us that, whatever we do, we shouldn't disrespect others. Every person has an inherent moral dignity that calls for respect and places a limit on our actions. And sometimes, too, we have a duty not merely to refrain from harming others but also to take steps to aid people who are in need.

Another helpful suggestion comes from Jeremy Bentham (1748–1832), a *utilitarian* philosopher, who claimed that the basic good was pleasure. Since he believed that everyone matters equally, he wrote that the morally right thing to do was to maximize the total amount of pleasure in the world (or, more precisely, the total balance of pleasure over pain).[9] Bentham called his method of calculating pleasure and pain the "hedonic calculus." It wasn't terribly scientific, but it served as a rough guide for individual behavior (as well as government policy, his true concern).

Is this what Superman should be concerning himself with: maximizing pleasure? Well, if pleasure strikes you as morally frivolous, we could use a more "serious" term such as *well-being*, or even simply talk about maximizing *the good*. That seems obvious: having more good (better lives, better outcomes, even more respect) does sound preferable to having less. Of course, if Superman exercises his practical reasoning by looking to maximize the good in every situation he encounters, it seems that there will only be time for the most urgent matters—and no life for Supes. Once again, we face the problem of the demandingness of morality: it's a waste of time morally for Clark to visit a fancy restaurant with Lois when Superman could instead be saving lives somewhere in the world.

But perhaps we can make better sense of these matters if we consider what philosopher Bernard Williams (1929–2003) called *deliberative priority*.[10] Saving lives is more important than a date with Lois, but that doesn't mean that Clark should never get to have a love life. Sometimes things of lesser importance have to take greater priority in our decision-making, especially if we're *committed* to them (as opposed to merely *caring* about them). At some point, as Superman decides what to do next, his commitment to Lois and to living his life will take priority over the people of Earth whom he (merely) cares about. We are, then, under no immediate pressure to accept a strictly utilitarian model of justification in practical reasoning, even if it might have its uses in certain contexts.

Faster Than a Speeding Bullet

Let's go back to our initial scenario. Superman is in a fight with General Zod and there are a number of people who he can try to help—but even Superman, fast as he is, can't help them all. So, he can perform a calculation and try to work out the balance of pleasure over pain in each scenario and see which action produces more good in the world.

If we had to do this for every action we ever took, it would be a daunting or even impossible task. Will the world be a better place if I buy energy-efficient light bulbs? Maybe, provided I dispose of them correctly when they eventually burn out. But will it be a better place if I give a certain sum of money to a homeless stranger on the street, or to a recognized charity? Will life go better if I chastise my friend for being selfish when she enrolls in an MBA program, or should I encourage her in her ambitions? I don't know. It's hard to know! And these problems don't go away simply by rejecting the utilitarian approach. A constant enumeration and assessment of our various reasons for action may simply be beyond us. We are often creatures of habit and, occasionally, creatures of impulse. And perhaps this is not a bad thing. We might draw up a list of pros and cons for an important decision, like a career change or the choice of college major, but we don't want to approach every practical decision as if it were a calculus test. It's just too much to manage.

But perhaps Superman can perform such constant feats of complex moral calculus. After all, Superman has a super-brain; like a computer with high processing power, he can handle a lot more material than we can. His super-brain has been a part of Superman's power-set since the 1940s and, while it is ignored much of the time, it does make itself known every now and then. For example, in one recent scene Superman manages to enjoy a popular novel and some demanding non-fiction at the same time by hiding entire books in microdots disguised as punctuation in the novel.[11] He might not be a deductive genius like Batman, but he is able to process information in a way that goes far beyond the usual human capacity.[12] Nevertheless, we may have reason to hope that Superman isn't a super-calculator when it comes to practical decisions. There is something a little inhuman about this, even for a Kryptonian—it seems more like a computer running sub-routines to work out its next response.

Moreover, we don't always see problems as a set of options to be evaluated and considered. To illustrate this point, Bernard Williams asks you to imagine that you are at a meeting with your business partner and she says of a rival, "of course, we could have him killed, but we should lay that aside right from the beginning."[13] Sure, it's not as bad as seriously considering this option, let alone actually deciding to do it. But isn't there something wrong if this idea comes up at all? Your business partner sees it as one of the options to be evaluated even if it can be dismissed very quickly. (In other words, watch out for her!) Williams believes that it is better if some possibilities just don't register as options at all. He calls this *deliberative silence*: for example, we don't ordinarily have to deliberate about whether or not to go next door and murder our neighbor's cat. That option simply doesn't figure in our reasoning at all.

The Virtues of Being Super

We can make a more general point about good—even virtuous—practical reasoning, drawing on Aristotle (384–322 BCE). A well-adjusted and fairly moral person will respond to the world in certain kinds of ways that go beyond making calculations of reasons. First, there is the issue of what they will count as a reason at all. A well-adjusted person is able to recognize pain in others as a reason to help, not to inflict more of it. Second, there is the matter of when serious deliberation is required at all. Just as we act out of habit in our usual daily routines, so too we can act out of habit in less routine matters. And these habits can be emotional too: for instance, pain in others disturbs us and causes us to feel sympathy. In the same way, injustice causes us to feel anger on our own or on others' behalf, exemplified by Grant Morrison's Superman-as-social-crusader in the new *Action Comics* (relaunched in 2011). We often don't have to spend much time thinking about what to do. When the circumstances make things clear, a virtuous person just acts.

In this sense, Superman is virtuous in his exercise of practical reason. He is a hero, yes, but he acts to help others as a matter of instinct. Being a virtuous agent, his emotions pull him in the direction of right action (helping the helpless) not the wrong direction (greedily exploiting the weak). Superman does not ask

"What's in it for me?" He does not act on a calculation of interest—instead, he acts because he cares, or because he has moral dispositions. He sees our need as a reason to help, and he sees injustice as a reason to step in. But more than that—because he cares about us he comes to need us. He needs Jimmy's friendship and Lois's love. Emotionally, Superman is Clark Kent: he was raised a good person (and a good human).

Despite his vast power, and his super-brain, Superman's practical reasoning is much like ours (or, at least, the best of ours). He is virtuous and caring, and he instinctively acts to do good, to right wrongs, to help the needy. And just as Superman is like us, so too we are like him. We are less powerful and perhaps less heroic, but if our instincts are true, we find that most of the time we can tell pretty accurately what we ought to do on a personal level.

So Whom Does He Save?

Let's get back to our opening scenario. How does Superman choose whom to save?

Consider the reasons he has. The orphans are innocent, defenseless children with great potential—and Superman is the only one in the position to save them. They are also in certain danger, but Jimmy may not be—his level of risk and need is unknown. And while Lois holds a special importance for Superman, she is a fearless and self-motivated investigative reporter. She knowingly put herself in her dangerous situation; moreover, there are heroes aplenty in Gotham who might be able to help. Regarding the genocidal war, this is a political matter that Superman has to be particularly sensitive to, and it may be better left to institutions like the United Nations.[11] Maybe he could fly to the Balkans later, helping those still in need without causing an international incident (or possibly such a mission is more appropriate for another hero, such as Wonder Woman).

So in the end, I think he should fight Zod and save the orphans. But I'm no Superman, and Superman may evaluate and assess his reasons differently. He is virtuous, astute, and thorough, and he always tries to do what is good and right. What more can we expect from a hero?

Notes

1. T.M. Scanlon, *What We Owe to Each Other* (Cambridge, MA: Harvard University Press, 1998), 17.
2. Philosopher Elizabeth Anscombe (1919–2001) investigated the nature and significance of intention, as well as the ways that people's reasons for acting make their actions intelligible in *Intention* (Oxford: Blackwell, 1957).
3. Joseph Raz, "When We Are Ourselves: The Active and the Passive," in his *Engaging Reason* (Oxford: Oxford University Press, 1999), 5–21.
4. This is the usual formulation; the idea runs throughout his moral philosophy, although Kant never used this exact phrasing. See especially Kant's *Grounding of the Metaphysics of Morals*, trans. James W. Ellington (Indianapolis: Hackett Publishing Company, 1785/1993).
5. This, I think, is the right way of reading Aristotle (384–322 BCE) on the subject. At any rate, what Aristotle considered just or virtuous does not vary based on the capacity of any particular agent to act justly or be virtuous. See his *Nicomachean Ethics*, trans. J.A.K. Thomson and Hugh Tredennick (London: Penguin Books, 1976).
6. *Batman: The Dark Knight Returns* #4 (June 1986), reprinted in *Batman: The Dark Knight Returns* (2002).
7. For more on Superman's responsibility to the world and to himself, see chapter 14 by Anton in this volume.
8. On the first question, see *Giving Well*, ed. Patricia Illingworth, Thomas Pogge, and Leif Weinar (Oxford: Oxford University Press, 2011), and on the second, see *The Problem of Moral Demandingness: New Philosophical Essays*, ed. Timothy Chappell (Basingstoke: Palgrave Macmillan, 2009).
9. Jeremy Bentham, *An Introduction to the Principles of Morals and Legislation* (Buffalo: Prometheus Books, 1789/1988).
10. See Bernard Williams, *Ethics and the Limits of Philosophy* (London: Fontana Press, 1985), 182–183.
11. *Superman*, vol. 1, #655 (October 2006), reprinted in *Superman: Camelot Falls* (2007).
12. And sometimes Superman is portrayed as a scientific genius as well, as recently shown in *All Star Superman* (2006–2008).
13. Williams, *Ethics and the Limits of Philosophy*, 185.
14. On related themes, see *Superman: Peace On Earth* (1999).

Chapter 3

Can the Man of Tomorrow Be the Journalist of Today?

Jason Southworth and Ruth Tallman

It's a typical workday morning. The *Daily Planet* bustles with activity as journalists busily type, take phone calls, and rush out the door in pursuit of stories. Amidst the chaos sits a fortress of solitude, Clark Kent's desk, empty once again. Superman saves the world and Clark Kent documents his exploits. But they are the same person. This dual identity is often the source of drama in the personal life of the Man of Steel, but seldom do we stop to consider how it affects his professional life as a reporter. This leaves us with the question: Can the Man of Tomorrow be the journalist of today?

The Face and the Voice

The most intuitive way to consider moral questions is in terms of individual *moral agents*. A moral agent is a being who has the ability to think about his actions and the actions of others in terms of right and wrong. Moral agents can consider whether a particular action would be right and then make a decision about whether to perform that action in light of its morality. This isn't to say that moral agents always do the right thing—a moral agent could choose to behave badly. Lex Luthor, for example, offers moral reasons (although we usually disagree with him) for his decision to oppose and try to defeat Superman.

Superman and Philosophy: What Would the Man of Steel Do?, First Edition. Edited by Mark D. White.
© 2013 John Wiley & Sons, Inc. Published 2013 by John Wiley & Sons, Inc.

What separates moral agents from amoral beings (like squirrels) is the ability to think about and make decisions in terms of right and wrong, rather than just acting based on instinct. Luthor clearly thinks carefully before acting and can offer rationales in support of his wicked deeds, making him a moral agent who makes immoral decisions.

Because moral agents have the ability to make moral (and immoral) choices, it follows that they can be praised or blamed in light of those decisions in a way that amoral beings cannot. Clark Kent is usually thought of as a good person. This is because he, more than regular people, has great power, which he could choose to use for good or for evil. (This is why another moral agent, General Lane, chooses to oppose him: he believes Superman poses a security risk because he wields such immense power yet refuses to declare his unwavering allegiance to the US government.) Because we believe that Clark is a moral agent—capable of considering different actions and making decisions about how to behave based on his understanding of right and wrong—it make sense for us to praise him for his decision to use his great power to be a hero, rather than using it to take over and control the world. On the other hand, a villain like Doomsday is simply a mindless aggressor. We want to stop him from wreaking havoc on the world, but we don't blame him in the way we blame Luthor and Lane, because he is simply an unthinking beast storming through life acting on his instincts—he lacks moral agency.

A Reporter's Story

When thinking about morality, however, it quickly becomes clear that moral rights and obligations don't exist merely at the level of individual moral agents. Most of us play many roles in our lives, and our moral duties are often contingent on which role we happen to be playing in a given situation. A helpful way to think about this is in terms of "moral hats" —or in Clark Kent's case, hats and capes. In a given day, Clark might start out wearing his basic "moral agent" hat, but over breakfast with his wife Lois he dons his "husband" hat. Then he goes to the office, where he takes on several "professional" roles, including "journalist," "co-worker," and "employee." When he gets word that

Doomsday is loose in Metropolis, Clark changes both clothes and names, in a very concrete acknowledgment of his role change. When he teams up with the Justice League, Superman takes on the role of "superhero teammate." Stopping in to visit Ma Kent at dinnertime, Clark takes on the role of "son," and so forth.

If you think that Superman just has a particularly role-filled life, consider your own typical day. You're probably as busy changing hats as he is: parent, spouse, child, friend, employee, student, supervisor. The average person plays many roles each day, and each one of these roles comes with their own sets of moral rules. But we might not realize the differing moral responsibilities of these roles until two or more of those "hats" come into conflict.

No matter how careful we are, we sometimes find ourselves caught, unsure which one of our roles should take precedence in a given situation. What do you do when your child is sick on a busy work day? Your mom and your partner are both texting you with crises— who do you attend to first? In many cases, the conflicts are reconcilable and can be decided on a case-by-case basis. When your child is sick, you and your partner compare notes and whoever has the least pressing work demands stays home. You read both text messages and make a judgment call about which crisis can wait longer. In such cases you make a judgment call regarding which role is more important in that instance—not rejecting the other one, but judging it less important at that moment.

Comics are filled with such examples. Conner Kent, the post-"Death of Superman" Superboy, learned that the decisions he had to make to promote himself as a celebrity were incompatible with being a superhero. John Henry Irons, the latest hero to go by the name Steel, gave up his hefty engineer's salary at AmerTek Industries because he could not be the good person he wanted to be while working for a company that created weapons used to kill innocent people.[1] It looks like Clark's situation is set up in such a way that there is an apparent conflict between his role as the mild-mannered reporter for the *Daily Planet* and his role as the Man of Steel.

The job of the press, the "fourth estate," is to inform the public regarding issues that affect their lives and of which they would otherwise be ignorant. We trust journalists to educate us about current events, government, business, and so forth. After all, they have the luxury of investing more time and energy into discovering truths in these areas than the rest of us do; that's their job and their role. We don't use the word "trust" here lightly. When it is discovered that a journalist plagiarized, manufactured a false story, withheld important information, or failed to disclose a conflict of interest, we feel violated.

The last son of Krypton is guilty of three of these four offenses. He has manufactured stories, describing "interviews" with Superman that never happened. In fact, he got the job at the *Daily Planet* by bringing Perry a staged photograph of himself as Superman with some (fake) kryptonite.[2] He fails to disclose conflicts of interest when he reports on Superman without telling us that he is Superman. More often than not, he withholds important information in his stories. Leaving aside his knowledge of who Superman is, he also knows but doesn't reveal the identity of the Gotham City vigilante who brutalizes criminals and brings children to gun fights. The problem isn't just that he does these things, but he seems to do them for self-interested reasons. This compromises his credibility; if he were ever discovered, all of his reporting about Superman would be called into question, even the information that was 100 percent unadulterated and accurate. This is not to say he might not be justified in these behaviors, but on the face of it, these look like serious problems—ones we would not tolerate from any other journalist.

The Reporter of Steel

Within our society, the concept of a *profession* carries with it certain assumptions. Professionals are people who have received specialized training, making them experts in their particular fields. Society places special trust in its professionals, and with each professional field comes a special set of privileges and responsibilities, specific to the profession. For example, doctors ask us the most personal questions, see us at our worst, and cut us open with sharp instruments. In exchange for these special "privileges," doctors are responsible for keeping the information we share with them private, not making us worse off than we were when we walked in their door, and so forth. These profession-specific obligations are referred to as *institutional duties*, and the professional organizations that back the members of particular fields often lay out their specific moral obligations in a formalized way. Doctors swear the Hippocratic Oath, lawyers follow the code of conduct established by the American Bar Association, and journalists, like Clark Kent, are bound by the Code of Ethics of the Society of Professional Journalists.[3]

The first professional organization of journalists was founded in 1909 under the name Sigma Delta Chi, which later changed its name to the Society of Professional Journalists (SPJ).[4] In 1926, the group adopted its first ethics code, adapted from the code already in use by the American Society of Newspaper Editors. These organizations were formed in response to rampant corruption and yellow journalistic practices that were prevalent at the time, in an effort to self-regulate the profession and to make the fourth estate an institution of integrity. The code has been rewritten several times over the years in response to changing moral concerns created by new forms of media, but the general sentiment of the code has remained intact. It is used in journalism classrooms and newsrooms nationwide and, although it lacks the force of law, a journalist who violates its precepts will have a very difficult time finding a job. As an example of how seriously the industry takes these standards, Lois Lane, a world-renowned, Pulitzer Prize-winning journalist who is now the executive producer of PGN's nightly news division, was recently nearly fired for authorizing the hacking of security cameras in order to get a story. The only thing that saved her was the discovery that the cameras were owned by PGN itself.[5]

Superman Confidential: Seek Truth and Report It

The SPJ's Code of Ethics divides the institutional duties of a journalist into four main categories, designed to capture the essence of what it means to be a good journalist: seek truth and report it, minimize harm, act independently, and be accountable. This part of the code requires, among other things, that journalists "identify sources whenever feasible," working on the assumption that "the public is entitled to as much information as possible."[6] We also know that journalists may reserve the right to keep a source's identity confidential, but this is to be done only out of great need, when the source's safety would be in jeopardy if revealed. Clark doesn't live up to this part of the code very well. In order to keep his dual-identity secret,

Clark obtains much of his information through the use of his own super-senses, though he never admits it. He also takes tips from Batman, Oracle, and other superheroes, and not only does he never disclose those sources to the public, he doesn't even register them with his editor, as is standard practice with anonymous sources. (Registering anonymous sources with one's editor is designed to discourage journalists from simply making up sources and reporting them as "anonymous.")

Some people might argue that Clark isn't really doing anything wrong here. After all, the code just asks reporters to disclose their sources "when feasible." Maybe it's not feasible in Clark's case. After all, his main reason for failing to disclose is to protect his secret identity and the secret identities of his fellow superheroes. But this seems like a little bit of a cop-out. After all, far less powerful heroes are "out" and do ok: for instance, Buddy Baker (Animal Man) has a wife and small children but still chooses to be a public figure. John Henry Irons let the world know his identity when he stepped forward as Steel to fill the void left in Metropolis after Superman's death. If heroes like these can do it, surely the most powerful hero of them all could disclose his secret identity and still keep his family safe.[7]

Additionally, Clark has other options. If he's so concerned about the safety of his loved ones that he feels he simply cannot disclose the fact that Clark Kent is Superman, he could choose to be a reporter as Superman. If he did this, the public would be aware of how he is obtaining his information but the personal relationships he has as Clark Kent would be protected. He could report his other superhero sources in this way as well, informing that he was tipped off by Oracle, for instance, without revealing her as Barbara Gordon. The *Daily Planet* and the public at large would then be free to accept or reject him as a reporter, knowing that he has a personal life that he keeps secret, but aware of the practices and sources directly related to his job.

The code also tells journalists to "avoid misleading re-enactments or staged news events. If re-enactment is necessary to tell a story, label it."[8] The rationale for this precept should be obvious: the public expects journalists to recount events that have actually happened, not to create works of fiction, so fabricated or altered stories that are presented as news are misleading. Yet Clark violates this part of the code all the time, conducting staged "interviews" with himself in order to have a venue for telling the public about events and information a non-powered being couldn't be present to directly report. Additionally, Clark has staged events in which he and the Man of Tomorrow were in the same place at the same time, using one of his robot supermen, a shape changer like the Martian Manhunter, or even Bruce Wayne disguised as Clark Kent.[9]

Reading further, the code instructs journalists to "Avoid undercover or other surreptitious methods of gathering information except when traditional open methods will not yield information vital to the public. Use of such methods should be explained as part of the story."[10] Clark's newsgathering is often squirrely. He could obtain information through "traditional open methods," but he chooses not to because his way is easier. Knocking on doors and asking questions is much harder than listening to everything in Metropolis with his super-hearing and looking through walls to spy on people. After doing things the easy way, he can "stumble onto" the evidence he needs—he is pretty lucky that way. The super-spying aside, *all* of Clark's reporting is under-cover work in a serious way. He is not exactly who he says he is, and the readers and the subjects of his reporting don't know it. Wouldn't you want to know, before you agreed to be interviewed, that the person conducting the interview was going to be listening to your heart beat to determine if a line of questioning made you nervous, and to determine if you were lying or not?

One final point of concern regarding the first section of the code is that journalists must maintain a clear distinction between "advocacy and news reporting."[11] Again it looks like we have a problem, as Clark doesn't take a "just the facts" approach to his stories. He is selling the readers of the *Daily Planet* a view about Superman being a hero and other people being villains. His Superman articles are about a hero saving the city or the world from some threat. Conveniently, he fails to report on the times Superman breaks into a LexCorp building or threatens its owner. There has probably never been a Clark Kent-penned story discussing the collateral damage Metropolis suffers when Superman battles the villain of the week. On the flip side, he does discuss how Superman helps rebuild the city after its destruction. There is a clear agenda to Clark's writing, and the only one who acknowledges that this is a problem is the person we least want to listen to: Lex Luthor.

The Big Forget: Act Independently

The code explains that, "Journalists should be free of obligation to any interest other than the public's right to know." They should also, "avoid conflicts of interest, real or perceived, remain free of associations and activities that may compromise integrity or damage credibility ... shun secondary employment ... and disclose unavoidable conflicts."[12] Clark's disregard for this section of the code seems to be the root of all his other violations. There is at the very least an apparent conflict of interest between him being Superman and reporting on Superman's exploits. His professional code calls for him to be unbiased and detached from the content and subjects of his stories, yet he cannot possibly be, since he himself is often the subject of the story as well! It would be one thing if Clark were Superman's pal, like Jimmy Olsen. There is an apparent conflict, but it seems possible that Jimmy could set aside any bias and at the very least, he is disclosing that they are friends. Things are a little trickier for Superman's girlfriend/wife, Lois Lane. In this case, the conflict is stronger, as she loves him. Still, she has brought herself to report on Superman's troubling behavior, and like Jimmy, she discloses her connection. With Clark, however, it isn't just that there is a closeness—they are literally the same person.[13] The temptation to skew coverage in his own favor seems too strong even for the Big Blue Boy Scout to overcome, as we have already discussed. Regardless, he does not disclose this conflict of interest, and that is a problem.

While it may seem like a smaller point, Clark's violation of the job restriction clause is also serious. Being a superhero often requires him to drop everything and rush off to the emergency, leaving his *Daily Planet* responsibilities unfinished, and his co-workers to pick up the slack and cover for him. Not only does this diminish his credibility in the *Daily Planet* news structure (because everyone else just thinks he's an irresponsible slacker), but it also reduces the overall quality of the *Planet*'s coverage. Clark being Superman first and reporter second means his reporting suffers. Because he is often at the epicenter of the incident as Superman, and not in the newsroom, he is frequently relegated to conducting after-the-fact, man-on-the-street interviews, rather than firsthand reporting. Even these interviews are put on the back burner, however, and are conducted well after most other reporters would do them. Putting more time between the incident and the interview means the firsthand accounts from residents are more likely to have inaccuracies and to be less detailed. Adding insult to injury, Clark has been known to neglect informing his editor that the interviews were conducted so long after the fact. So Perry is unlikely to value them appropriately compared to similar interviews from other *Planet* reporters. His obligations as Superman continually put Clark in a position where he compromises his journalistic integrity in the name of his superheroics.

Wicked Business! Minimize Harm

Clark does pretty well with respect to the section of the code that concerns treating "sources, subjects and colleagues as human beings deserving of respect."[14] No one disputes that Clark's a pretty good guy (even if he's not a good journalist), and he treats most people with kindness and care. The only problem is, Superman's super-hatred of evildoers can cloud his journalistic need to "be judicious about naming criminal suspects before the formal filing of charges," and to "balance a criminal suspect's fair trial rights with the public's right to be informed."[15] In his crusade for justice, Clark can be a bit too quick to name villains and declare their guilt, in a way not befitting a journalist committed to preserving the rights and privacy of the accused until they are proven guilty in a court of law. This is especially true in a world where mind control and shape-changing are prevalent. Given that Superman himself has done some pretty terrible things while being mind-controlled by Maxwell Lord,[16] he should perhaps be more hesitant to publically accuse others without certainty that they are acting of their own volition, and that he is not sullying the reputation of someone whose shape has been adopted by a villainous white Martian.

Finally, journalists are charged with revealing "unethical practices of journalists and the news media" and abiding "by the same high standards to which they hold others."[17] Here again, it looks like Clark falls short. He certainly would not be cool with other journalists engaging in the kind of shady practices he engages in. Sure, he knows he's on the "right" side, but how does the rest of the world know that? Moreover, he should probably be reporting Lois and his pal Jimmy Olsen for some of *their* unethical practices, but of course he won't, because their questionable behavior is almost always done in an effort to protect him! Yet, we see him scolding Kat Grant for her biased treatment of Supergirl in her stories, but her bias against Kara is far less extreme than the bias of Lois and Jimmy in favor of Superman.

As we acknowledged earlier, personal moral conflicts arise any time we must balance our varying moral hats. Sometimes these conflicts are resolvable, and it looks like there are ways Clark could seek to acceptably balance his roles.[18] But he is not currently doing what is needed. If he chose to disclose his identity, or at the very least his sources, perhaps an acceptable balance could be reached. Another option might be for him to request a different beat, so that he was reporting on, say, politics, rather than his own exploits as Superman. If he is unwilling to make such changes, however, it seems the only moral option is for him to give up being a reporter, as his current practices violate his journalistic integrity. After all, shouldn't the guy with the reputation as the world's most moral superhero want to be good in other aspects of his life as well?

Fatal Flaw?

Clark Kent's dual life and the choices he makes as Superman keep him from meeting the minimum standards of journalistic ethics. While there are always tensions between working for a living and saving the world, journalism is a profession, and the job of a reporter carries with it certain responsibilities that go above and beyond those expected of a clerk in a flower shop or a bartender. Much is made of the moral character of Superman and the example he sets for the superhero community. By taking seriously the ethical standards of his profession, Clark could set an example for the journalistic community as well. If he is unable or unwilling to meet those standards, he ought to resign from the *Daily Planet* and take a job that does not place him in direct conflicts of interest. Now *that* would be a front-page story!

Notes

1. For the beginning of both superhero careers, see *The Return of Superman* (1993).
2. *Action Comics*, vol. 1, #257 (October 1959).

3. See http://www.spj.org/ethicscode.asp.
4. See http://www.spj.org/spjhistory.asp.
5. *Superman*, vol. 3, #2 (December 2011).
6. http://www.spj.org/ethicsfaq.asp.
7. For more on the ethics of Superman's secret identity, see chapter 5 by Malloy in this volume.
8. Ibid.
9. *Superman*, vol. 1, #128 (April 1959).
10. http://www.spj.org/ethicsfaq.asp.
11. Ibid.
12. Ibid.
13. Or are they? See chapter 18 by Michaud in this volume.
14. http://www.spj.org/ethicsfaq.asp.
15. Ibid.
16. *Superman: Sacrifice* (2006).
17. http://www.spj.org/ethicsfaq.asp.
18. For more on practical judgment, see chapter 2 by Feltham and chapter 1 by White in this volume.

Chapter 4

Could Superman Have Joined the Third Reich?
The Importance and Shortcomings of Moral Upbringing

Robert Sharp

It's 1926, and on a small farm with a few fields of wheat, a meteorite has just charred its way through a good bit of the crop. The farmer who owns the land is dismayed. His life has been hard since the Great War, even though prices for his food have skyrocketed, at least in terms of the actual bills carried around. In fact, one of his neighbors joked that he needed a wheelbarrow to carry around the cash to buy a loaf of bread, given how worthless the money had become. He and his wife are barely scraping by. Perhaps it is just as well that they had not been able to have children. Where would they find the money? His wife is fond of saying, "God will provide," but sometimes he has doubts. And now a large part of his best field has been destroyed by a rock from space!

As the farmer heads toward the damaged area, he calls back to his wife to bring a shovel in case there are any scattered fires to smother. He can see the hot smoke from the house, though the meteor itself is buried. His wife is almost half way to him when he reaches the crater, his eyes widening. "Magda!" he shouts, with a mixture of awe and anxiety, "Magda, bring a blanket! There is ... a child!" The words seemed distant from him, as though said by someone else. His wife, believing she has misheard, runs toward him, shovel in hand.

Superman and Philosophy: What Would the Man of Steel Do?, First Edition. Edited by Mark D. White.
© 2013 John Wiley & Sons, Inc. Published 2013 by John Wiley & Sons, Inc.

"Jonas? What is it? What is wrong?" she asks, her hands trembling. As she nears her husband she can see him, just emerging from some sort of space pod—a small boy! A gift from God! Her prayers are finally answered. Here in the German heartland, a miracle occurs, one that will soon have profound consequences for the world at large. The small child that had landed on Jonas and Magda Kuhn's farm was the *Übermensch* himself, a "super man." The *Übermensch* would vindicate Hitler's claim that the New World Order would arise in Germany and prove that nation's superiority.[1]

Only three years later, young Karl Kuhn, as he was named in the adoption papers, would join the Hitler Youth. Indoctrinated into the cause, his character was formed by the Nazi Party. He never knew any other life, and when the war finally came, Hitler used his young prodigy as the ultimate super-weapon. The war was over before it had begun, as the Allies had no counter to such raw power. A farm boy from the middle of nowhere had helped the Nazis take over the world.

... Or Not

If this alternate history seems unlikely, take a moment to consider how important Superman's childhood in rural Kansas is to his character. As portrayed in decades of comics, television shows, and movies, Jonathan and Martha Kent represent the core values of hard work and simple goals. They teach their son Clark to value "truth, justice, and the American way." While Superman's fantastic abilities make him the most powerful being on Earth, his upbringing on the Kents' farm is what makes him a hero. As with Clark, a great deal of each person's character is developed during childhood when our brains and minds are developing and malleable. Personality traits can often be traced back to childhood experiences, some of which we may not even remember, but which nevertheless profoundly influence who we become.

Unfortunately, moral philosophy often understates the importance of such character. One popular approach to ethics, *utilitarianism*, asks us to act in ways that maximize the happiness or well-being of all the people affected. So, if Superman were a utilitarian, he would refrain from robbing banks because he would recognize that his own pleasure in having more money would be outweighed by the pain felt by society at large (through the loss of wealth, the fear of being robbed, and so forth). While a good upbringing might help people make such decisions in a thorough and comprehensive way, the utilitarian emphasis is on making a mathematical calculation, one that should result in the same answer for anyone who has the same information about potential results. An opposing viewpoint to such utilitarianism, known as *deontology*, focuses on the intent of the act rather than the results. The most prominent form of deontology, based on the work of Immanuel Kant (1724–1804), asks us to determine whether the act could be willed as a universal law for all rational beings. As with utilitarianism, every person who understands this reasoning should reach the same conclusion about right action (and duty); little is said about upbringing, except for the need to encourage use of reason.

There is, however, a third approach to ethics, one that recognizes the importance of how we are raised: *virtue ethics*, dating back to the ancient Greeks. Aristotle (384–322 BCE), a central figure in virtue ethics, wrote that ethics was the pursuit of *eudaimonia*, a conception of happiness more like deep fulfillment than momentary pleasure, which comes in part from having good or virtuous character. Aristotle argued for the *golden mean*, the ideal middle spot between two extremes.[2] Personality traits or dispositions fall on a scale from deficiency to excess. Vices develop when we're at one extreme or the other. Virtues develop when we regularly do certain things "to the right person, in the right amount, at the right time, for the right end, and in the right way."[3] Think of it as the "Goldilocks and the Three Bears" approach: you don't want to eat the porridge that's too hot and too cold, but rather the one that's "just right."

Of course, that's more easily said than done, but consider an example. Bravery is a virtue, because it tends to contribute to a good life, and is the mean between two extremes. If you have no fear at all, you are reckless, which is dangerous and foolhardy. But if you have too much fear, you are cowardly, which is problematic in another way: rather than avoid danger, you'll avoid many life opportunities that are safe and contribute to a fulfilled life. Furthermore, what actually counts as bravery may differ from person to person: for a young child, saying "hi" to a new person might be seen as brave, but it would be considered normal for an adult. Likewise, standing up to a man with a gun would be considered reckless for a normal person, but the action would not even constitute bravery when bullets bounce off your chest. Fighting villains like Doomsday, who famously killed Superman, is brave—and perhaps a little foolhardy, even for Supes![4]

Aristotle lists many such virtues which together constitute necessary ingredients of a fulfilled human life.[5] Repetition and practice are the keys to acquiring and maintaining these virtues, since they are basically good habits or dispositions (along with the knowledge of what makes them good). This explains why upbringing is so important to Aristotle. We are not born with virtues (or vices), and this is critical for understanding Superman's heroic personality. As Aristotle explains, "the virtues arise in us neither by nature nor against nature. Rather, we are by nature able to acquire them, and reach our complete perfection through habit."[6] If being virtuous were part of our nature, we would not be able to avoid it or change it. But, in fact, we can change our character traits. Mostly this is done through repetition, but there must also be some intention behind the habit. Robots are not virtuous no matter how many times they repeat actions that would appear to be virtuous. Raising a child thus calls for instilling good habits while also teaching the principles behind those habits.

The Moral Education of a Superman

With this in mind, consider Superman's first days on Earth. In the canonical version of his origin, the Kents found Kal-El when he was a baby or toddler, at least by human standards. Clark (as the Kents name him) then continues to develop, physically and emotionally, alongside his peers at school in Smallville. So let's assume he was six years old at the time. He was put in the rocket as a baby, so he has aged a bit on the way.

Now, in some stories, Superman is taught some information on the way by the computers on his ship. In the Superman movies from the 1970s and 1980s, his Kryptonian father Jor-El charges him with helping the people of Earth. There are suggestions that he is taught language, ethics, and details about Earth along the way. This is a critical time in child development, and if Kal-El had not been taught anything during these years, his intellectual growth would have been permanently stunted (assuming similar brain development among

Kryptonians and humans). And yet, in some stories, he does not seem to know that he is an alien until later.

Let's assume he was taught some form of ethics by his Kryptonian father. Could that training be overcome by the Nazis? Most likely, yes. Virtues are tied to our habits, and our habits can be changed by our circumstances. Even if Kal-El was started on the road to being a good person while *en route* to Earth, he still arrives at a young enough age to change that. Once in the Hitler Youth, indoctrination would have begun immediately. In Hitler's own words, "this youth does not learn anything else other than to think German, to act German and when those boys at the age of ten come into our organization … they will never be free for the rest of their lives."[7] Hitler is referring to a systematic approach to ensuring that all members of the Hitler Youth are fully committed to the cause. As former Hitler Youth member H.W. Koch points out, this indoctrination was not actually as all-encompassing as Hitler implied, but there was still "a deliberate attempt to eliminate as far as possible the notion of the existence of a private life."[8] By keeping its members isolated from mainstream society and busy with German-centered tasks, the Hitler Youth prevented exposure to outside ideas and maintained the kind of discipline that is necessary to instill and maintain strong habits and character traits—even against one's earliest moral education, say, in a rocket.

What would this do to Superman? One might be tempted to say that the normal rules of upbringing do not apply to him, because his powers will prevent him from being just another member of the Hitler Youth. To some extent, this may be true. Superman is not human, and we have no clue how his psychology differs from ours. However, this may imply that the Nazis would work even harder to indoctrinate the values of the Reich. So for the sake of argument, let's assume that young Kal-El would not be immune to Hitler's propaganda machine, even if it did take extra effort or innovative methods to do it.

The Nazis were masters of propaganda and psychology. They were able to convince the German people to support a war that ultimately led to disaster for the nation. After the war, some people believed that the Germans were particularly susceptible to authority, but the famous "Milgram experiment" showed that they were no exceptions.[9] In this experiment, designed and conducted by Yale University psychologist Stanley Milgram (1933–1984) in the early 1960s, an authority figure (a researcher in a lab coat) would tell subjects to continue to administer what appeared to be increasingly painful shocks to a person in another room. (The person was a researcher and the shocks were faked.) While the subjects did object at first, after mild encouragement from the researcher to continue the shocks, 65 percent of the subjects went through with the highest level of shock possible. This experiment, conducted on Americans, showed that nationality was not a key factor in a person's submission to authority.

Superman: Son of the Third Reich

The question of how Superman's upbringing would be affected by landing in another nation was explored in Mark Millar's *Superman: Red Son* (2004). This story presents an alternate version of the Superman legend in which Kal-El lands in Soviet Russia and grows up to follow Stalin's approach to governing. Millar's Superman does not seem that different from the one we know, at least where core values are concerned. He still wants to help people, but his ideas regarding how to do this are shaped by his Communist upbringing, which tells him that such help should come through government agency. In case you haven't read it I won't give any spoilers. Suffice it to say that ultimately, Millar's Soviet version of Superman does not seem that foreign. His methods are different, but his overall goal of helping people is basically the same.[10]

Perhaps Millar believes that Superman's character traits are inborn, although this would contradict the opinion of most virtue ethicists. Consistent with Aristotle, contemporary philosopher Alasdair MacIntyre argues that the stories we learn in childhood help dictate the narrative that we use to understand the world.[11] Our conceptions of the good and the virtues we develop in our pursuit of that good depend on the story that our cultures have created for us. We are co-authors of that story, of course, and Superman would play a key role in the story of whatever culture he entered. But we are nevertheless inheritors of "an image of the future which always presents itself in the form of a *telos* [goal]—or of a variety of ends or goals."[12] This narrative and its accompanying goals influence our visions of ourselves, limiting what we perceive as acceptable paths in life and means we can use to follow those paths to our goals.

Millar provides some continuity between Superman's Kansas upbringing in his standard origin and the retelling in *Red Son* in which he grew up on a collective farm in the Ukraine. It would be easy to assume that his humble farmboy upbringing, either in Kansas or Russia, makes Superman wholesome, but this is far too simplistic. Ed Gein, the real-life basis of the character of Norman Bates from the movie *Psycho*, grew up on a farm in rural Wisconsin. Gein was at least partly the product of his mother's abuse; she isolated him from the rest of society and contributed heavily to his twisted mind. While Superman is probably immune to physical abuse (although, in some versions of his origin, his powers only develop after a few years of exposure to our yellow sun), mental abuse of the type Gein endured may still affect him.

Such mental abuse is likely to be introduced to him at an early age in the Third Reich. As soon as Hitler learns about this young *Übermensch*, he would recruit him into the Hitler Youth program, which was basically preparation for joining the *Sturmabteilung*, the paramilitary organization that later gave way to the more famous *Schutzstaffel* (the SS). Boys and girls as young as ten years old would be recruited into the program and indoctrinated into the ways of the Third Reich. Once Hitler had seized full power, joining the group became compulsory for all German children. The children would be taught the values of the Reich, including anti-Semitism and total obedience to Hitler.

Imagine young Karl Kuhn, a child of Krypton, in such a program. How would his life be different from the version we know? The most obvious difference would be in his core goals. Instead of truth, justice, and the American way, Hitler's Superman would value the totalitarian ideals of propaganda, obedience, and serving the führer. As philosopher and political theorist Hannah Arendt (1906–1975) explained, the totalitarian state Hitler created saw itself as part of a grand history, one which elevated humans by forcing them to become part of a political machine in which every individual becomes subsumed by the broader goal of the greatness of the state and its place in history.[13] This would be similar to Millar's Soviet Superman, though the goals of a Nazi version would focus not upon the proletariat but rather on the development of an elite class of men who would be seen as better than others, as masters of the human race by virtue of innate superiority enhanced by a scientifically exact upbringing.

Physically speaking, Superman already has the innate superiority due to his amazing powers. All that remains is to train him properly. For instance, the Nazis would demand that he recognize that his superiority entitles him to treat others as inferior. As Hitler's right-hand man and head of the SS, Heinrich Himmler, explained:

> The SS man ... must be honest, decent, loyal, and comradely to members of our own blood and to no one else. What happens to the Russians, what happens to the Czechs, is a matter of utter indifference to me ... Whether the other peoples live in comfort or perish of hunger interests me only in so far as we need them as slaves for our culture.[14]

For Himmler and those he would train, only Germany mattered. Every other nation and people was destined for slavery to the Reich. This is the mindset that Superman would have learned, and it is the one he would have followed, if the Nazi indoctrination were successful.

In the End, Hitler Still Loses

Imagine how some of the major events of World War II may have been different had Superman been involved with Hitler's cause. The Night of Broken Glass, which took place in late 1938 and saw the Nazis destroying the shops and homes of Jewish citizens, would have been even worse. The destruction Superman could have caused would have devastated Jewish communities. The Night of the Long Knives a few years earlier, in which Hitler destroyed the SA in order to transfer its powers to his more loyal SS, would have happened before Superman was 18 in the story we are telling here. Even so, if he were fully in Hitler's power by this point, I doubt the führer (as he became a month after this incident) would have been able to resist using his young protégé in the attack. Perhaps knives would no longer be involved at all, and the event would be known as the Night of the *Übermensch*. Having Superman on board would have been a game changer for Hitler.[15] Once fully indoctrinated, Superman would be the ultimate weapon, exploited to the fullest. No doubt, Hitler would also have kept some kryptonite on hand, just as Batman does, in case things went wrong.

At some point, a confrontation would have been inevitable. By teaching Superman that he was part of a superior race, a moment would eventually arise in which he would wonder why he bothered to serve a lesser man. This was a common worry for Hitler, who became increasingly paranoid toward the end of the war. In many cases, he was right to worry—and he would have been right to worry about Superman. While he would have been trained to be loyal, he would also develop a superiority complex that would threaten Hitler's authority over him. Ironically, Hitler would have to hope that some of Superman's virtuous character *had* been formed in that rocket and was *not* easily changed. He would need Superman to be a hero, but paradoxically, a hero who would ultimately stop his evil plans.

Notes

1. For more on philosopher Friedrich Nietzsche (1844–1900) and his conception of the *Übermensch*, see the chapters by Bogaerts, Gadon, and Barkman in part 3 of this volume. (Barkman comments specifically on Hitler's misreading of Nietzsche.)
2. Aristotle, *Nicomachean Ethics*, trans. Terence Irwin (Indianapolis: Hackett, 1985), book 1, section 2. (This will be the translation used for quotations, but the chapters, sections, and page number are standard in any version of the book.)
3. Ibid., 1109a.
4. Doomsday killed Superman in the classic *Superman*, vol. 2, #75 (January 1993), reprinted in *The Death of Superman* (1993).
5. Aristotle, *Nicomachean Ethics*, book 1, section 2.31.
6. Ibid., 1103a.
7. As quoted in H.W. Koch, *The Hitler Youth: Origins and Development 1922–1945* (New York: Cooper Square Press, 2000), 127.
8. Ibid., 128.
9. The experiment is described in full in Stanley Milgram's 1974 book *Obedience to Authority: An Experimental View* (New York: Harper Perennial, 2009 reprinted edition).
10. For more on *Superman: Red Son*, see chapter 13 by Jensen in this volume.
11. Alasdair MacIntyre, *After Virtue*, 3rd ed. (Notre Dame: Notre Dame Press, 2007), 211–220.
12. Ibid., 215.

13. Hannah Arendt, *The Origins of Totalitarianism*, 2nd ed. (Cleveland: Meridian, 1958), available at http://archive.org/details/originsofto talit00aren.
14. Heinrich Himmler, "Speech in Poznan, October 4th, 1943," *International Military Tribunal*, Vol. XXIX, 1919.
15. Compare to how the presence of Dr. Manhattan in *Watchmen* (1987) changed the outcome of the Vietnam War in that alternate version of history.

Part Two

TRUTH, JUSTICE, AND THE AMERICAN WAY
WHAT DO THEY MEAN?

Chapter 5

Clark Kent Is Superman!
The Ethics of Secrecy

Daniel P. Malloy

I have a secret or two. So do you. Our secrets may be big or small, important or trivial—it doesn't matter. For one reason or another, there is some information we won't share with others. We keep our secrets in a variety of ways and for a variety of reasons. Some secrets are kept to avoid bad consequences, and some are kept out of loyalty or fear. Sometimes keeping them only requires keeping our mouths shut, and other times it requires bald-faced lying. I'll bet that few of our secrets compare with Clark Kent's big one: he was born on an alien world and has abilities far beyond those of mere mortals. Clark, in a word, is Superman—and that's one hell of a secret.

Some secrets are fine to keep to ourselves, and others are not. At first glance, Clark's secret seems to be fine, but it may not be if we look further into it. What about other people who know Clark's secret? What obligates them to keep it and what conditions, if any, would relieve them of that obligation? Lois Lane is an especially complicated case because she works as a journalist. On the one hand, Lois is obligated to Clark to keep his secret. But on the other hand, as a journalist, Lois has a professional duty to seek out and expose the truth.

Superman and Philosophy: What Would the Man of Steel Do?, First Edition. Edited by Mark D. White.
© 2013 John Wiley & Sons, Inc. Published 2013 by John Wiley & Sons, Inc.

What Is the Secret?

We all know Clark's big secret: he is Superman. Secrets always belong
to someone. This is one of the things that distinguish secrets from
information we simply don't have. For example, I don't know why
you're reading this book: maybe you're interested in philosophy and
comics, maybe you're taking a class, or maybe you're stalking me.
This information is simply not available to me, but none of it is secret
(except maybe the last). It only becomes a secret when someone
decides that it should remain hidden. A secret must be hidden, and the
act of hiding must be a decision. As contemporary philosopher Sissela
Bok defines it, a secret is a piece of information that is intentionally
concealed.[1]

We have to distinguish secrets from some concepts that are often
linked with them. First, secrets are not lies. Lies may be told to keep
secrets—Clark lies all the time.[2] In order to keep his secret, Clark has
to try to get people to believe things that aren't true; he has to lie. But
Clark, being the world's oldest Boy Scout, tries to avoid lying whenever he can. If he has the option he simply avoids the question or
changes the subject or just clams up. All of these are perfectly valid
techniques, but sometimes keeping the secret necessitates telling a lie.

The other closely linked concept we must distinguish from secrecy
is privacy. The essential difference between secrecy and privacy is that
privacy is often thought of as a right, whereas secrecy is a method.
There are certain things we all have a right to keep to ourselves that
do not require secrecy. Perry White has a private life away from the
Daily Planet, but not a secret life. Clark, on the other hand, has both
a private life and a secret life. In his private life, he does a lot of the
things we all do in our private lives: he watches movies, goes on dates,
eats meals, shops for clothes, visits his parents, and so on. In his secret
life, he does things most of us would like to do, but can't, like leaping
tall buildings in a single bound.

The right to privacy is somewhat controversial. Legally, at least in
America, it has been established through precedent and interpretation, but cannot actually be found in the US Constitution.
Contemporary philosopher Judith Jarvis Thomson, along with some
other philosophers, has argued that the right to privacy isn't a moral
right either. Instead, Thomson argues that what we take to be the

right to privacy is actually an amalgam of rights that a person has over herself and over her property.[3] Still, privacy does have some moral grounding. Secrecy, on the other hand, is not morally grounded. We have no right to keep secrets.

Secrecy, then, is morally neutral. It is not presumed to be immoral, as lying is. Nor is it presumed to be a moral right. Secrecy is a tool, and sometimes it is the right tool for the job. Just like any other tool, its rightness or wrongness depends on the use to which it is put. A hammer can be used to build a house for a poor family or to kill a mime.[4] Neither use has any effect on the hammer itself—it's just a hammer. In the same way, secrecy can be used for good or bad purposes. You can keep a secret so that you don't spoil a surprise party or so that you get away with a crime.

Superman for President!

In a story in *Action Comics*, vol. 1, #900 (June 2011), Superman renounces his US citizenship. This is quite dramatic, except for one thing: Superman is NOT a citizen. He wasn't born in the United States, and he has never been naturalized. Setting that aside, the Superman persona is not one that can have citizenship. Clark Kent is a citizen (sort of), but Superman is purely a public persona—a mask, if you will. To claim that he is a citizen is like saying that Ronald McDonald and the Pillsbury Doughboy are citizens.[5]

This incident demonstrates that Superman is a public figure. To a lesser extent, so is Clark—he's a reporter and columnist for the *Planet*, after all. This is important because the rules of privacy are somewhat different for public figures than for private individuals— but it is controversial just how different they are. At one extreme, the paparazzi might argue that a public figure has no reason to expect privacy. At the other extreme, some public figures might claim that they should have the same expectation of privacy that everyone else has. In the middle is the recognition that someone like Clark invites his readers into his world by writing a newspaper column. This broadcasting of one's opinions necessarily blurs the lines between public and private. With other public figures, that line is even blurrier. With Superman, it is non-existent—he *only* exists in public.

The rules are different for public figures because they voluntarily put themselves in the public eye, thus inviting the public to share in certain parts of their private lives. In Clark's case, the public shares in his "secret" life. Think about it: before Clark put on the cape, he was doing the same kind of things, only much more covertly. He still used his powers to help people, he just didn't draw any attention to himself; he took special pains to ensure that he and his abilities remained hidden. With the invention of the Superman persona, that kind of secrecy became unnecessary. Superman could do all of that stuff in plain view—even be photographed! (Thanks, Jimmy!) But now a new kind of secrecy was needed—Clark had to keep his connection to Superman out of public view.

So now we have two separate cases. In his early days of adventuring, Clark was doing good works, but keeping out of the public eye. Once he donned the cape, he was doing good works in the public eye, but under an assumed name and identity. Both are cases of secrecy, but they may not both be justified. In the first case, Clark was fully justified in acting secretly. The case is parallel to giving anonymously to charity: you do something good, but you don't want recognition for it. We may not like or approve of such anonymous good deeds—if done publicly, they might encourage others to act similarly—but it is well within an individual's rights to keep this information private. If that means concealing the information, so be it.

The case of the cape is more difficult, particularly because it is hard to see any real-life parallels to Clark's actions. It's rare that someone would do a good deed in full view of the public, and then deny responsibility for it. It's one thing to be modest after saving a child from drowning in a pond—"Anyone would have done the same thing!"—but it's quite different to deny that you did it. But that is precisely what Clark does when he puts on the cape. He's created a distinct identity to get credit for his actions. The closest parallel is when someone does a bad thing in public and then denies having done it. For instance, growing up my brother and I had an invented friend—not much of a friend, really. Or at least, we weren't good friends to him. We called our invented friend "Mr. Nobody" and he got the blame for anything we might get in trouble for. Unfortunately, Mom didn't believe in Mr. Nobody (parents can be such skeptics sometimes), so whenever one of us invoked him we both got in trouble.

Mr. Nobody was our version of Superman: we invented him to keep something secret. The difference, of course, is that Mr. Nobody was about avoiding blame. We never invoked him to avoid praise. And that may be why our secrets wouldn't have been covered by any expectation of privacy—what we were trying to keep secret was the fact (in most cases) that we'd done something we knew we shouldn't have. This is a relevant difference from the case of Clark and Superman. Posing as Superman, Clark keeps his powers and abilities a secret. He does good things with them, and in full view of the public, but the public does not connect those good deeds to Clark.

If good deeds can be considered private—as it seems they can— what about abilities? In general, our skills and abilities are our business and ours alone. Some skills you might even be encouraged to keep to yourself: remember the kid in school who could belch the alphabet, or the one who could turn his eyelid inside-out?[6] Others you might want to keep to yourself for a variety of reasons. Maybe you spent years mastering the art of mime, only to realize that mimes are the embodiment of all that is evil and loathsome in the world. Or maybe you are a skilled ventriloquist and don't want anyone to know so you can pull a few pranks. Whatever the reason, you do have the right to keep your skills and abilities private. How you use them may be a different story: a skilled safe-cracker can keep that talent quiet, unless she uses it to steal kryptonite. In Clark's case, though, he uses his abilities to help people, so I don't think we can begrudge him a bit of privacy.

If you think about it, that describes Clark and Superman's super-secret. The secret is the relationship between the two. If we have a right to keep good deeds and abilities private, then Clark has the right to keep his alternate identity as Superman private, since that's really all Superman is—good deeds and superpowers. Since the secret falls within the realm of privacy, Clark is doing nothing wrong in keeping the secret. That's his right. How far he goes to keep the secret may be another story. And it gets even more complicated when we're talking about other people's secrets.

The Secret Revealed!

In *Superman*, vol. 2, #2 (February 1987), Lex Luthor figured out Superman's secret. To be precise, a computer program figured out Superman's secret. When it proclaimed that Clark was Superman, Lex rejected the notion out of hand—luckily for Clark. Lex's reasoning is a bit revealing: he proclaims that Superman would never disguise himself as such a bumbling oaf.[7] In Lex's mind, a being as powerful as Superman would never wish to disguise himself.

Lex isn't the only villain to have unlocked the secret of Superman's identity. It's happened quite a few times, but for various reasons the villains never take full advantage of the information. Manchester Black used it to torture Supes, up to the point of making him believe that Lois was dead, but when Big Blue proved he was the Boy Scout everyone thought he was, Black erased the knowledge from those he'd given it to, including Lex.[8]

In dealing with other people's secrets, it is important to consider how they are learned. For instance, in the case of the villains who have learned Superman's secret, they're not let in on it by Clark himself. The whole point of a secret identity is to keep friends and loved ones safe by keeping it secret. So, the villains must discover Clark's hobby in some other way. Usually this discovery involves violating Clark's privacy. Now, a villain who has violated someone's privacy to discover a secret is not likely to feel any obligation to keep that secret—but that doesn't mean the obligation doesn't exist.

Imagine a scenario where, instead of a villain, one of Clark's friends stumbles upon his secret identity. Is this person obligated to keep Clark's secret? Yes, the friendship would seem to include a duty to keep the secret. But, actually, even a stranger might be obligated to keep the secret. Inadvertent invasions of privacy are still invasions of privacy, and still wrong.

Opening the Shirt

Setting aside those with a vested interest in discovering Superman's secret and those who have similar secrets of their own, there are normally only a handful of people who know that Clark Kent is Superman—Jonathan and Martha Kent, Lana Lang, and (depending on where we are in the continuity) Lois Lane. Superman has confided his true identity to the Kents and Lana (though he didn't have much of a choice with Jonathan and Martha).

Clark entrusted Jonathan, Martha, and Lana with his secret. That sort of trust creates an obligation. But an obligation can't be created unilaterally. That is, if I confide a secret with you that you don't want to know, I haven't necessarily placed you under any obligation to keep my secret. There has to be an understanding of some sort. With Ma and Pa Kent, it's easy to see the source of this understanding; in a very real sense, Clark's secret is also theirs. This is an example of a shared secret. A secret has to belong to someone, but it doesn't have to belong to just one person. In fact, sometimes it can belong to quite a few people. Think about a surprise party—there is only one person, the guest of honor, who must be kept in the dark. Everyone else in the world could know about it, but as long as the party is being intentionally concealed from someone, it remains a secret.

This type of shared secret carries with it a sense that we are morally bound to keep it. To blab would be to betray the secret and the others keeping it. In a sense, blabbing is not playing fair. I tell you a secret, expecting that you will keep it. You tell me a secret on the same basis. If I then turn around and reveal your secret, I have not abided by the rules that I still expect you to abide by. There are, of course, exceptions. As we saw earlier, secrecy is morally neutral and can be used for good or bad ends. In the case we're looking at, the Kents are keeping their collective secret for good reasons. Initially, they kept the secret of Clark's origin because they wanted their adopted son to have a good life. The secret has remained in order to protect Clark, themselves, and anyone else who might be put in danger were Superman's true identity to become public knowledge.

Lana's case is a bit different. She wasn't in on the secret from the start; she was let in. To see whether this creates any obligation for her, we have to look at the circumstances. At least in John Byrne's 1986 re-imagining of Superman's origins, Clark told Lana about his abilities soon after their graduation from high school.[9] He wanted her to know why he was leaving Smallville. What options did he have? Aside from telling Lana his secret, there were three possibilities: disappearing, lying outright, and shading the truth. Disappearing would have been cruel and impractical. The Big Blue Boy Scout isn't good at cruelty, so that option is out. Lying faces the same problem. Shading the truth, or telling what philosophers call a lie of omission, is a little better. In this option, Clark could have told Lana that he was leaving Smallville because he felt he could accomplish more elsewhere—perfectly true, but it leaves out one vital piece of information: that he's going to accomplish a lot because he has superpowers.

As we know, Clark went with the truth, and in doing so burdened Lana with a secret that wasn't her own. It was the least cruel thing Clark could do—anything else would have left Lana wondering what had happened to him, or worse, what she had done to drive him away. But now that she has this knowledge, does she have an obligation to keep the secret? I don't think so. She has obligations to Clark and to the Kents, to protect them and keep them safe, so far as that is in her power. Those obligations entail keeping the secret. But because she was let in on the secret without her consent, the secret itself carries no obligation.

Put it like this: suppose Clark's secret posed no danger to himself or others. He simply wanted it kept because of some notion of modesty. In those circumstances, Lana wouldn't have any obligation to keep the secret. In the actual circumstances, Lana's duty to keep the secret is an indirect duty that has its origin in her duty to protect Clark, Jonathan, and Martha—a duty that is not special to them. It's a duty we all owe to each other, to varying degrees.

Letting in Lois

And so, at long last, we come to Lois. Lois deserves special consideration for a couple of reasons. First, there is her importance in Clark/ Superman's life. Second, there are the great lengths Clark went to for a very long time (though how long it was in comic-book time is anyone's guess) to keep her from discovering his secret. Most importantly, Lois requires special consideration because of two things: her knowledge of Clark's secret and her job.

Lois learned of Clark's double life only when he told her—after proposing, which seems risky.[10] Being let in on Clark's secret presents Lois with a conflict of duties. On the one hand, she owes a duty to Clark to keep his secret—to let it out would be to endanger quite a few people unnecessarily, including herself. On the other hand, Lois has a professional duty to tell the world. Lois is an investigative journalist. Her job is about getting the truth and publicizing it. But this isn't just a job description; it is an ethical duty. As a journalist, Lois has no more right to conceal the truth from her readers than a doctor has to refuse to treat blue-eyed patients. Nor can she ethically choose what to report and what not to. The only questions involved in decisions about what to publish and what not to are questions of importance and relevance. A newspaper has no duty to publish the nonsensical "human interest" pieces that are designed to give us all warm, fuzzy feelings (similar, in my experience, to nausea) because those pieces do not give relevant information. It does not matter to anyone if Mr. Siegel's cat gets stuck in a tree or Mr. Shuster's dog had 25 puppies. It does matter if the police go on strike or the local government plans to raise sales taxes.

So, with Superman's secret identity, the question is: does it matter to the public? This question is not as easy as it seems because of the ambiguity of the word "matter." There are two ways we can understand it. First, things matter if they have practical impact on people's lives. Thus police strikes and sales taxes matter because the one makes people less safe and the other means higher prices on goods and services. In a second sense, things matter if people care about them. The reason for the ambiguity is that these concepts often overlap: if something is going to have a practical impact on your life, you tend to care about it.

But the two senses of "matter" do not always overlap. There are plenty of things that will have practical impacts on our lives that we can't bring ourselves to care about, and, conversely, many things that we care about that have no conceivable practical impacts on our lives. For instance, most people aren't overly concerned about banking regulations. And yet banking regulations have a direct impact on loans, credit, and economic stability, all things that have practical impact on most of us. On the other hand, many people are very concerned about the lives of fictional characters. A comic-book company can't kill off or significantly change any of its well-established characters without attracting news coverage (which, naturally, is a large part of why they kill off or significantly change well-established characters). See, for instance: the "death" of Superman, Batman breaking his back, Green Lantern going insane, the "death" of Batman, and so on. While we care about these things—and I'm assuming you do, since you're reading a book about Superman—they really don't have a practical impact on our lives, because they concern *fictional* characters.

The job of an investigative journalist like Lois Lane is to report information that matters in the first sense—that has a practical impact.

So in figuring out whether to reveal Clark's secret, Lois has to decide whether Superman's true identity really has a practical impact on her readers' lives. There is no doubt that the public would be interested to know. But there is some room to doubt whether the public has a right to know. The right to know is associated with practical impact. For instance, I have no right to know how you spend your money. It's your money, after all. Spend it as you like. But if I give someone money for a particular purpose, or if I invest money in a company, then I do have a right to know how that money is spent. Similarly, we all have a right to know how the government spends our money.

In the case of Superman, you might argue that we have a right to know everything about him because of his status as a public figure. But, in fact, his status as a public figure is what creates the desire to know everything about him—not a right. Superman, remember, is the ultimate good Samaritan.[11] As such, he is not really a public servant; he's more of a volunteer. Every time Clark dons the cape, he is going above and beyond. The right to know is tied to obligations of public servants. We have the right to know about the president, the mayor, and so on. When a cop gives you a ticket, you have a right to know his badge number. But you have no right to know about the passerby who pulled you from the burning wreckage.

Given this limitation on the public's right to know, it seems that Lois doesn't have any duty to reveal Clark's secret. Even an investigative journalist has an obligation to respect privacy. So it seems Clark's secret is safe.[12]

In the Vault

Secrets can be good or bad. Some must be kept at all costs. Some should only be kept in the absence of compelling reasons to reveal them. And some shouldn't be kept. Clark's secret is decidedly not one of those, but it might be difficult to decide if it should be kept at all costs or only in the absence of compelling reasons to reveal it. That is, until we reflect on it a bit. Secrets have purposes, and where they fall on this spectrum will be determined by those purposes. Lex Luthor wants to keep his criminal enterprises secret because exposure would mean imprisonment, among other things—it is that purpose that dictates whether the secret ought to be kept.

In Clark's case, there are several reasons for his secret, but the most compelling one is to protect his loved ones. Given that this is the purpose of keeping the secret, we can easily say that the secret must not be kept at all costs. If a situation arises in which Clark is compelled to reveal his secret to keep his loved ones out of danger— and they do so tend to get into danger—then he has to reveal his true identity. If Clark lost all of his loved ones at once, this reason for keeping the secret would disappear. Certainly the Boy Scout has other reasons for keeping his secret, but those are about personal preferences more than moral obligations. Clark knows that it is dangerous to be Superman—dangerous to him, of course, but more dangerous to the non-super-powered people associated with him. He has an obligation to keep them out of danger, and that obligation is at the root of the secret. So Clark's right to his secret is not absolute. Because secrets are means to particular ends, the right to keep them depends solely on the morality of those ends. And given the danger in which their crime-fighting put their loved ones, heroes such as Superman would seem to have a sound moral reason to keep secrets. (So don't tell anybody!)

Notes

1. Sissela Bok, *Secrets* (New York: Vintage 1989).
2. Can you *believe* that Jimmy Olsen is still in the dark? Others I get, but *Jimmy*? He takes pictures for a living and he *still* can't see that Superman and his pal Clark have the exact same facial features? What is he, the world's only blind photographer?
3. Judith Jarvis Thomson, "The Right to Privacy," *Philosophy and Public Affairs* 4 (1975): 295–314.
4. He'll make a noise!
5. For more on the issue of Superman and citizenship, see chapter 7 by Terjesen in this volume.
6. If you are either of these kids, stop it!
7. Lex's rant here is actually an interesting precursor to Quentin Tarantino's analysis of the Clark Kent identity in the 2004 movie *Kill Bill: Vol. 2*.
8. *Action Comics*, vol. 1, #796 (December 2002).
9. *The Man of Steel* #6 (December 1986), reprinted in *Superman: The Man of Steel Vol. 1* (1991).

10. The proposal was in *Superman*, vol. 2, #50 (December 1990). Clark told Lois about his secret identity in *Action Comics*, vol. 1, #662 (February 1991).
11. In Kurt Busiek's *Astro City* series, his version of Superman is actually called "Samaritan."
12. For more on journalistic ethics, see chapter 3 by Southworth and Tallman in this volume.

Chapter 6

Superman and Justice

Christopher Robichaud

We all know that Superman stands for truth, justice, and the American way. Most of us take the meaning of these words for granted—but not philosophers! We ask things like: what's Superman's precise relationship to the truth? And is there such a thing as *the* American way? Both these questions are worth pursuing—and are pursued elsewhere in this book—but in this chapter, we'll focus on justice, a term just as vague as the other two.

To explore what kind of justice Superman should stand for, we will explore two alternate theories from contemporary political philosophy. On the one hand, according to *libertarianism*, justice means that the state should ensure that our personal liberty is protected. On the other hand, according to *liberal egalitarianism*, justice involves the state ensuring not only that individual rights are protected but also that there is a fair distribution of opportunity and resources among us. Superman obviously isn't a political entity like the state, but if he claims to stand for justice, then he should do it ... well, he should do it justice!

It's All About Personal Liberty

One of the most important contributions to contemporary political philosophy—and also a foundational text in contemporary libertarian thought—is *Anarchy, State and Utopia*, written by philosopher

Superman and Philosophy: What Would the Man of Steel Do?, First Edition. Edited by Mark D. White.
© 2013 John Wiley & Sons, Inc. Published 2013 by John Wiley & Sons, Inc.

Robert Nozick (1938–2002).[1] In this book, Nozick imagined a "minimal state" empowered to protect us from various acts of aggression and violence, as well as to enforce contracts that we freely enter into with each other. It's not empowered to do much of anything else. It's not allowed, for instance, to tax people in order to provide for public education, to offer public healthcare, or even to help with infrastructure issues like the provision of public roads and of transportation. Taxes can only be collected for the purpose of basic police and court functions.

Why should we accept this limited conception of the state? The most famous line of reasoning Nozick offered on its behalf was his "Wilt Chamberlain argument." Nothing against the basketball legend, but we'll use a slightly different version of it. Suppose that as Clark Kent grew up here on Earth, he decided that he didn't want to be a superhero. Instead, he wanted to be an entertainer, the amazing, the astounding, the unbelievable Superman! He wanted to use his powers to awe crowds wherever he went—and awe them he would, since his powers are absolutely amazing. People would drive hundreds of miles to see him wherever he performs.

Now suppose he wanted to charge people money to view him run faster than a speeding bullet, leap buildings in a single bound, and show us that he is indeed more powerful than a locomotive. We can reasonably predict that Superman will quickly become one of the wealthiest men on the planet. If people will travel from around the country to see him, they'll certainly pay to see him as well. If sales ever slow, Superman will no doubt find some new feat to perform to fascinate his fans all over again.

Nozick would now ask us to consider what taxes the state may justifiably collect from Superman. The reason the focus is on taxes is because taxation is considered to be one of the primary coercive powers of the state (along with prosecution and incarceration), and whenever the state acts coercively, we should ask whether it is just. Superman made his money using his own talents, freely entering into a contract to collect payment for putting on a show. And many people freely chose to hand over their own money—earned from the free exercise of their own talents—to see him perform super feats. The money Superman now has is his property, acquired through voluntary transactions and the free exercise of his own talents. The state, therefore, if it is truly invested in preserving personal liberty, can only take money from Superman if it has good reason to. And the only good reason available to it, on this view, is the need for funds in order to protect the personal liberties of the citizens of the state.

Nozick thought it was intuitive that collecting taxes to be used for security and for the enforcing of contracts are the only legitimate uses of the state's coercive power of taxation, because security and contract enforcement are the only things that *all* people need in order to exercise their personal liberty.[2] What reason could the state possibly give to justify taking more of Superman's property than what is required to preserve personal liberty? After all, people *freely* gave him money to see him perform and he was *freely exercising his own talents*. People gave Superman what they were willing to give him to see him do something that he freely chose to do. The state cannot just step in after that and take from him what people freely gave to him for whatever reason it sees fit. Superman can be taxed, to be sure, but he won't be taxed for any of the social programs we currently enjoy in this country, such as roads, education, and healthcare for the poor and elderly, none of which are necessary to preserve personal freedom.

It is important to understand that Nozick wasn't claiming that affordable education, well-maintained bridges and highways, and affordable healthcare aren't important. What he is claiming is that it is not the business of the *state* to provide for these things. Sure, these are important social goods, but they're not necessary to preserve liberty. If people want affordable education, for instance, they should engage with the private business of offering affordable education, which would provide an important social good while also preserving personal freedom. If Superman wants to take his pile of money and go into business building roads and setting up schools, that is his choice. But by taxing him to establish these things, we rob Superman of his choice and thus curtail his freedom. And that is an injustice, according to Nozick's libertarian view.

Truth, Libertarian Justice, and the American Way

If we accept this libertarian conception of justice, that puts a premium on personal liberty above all other things, then what would it mean for Superman, as a superhero, to stand for justice? As it is, much of what we see Superman doing in the comics is consistent with him standing for justice of this sort. After all, Superman is mostly concerned with protecting us from all sorts of threats to our security, from the nefarious plots of Lex Luthor to the devious schemes of General Zod. Superman can see himself as an extension of the state in this regard, providing security for us so that we may go about exercising our personal liberty and stepping in only when we choose to exercise that liberty in a way that violates the liberty of others.

Of course, if Superman truly embraced this libertarian conception of justice, he could go much further. After all, he should look at the United States, where he was raised, and recognize that it is currently up to its eyeballs in injustice (according to libertarianism). For example, the state unjustly coerces individuals through taxation to pay for all sorts of social goods. If Superman really stood for libertarian justice, he could use his unique position to put an end to unjust government activity. At the very least, he could put his "brand" behind politicians who share his libertarian sensibilities. More directly, he could become extraordinarily wealthy and provide these goods himself in the private sector. If Superman got into the business of laying down roads, for instance, he could do a heck of a job at a fraction of the time it usually takes. He could probably do it for free, but that wouldn't send the message about libertarian justice that he wants to send. He would want road construction to be a business in order to show how the private sector can provide this good more successfully—and more consistent with justice—than the government can. And that, presumably, would pressure the state to abandon collecting taxes for these purposes.

Not everything would be as easy for him as laying down roads, of course. But Superman could certainly offer a wide range of skills to those interested in privatizing other social goods, like education and healthcare. Admittedly, conceiving of Superman as some big businessman, as well as a protector of the people, might strike many as being incompatible with conceiving of him as a superhero. That's not so obvious, however; libertarianism, after all, regards unwarranted state coercion as an extremely serious injustice. Fighting it in the way we've just described may not be as glamorous as flinging nuclear missiles into space, clobbering Doomsday, or even giving a speech at the United Nations. But if Superman is serious about standing for libertarian justice, it is a fight he may not in good conscience walk away from, even if it requires him to establish SuperCorp to do it.

Great Rawls!

Many of us think that justice involves taking personal liberty seriously, but perhaps not so seriously that taxing people to promote social welfare programs is considered to be unwarranted coercion. A popular alternative to libertarianism was provided by John Rawls (1921–2002), the most influential political philosopher in the last hundred years, in his famous book *A Theory of Justice*.[3] In it, Rawls argued that we ought to conceive of justice as fairness. When asking whether political institutions and the distribution of social goods are just, we should ask whether they are *fair*. And, most important, Rawls gave us a way of answering that question and reaching conclusions about what fairness amounts to.

The best place to put Rawls in conversation with Nozick concerns our talents and what we deserve to gain when we exercise them. Nozick, remember, thought that we have a nearly absolute claim on the fruits of our labor, and the only justification for taxation is to provide for security and the enforcement of contracts. Rawls agreed that the state needs a justification to tax its citizens, but disagreed with Nozick regarding how much people deserve to keep out of what they earn. He points out that what we earn is, in part, determined by the natural talents we possess, which we cannot claim as "deserved." We were merely born with them, a result of a natural lottery, a mixing of genes, aided by the environment in which you grew up. In other words, your raw talents are based on one part biological determination, one part upbringing, and one part luck. If you are born with high intelligence, or great looks, or tremendous athleticism, you most assuredly didn't *earn* those traits by doing something. It's just a result of how the dice landed for you. This applies to Superman, too; Kal-El didn't earn the powers he has. It was a combination of what he was born with and that his parents chose to send him to our planet.

We do, of course, play a large role in taking those talents, developing them into skills, and using them toward our goals and dreams. While all of us must work with what we are given in terms of raw talent, we must contribute effort and drive to make something from it. Based on this, Rawls did not say that we don't deserve *any* of the fruits of our labor; that would be absurd. But he points out that it's just as absurd to say we deserve *everything* we earn from the use of our inborn talents, which are in part the result of sheer luck. While we have a legitimate claim on whatever part of our success comes from the effort we put into creating it, we have no claim on the part that resulted from luck.

The end result of this is that if we do not deserve the entirety of the fruits of our labor, then we have less reason to argue against taxation for the purpose of supporting social programs. If Superman does not "deserve" the powers that enable him to become rich as an entertainer, then he has less claim on them when the government comes to collect taxes for reasons above and beyond security and contract enforcement.

Behind the (Lead-Lined) Veil of Ignorance

Starting with the role of luck in determining our natural talents, Rawls developed one of the most well-known ideas in political philosophy: the *original position*. Like Nozick's Wilt Chamberlain argument, Rawls intends the original position argument to capture our intuitive judgments about what fairness—and, therefore, justice—involves.

Let's say we want to establish what kind of a society will be fair. We'll have to decide what political and social institutions to adopt; what liberties they will be designed to protect and promote; which social, economic, and political goods to distribute and how; and what this distribution of goods will look like. In order to be fair—to consider the interests of all people equally—we decide to think about this ideal justice as if we were behind a "veil of ignorance." What that means is that we should think about these questions as though we weren't aware of what our natural talents are, as well as our race, sex, or other attributes we're born with—which Rawls called the "original position." If we don't know what our actual position in society will be, we'll design a society that respects the rights and needs of everybody, since each of us could potentially be anybody—Lois, Jimmy, Lex, or even Clark. We'll make sure that we don't stack the deck in our favor by creating a society in which those with our talents and attributes will be privileged at the expense of others.

Ideally, this thought process will result in a fair society, one that we can justify to everybody regardless of their natural talents or lack thereof. Furthermore, once we imagine ourselves behind the veil of ignorance, unaware of what position we'll hold in society, we can base our institutional design on our own self-interest. Despite the hypothetical nature of the veil of ignorance and the original position, this grounds Rawls's theory in reality. Rather than arguing that the ideal society is one that people *should* want, or one that people should recognize is good for *other* people, it speaks to people's own interests: this society will be the best for you if you don't know if you'll be smart, beautiful, athletic, and so forth.

Rawls believed that if we agree to think about society as if behind a veil of ignorance, we'll create a society that conforms to two key principles—principles which, in his opinion, inevitably flow from our own self-interest. The first principle—which would be familiar to Nozick and other libertarians—is that our society must have strong institutions in place to protect basic liberties like freedom of speech, of the press, and of conscience. This principle, as a matter of self-interest, would take priority over the second principle, which deals with equality of opportunity and resources; after all, having opportunity and resources means little if you don't have the basic freedoms to make use of them.

The second principle is both better-known than the first and more controversial. It says first that we must create institutions that promote equality of opportunity, so that anyone with the same talents will have the same professional opportunities open to him or her. The second part deals with the distribution of basic social goods, which Rawls called *primary goods*, such as food, clothing, and shelter, which are essential to making the most of one's opportunities. From behind the veil of ignorance, what institutions will we want in place to determine the distribution of these primary goods in society? Since we are just as likely to be born talented or untalented, to a rich family or a poor family, in a peaceful country or a war-torn one, Rawls maintained that we would want to pay particular attention to making sure the worst-off members of society are cared for the most.

As a matter of self-interest, then, we will adopt what has come to be called the *difference principle*: we will design institutions to distribute primary goods in such a way that benefits the worst-off first, therefore lessening the difference between the worst-off and the best-off. What they choose to make from those extra resources is up to them, but at least they get a little extra help getting started, to make up for their other disadvantages. According to Rawls, this is what we'd want society to do if we were the worst-off, and behind the veil of ignorance, each of us could be in that position.

Occupy Metropolis

What would it mean for Superman to stand for Rawlsian justice? Much of what Superman does already is consistent with Rawlsian justice, including the things that a libertarian Superman would do; this is natural, given that both systems place value on freedoms. For instance, promoting security is crucial to defending our basic liberties. By battling Luthor, Bizarro, and Brainiac, Superman helps the state perform its role in keeping us safe so that we may speak freely, worship as we please, and so forth.

But what about making sure that primary goods are distributed according to the difference principle? As we saw, Superman could start a business to promote libertarian justice, but that won't work for promoting Rawlsian justice. For Rawls, distribution of primary goods is a problem to be handled by government institutions, and unless Superman takes a position in the US government, he can't have a direct impact on how this is done. He must address distributional injustice differently, to the extent that it exists—and when it comes to the United States, where he was raised, it seems there is much Rawlsian injustice that needs to be addressed.

So what's the Man of Steel to do? March with Occupy Metropolis? Actually, he could do that: as the most powerful superhero on the planet, who is respected by people and nations around the globe, Superman is in a unique position to promote economic justice by advocating for it. His voice can literally be heard across oceans and continents. As Clark Kent, he can focus on news stories for the *Daily Planet* that bring to light the economic injustice that exists in our country. Perry White would surely run them—in his own self-interest, of course. Superman, however, can speak out against economic injustice, throwing the weight of his stature behind efforts to improve things. He can lobby for it to be changed. He can help put legislators into office who will address the problem.

But he can't *force* our country, or any country for that matter, to change. That would perhaps take him down a dangerous road of using his might to steer human affairs rather than help them along the path they've chosen for themselves. Superman can help us avoid natural disasters and invasions from outer space, and help improve conditions on Earth to some degree, but past that he has to let humanity determine its own way. Rawls's system of justice definitely has more room for government action than libertarianism, but it is actually rather limited. The government ensures basic liberties and helps the downtrodden get a head-start in life and some continued aid, but each person is still responsible for making something of his or her life using the help received. Superman is simply treating humanity the same way.

Superman's Greatest Foe?

It may seem underwhelming to suggest that Superman fight certain forms of injustice by marching in the streets. This is the guy who can fling a radioactive asteroid into the sun, and carrying a protest sign is the best he can do to combat injustice? When it comes to addressing certain institutional forms of injustice, however, that indeed may be the most effective thing he can do. As he says when defending his participation in protests in the Middle East by simply standing still in the middle of the crowd,

> I'm good when it comes to fighting apocalyptic threats. But the everyday degradations that humans suffer? Dying of thirst? Hunger? People being denied their basic human rights? I've never been very effective at stopping things like that.[4]

He can't pummel injustice with his super-strength or blast it with his heat-vision. In this sense, institutional injustice is as much of a challenge to Superman as Doomsday was, one that all the brute power in the world isn't enough to beat. It has more in common with Lex Luthor, a formidable threat who cannot be fought with mere force, but requires reason, strategy, and heart. In order to put the "justice" in "truth, justice, and the American way," Superman will gladly go behind the veil of ignorance (without his x-ray vision). Will you?

Notes

1. Robert Nozick, *Anarchy, State and Utopia* (New York: Basic Books, 1977). The discussion that follows also draws upon Will Kymlicka's discussion of libertarianism in his book *Contemporary Political Philosophy: An Introduction*, 2nd ed. (Oxford: Oxford University Press, 2001), 102–165. (I would be remiss if I didn't mention that Nozick came to reject the arguments he made in *Anarchy, State and Utopia*; see Stephen Metcalf, "The Liberty Scam: Why even Robert Nozick, the philosophical father of libertarianism, gave up on the philosophical movement he inspired," *Slate*, June 20, 2011, available at http://www.slate.com/artcles/arts/the_dilettante/2011/06/the_liberty_scam.single.html.)

2. There's an obvious complication to point out here, which is that Superman himself doesn't really need the state to perform these functions for him. But we can safely presume that Nozick didn't design his theory with Superman in mind!

3. John Rawls, *A Theory of Justice* (Cambridge, MA: Harvard University Press, 1971).

4. *Action Comics*, vol. 1, #900 (June 2011). For more on the fallout from this intervention, see chapter 7 by Terjesen in this volume.

Chapter 7

Is Superman an *American* Icon?

Andrew Terjesen

Superman caused a bit of a stir in the real world when he announced, in the landmark 900th issue of *Action Comics*, that he was going to renounce his US citizenship in the fictional DC Universe. One conservative activist told Fox News that Superman's actions displayed a "blatant lack of patriotism" and that Superman was "belittling the United States as a whole."[1] Though this seems to be mostly an example of media overreaction during a slow news cycle, it does raise some important questions about Superman's relationship to the United States, the "American way," patriotism, and cosmopolitanism.

Before we address those questions, however, let's get a simpler matter out of the way: even if this humble back-up story in an oversized anniversary issue is taken to be canon or "in continuity," it will have very little effect on anything. As almost everyone knows, the man we call Superman began life on the planet Krypton as Kal-El, the child of Jor-El and Lara, but was raised on Earth by Jonathan and Martha Kent as their son Clark. As he grew, Kal-El developed amazing abilities under our yellow sun, but as Clark Kent, he pretended to be an average human being (even wearing—*gasp*—glasses). Even though he now serves the people of Earth as Superman, Clark Kent is still the one who pays income taxes to the US government, who renews his driver's license in Metropolis, and who is (sometimes) married to Lois Lane.

Superman and Philosophy: What Would the Man of Steel Do?, First Edition. Edited by Mark D. White.

Most important for our purposes, Clark Kent is the one who holds US citizenship. Superman has no legal documentation with which to procure such legal status; his "long-form birth certificate" was destroyed with the rest of Krypton. Superman has no legal citizenship to give up, and unless Clark Kent renounces his citizenship, what Superman does is purely symbolic. So why has it caused such a stir?

Is Superman Giving Up on the American Way?

For decades, Superman has been seen as a distinctly American super-hero; after all, he fights for "truth, justice and the American way." Although Superman has been famously associated with that phrase through his radio and television incarnations, it wasn't always that way. The early radio programs stopped with "truth and justice." The "American way" part was only added in 1942 when the United States was in the thick of World War II.[2] And it didn't really become a popular phrase until the 1950s television show starring George Reeves.

Nonetheless, the idea that Superman is a distinctly American super-hero deserves close scrutiny. What exactly is the "American way" that he is fighting for? It can't be the same as "truth" or "justice," because those are both listed as distinct concepts. Is it democracy, equality, liberty, or the pursuit of happiness? While one could argue that all of these concepts can be found throughout American history and litera-ture, the particular notion of the "American way" as something that we need to fight for seems to have gained a lot of momentum in the mid-twentieth century, especially during the Cold War.

Since it was contrasted with the totalitarian Communist government of the USSR, it should not be surprising that the "American way" was very strongly associated with capitalism and individual freedom. In 1955, the conservative thinker Will Herberg summed it up as follows:

> The American Way of life is individualistic, dynamic, pragmatic. It affirms the supreme value and dignity of the individual; it stresses incessant activity on his part, for he is never to rest but is always to be striving to "get ahead"; it defines an ethic of self-reliance, merit, and character, and judges by achievement: "deeds, not creeds" are what count ... The American believes in progress, in self-improvement, and quite fanatically in education. But above all, the American is idealistic.[3]

This definition of the "American way" seems as good as any because it hits the same high points as most other discussions of "what makes America great." Yet, it does not identify anything that seems unique to America; certainly, we can find other countries that seek to protect individual dignity and promote self-reliance.

In a story that appeared just weeks after *Action Comics* #900 (albeit by a different writer), Superman explains what the American way means to him. After keeping the villain Livewire from destroying the Vegas Strip, Superman favors giving her a light sentence. Jimmy Olsen is outraged that Superman would turn a blind eye to the danger she had posed, but Superman answers him with a speech in defense of second chances:

> That's what America is about, really. That's the American way. Life, liberty, the pursuit of happiness—and second chances. None of us are forced to be anything we don't want to be … People from all over America—from all over the world—who went to the city to live the lives they wanted, to be the people they wanted to be. That's the idea that America was founded on, but it's not just for people born here. It's for everyone.[4]

This statement dovetails very nicely with what Superman said when he threatened to renounce his citizenship: "I can't help but see the bigger picture. I've been thinking too small. I realize that now."[5] Superman may have meant that the values of America are not limited to America, in which case it's not clear why renouncing his citizenship is so controversial. Superman is just trying to show how universal those values are, and that there is no reason why one has to be an American in order to stand for them. If anything, renouncing his citizenship would serve as a message to the world that those values are for everyone.

My Country, Right or Wrong–But Mostly Right

In giving up his American citizenship, Superman appears to be denying *exceptionalism*, the belief that one nation—in this case, the United States—is qualitatively superior in some way to other nations. Perhaps Superman's critics could take solace in the fact that he is not defecting, nor is he choosing to ally with another nation; he's simply saying that America is no more important to him than any other nation.

It shouldn't be so offensive to say that all nations are equal, but some critics are worried about how Superman's actions could undermine young children's belief in American exceptionalism—in other words, their patriotism.

Contemporary philosopher Alasdair MacIntyre explores the ethics of patriotism in a short work entitled *Is Patriotism a Virtue?*[6] MacIntyre points out that true patriotism has to involve a non-rational commitment to one's country, since there can't be a legitimate reason why one's country is superior to all others. If America actually were the only place where equality could be achieved, then one would have a good reason to defend it—but it's not. Someone who only supports their country when it is in the right is considered a fair-weather citizen compared to the "true patriot," who believes in "my country—right or wrong." Patriots are committed to their country because it is their country and for no other reason. Since patriotism requires people to support their country even when it does the wrong thing, it seems like patriotism is morally wrong. The fact that one was born or lives in a particular geographic location is not morally relevant when judging its actions. It would be wrong to excuse somebody's behavior just because he or she is our neighbor, so why should excusing one's country in the name of patriotism be any different?

MacIntyre suggests there is a reason why patriotism is different. We need a community to embody and pass on our values, and real communities are only preserved if people are dedicated to the community as a community, rather than as an ideal or based on the benefits of being a member of that community. If people love something other than their community (or country), then someday they may choose that thing over their community. People who fight for a country just because they are paid to do so are mercenaries, and they have no problem switching sides if it serves their interests (Lex Luthor is a classic example). A similar problem exists with communities dedicated to achieving certain ideals, like spreading democracy: groups that are dedicated to a cause will cease to be once that cause is achieved. For a community to be stable enough to produce generations and generations of mature adults, it needs to be dedicated to self-preservation, valuing its particular social structure (warts and all) and striving to protect it.

The "irrationality" of patriotism is precisely what concerns many modern thinkers and causes them to question its value. We can certainly see some of the excesses of patriotism. For instance, not everyone who fought for the Confederacy during the American Civil War was trying to preserve the institution of slavery. Some were patriots trying to preserve the way of life in their states, and preserving that way of life meant preserving both the good and the bad parts of it. This may be what Superman meant when he talked about thinking small: patriots tend to focus on preserving their country even if it is not a good thing for the rest of the world. From the perspective of an alien, the conflicts between America and Europe, or America and China, can seem like petty squabbles.

Can Superman Be a Citizen of the World?

The idea that we should think in global terms is known as *cosmopolitanism*, a word that combines the Greek words for the world (*cosmos*) and city-state (*polis*). Cosmopolitans are people who see themselves as part of a worldwide community and who try to experience and understand the larger world. As a philosophical view, cosmopolitanism is the idea that we should organize society in order to create such a worldwide community. Nations should be united under a single governing body that resolves disputes peacefully through dialogue and a commitment to a shared set of values. The United Nations and its predecessor, the League of Nations, are both products of cosmopolitan philosophy. Cosmopolitanism represents a range of views: some cosmopolitans think we simply need a set of rules that govern international politics, while others believe we should work toward a society in which national affiliations are incidental and we're all global citizens following the same laws and answering to the same institutions. Despite their differences, however, cosmopolitans all embrace global unity among the nations of the world as a means toward peace.

Superman's decision to renounce his US citizenship seems to reflect a very moderate form of cosmopolitanism. When explaining his decision to the American president's national security adviser, he says, "Truth, justice and the *American* way—it's not enough anymore. The world's too small. Too connected."[7] It seems that Superman is acknowledging that modern technology has made it almost impossible to be isolated from each other. Our actions affect people all over the world and as a result we need to stop focusing only on our national self-interest. Superman knows that we can't become cosmopolitans overnight, but his symbolic renunciation of American citizenship can inspire people around the world to come together as fellow human beings and stop treating each other merely as Americans, Russians, Chinese, and so forth.

One example of the subtle ways in which the world is becoming more cosmopolitan is that cultural influences are easily spread through the Internet and other media. Superman has fans all around the world who like to read his comics and watch his movies. In terms of the real world, Superman's cosmopolitan decision could be interpreted simply as DC Comics attempting to appeal to the global market for Superman stuff. Less cynically, though, one blogger said, "it's refreshing to see an alien refugee tell the United States that it's as important to him as any other country on Earth—which, in turn, is as important to Superman as any other planet in the multiverse."[8] Whether intended or not, American exceptionalism implies international inferiority. Patriotism will always be a barrier to international cooperation. If people around the world can find shared interests and shared values—even in the form of Superman—then maybe they can progress to a point where cooperation is common and patriotism recedes into the background.

Cosmopolitanism Then and Now

Many of the ancient Greek and Roman stoics endorsed a cosmopolitan worldview according to which the entire universe was a sentient and rational being that made sure everything happened in a rational manner.[9] From the Stoic point of view, patriotism was exactly what Superman described—a narrow perspective that neglected the larger God's-eye picture of the universe. Endorsing a strong form of cosmopolitanism, the Stoics sought to supplant particular cultures with a universal rational culture.

In his book *Cosmopolitanism: Ethics in a World of Strangers*, contemporary philosopher Kwame Anthony Appiah argues for a modern form of cosmopolitanism.[10] Instead of claiming that we are all part of one rational being or creature, like the Stoics did, Appiah appeals to the fact that we need to be responsible for the effects our actions have on people around the world. Appiah emphasizes connectedness, like the Stoics did, but he does not appeal to a single standard of the good. Instead, Appiah embraces the idea that there is more than one way to live a good life, and explains that cosmopolitanism has to find a way to balance the interconnectedness of peoples, and the obligations between them, with mutual respect for their differences.

Critics of cosmopolitanism fear that respecting everyone else's life choices would create a community based entirely on twenty-something hipster irony. Instead of patriotically defending their community from threats, people would "patriotically" defend their community, going through the motions but not really believing that it was truly worth saving. Since the members of the community can't fully commit emotionally to its defense, it is likely that they would not fight as vigorously as they otherwise would. Moreover, they would not be able to transmit any standards to new members of the community. In the end, a lack of patriotism means a lack of cultural preservation, and since MacIntyre claims that every moral system is embedded in a culture, a lack of culture would mean a lack of morality. MacIntyre does not say, however, that this is proof that we need to be patriots. Rather, he raises the issue of how we balance the problems of overzealous patriotism (or *jingoism*) with the dangers of having no commitments that are beyond question.

Despite what some commentators in the media may say, Superman has not rejected America. His renunciation of citizenship is a symbolic denial of American exceptionalism, but it is not an abandonment of America or the values that it—but not it alone—represents and promotes. If he truly wanted to make a break from the American way of life Superman would need to renounce his citizenship and reveal his secret identity. He would need to renounce being Clark Kent. As long as Clark Kent still lives in Metropolis, Superman will favor Metropolis and the country in which it is located. He can claim to be a citizen of the world, but it's not really true. He still has commitments to a particular part of the world that make him more involved in its way of life. But if Superman's actions are not meant as a repudiation of America or an endorsement of strong cosmopolitanism, than what is he trying to accomplish?

The Appearance of Impropriety

In all of the brouhaha (as opposed to "bwa-ha-ha") surrounding Superman's decision, very little attention has been paid to the context in which he says he is surrendering his citizenship. In *Action Comics*

#900, we see Superman talking to the US national security adviser who is very upset because Superman created a national incident when he traveled to Tehran to support anti-government protesters. Rather than throw his weight around, he took no actions against the government forces, even when it seemed that they would hurt the protesters. Instead he merely stood in the public square for twenty-four hours in tacit support of the protesters. The Iranian government nonetheless interpreted this as the American government, acting through Superman, supporting the protesters, and *voila*—we have an international incident and a further erosion in US–Iranian relations.

Superman feels compelled to renounce his citizenship because as long as the most powerful being on the planet appears to be affiliated with a particular government or nation, he is always seen as acting in its best interests rather than those of the world in general. As he says, "I'm tired of having my actions construed as instruments of U.S. policy." Superman sought to be a moral force in Iran, putting pressure on both the government and the protesters to resolve their issues peacefully. But in order to exert moral authority he needs to demonstrate the essential traits of a moral person, especially impartiality.

In today's world we tend to think of an impartial person as having an abstract point of view that transcends any particular feelings, like someone who does not get upset when he sees a couple send their only child into space before their planet explodes (just an example, of course). There is, however, another way to think about impartiality. In *The Theory of Moral Sentiments*, philosopher Adam Smith (1723–1790) proposed a theory of moral judgment that hinged upon what he called the "impartial spectator," but this meaning of "impartial" is not unemotional.[11] Instead, Smith's sense of "impartial" simply refers to someone who does not have a particular interest in the outcome or any connections to anyone who is affected by the outcome. Notice that Smith did not call for us to imagine an "unemotional spectator." In fact, Smith thought that our emotions conveyed important information, although our emotions need to be pure in order to give us the right picture of the situation. If we are personally interested in the outcome, we might not feel the right way about it.

Whenever we think that someone has a particular interest in something, we begin to question their judgments on that topic. As one blogger pointed out, as long as Superman is viewed as a US citizen "it would indeed be impossible for a nigh-omnipotent being ideologically aligned with America to intercede against injustice beyond American borders without creating enormous political fallout for the U.S. government."[12] Anything that Superman did that had indirect benefits for the US government would be called into question. Superman's presence in Tehran could be viewed as support for a democratic movement or it could be viewed as an American attempt to destabilize an unfriendly government.[13] So the question we need to consider is whether Superman should feel morally obligated to avoid the appearance of impropriety.

To answer this question we need to recognize that impropriety is an unavoidable fact of life if one is to maintain any commitments or close ties at all. Rival newspapers undoubtedly think that Superman is "in bed with" the *Daily Planet*, but the fact that he often grants them interviews and that they tend to portray him in a favorable light is more a function of his close contact with the members of the staff (one in particular). If we want to avoid the appearance of impropriety altogether, we would need to shun any commitments that would produce normal associations. That, of course, is impossible since our connections and associations are part of who we are.

Even so, Superman does have a moral responsibility to make sure that he is not too closely involved with the American government. In many professions, conflicts of interest are dealt with by creating a so-called "Chinese Wall" that blocks the flow of information between different parts of an organization. Superman needs to maintain a wall between himself and the US government so that he does not appear to be receiving national secrets or taking marching orders from the president. He doesn't want to appear to be a secret tool of American policy like he did in Frank Miller's *The Dark Knight Returns*. (That didn't turn out so well, did it?)

Act Locally, Think Globally

Superman is inescapably an American icon in that he is deeply embedded in American society. More accurately, he's an icon who *happens* to be American. To some extent he will always favor America, but not because there is any clear set of distinctly American values that only America promotes or embodies. Still, Superman has to avoid creating the impression that his commitment to America is also a commitment to US foreign policy and its national interests. So the symbolic gesture of renouncing his citizenship might help in distancing himself from the American government in people's minds.

The renunciation is not enough on its own, however. Superman needs to show that he does not take national interest into consideration when he acts, and the best way to do that would be to spend more time helping on a global scale.[14] Appiah's modern cosmopolitanism encourages us to broaden our perspective without giving up the culture that makes us who we are. Superman can affect the world in ways that far exceed Appiah's examples of interconnectedness, so the argument for cosmopolitanism is much more compelling for Superman. If nothing else, the symbolic act of renouncing his citizenship would help Superman to think like a modern cosmopolitan when he looks at the world's problems—or, as the bumper sticker says, he should act locally while thinking globally.

Notes

1. Hollie McKay, "Superman Renounced his U.S. Citizenship in the 900th issue of Action Comics," FoxNews.com, April 28, 2011. http://www.foxnews.com/entertainment/2011/04/28/superman-renounces-citizenship-00th-issue/.
2. Brian Cronin, "Comic Book Legends Revealed #276," September 3, 2010. http://goodcomics.comicbookresources.com/2010/09/03/comic-book-legends-revealed-276/.
3. Will Herberg, *Protestant, Catholic, Jew: An Essay in American Religious Sociology* (Chicago: University of Chicago Press, 1955), 79.
4. *Superman*, vol. 1, #711 (July 2011), reprinted in *Superman: Grounded, Vol. 2* (2011).
5. *Action Comics*, vol. 1, #900 (June 2011).
6. Alasdair MacIntyre, *Is Patriotism a Virtue?* (Lawrence, KS: University Press of Kansas, 1984).
7. *Action Comics*, vol. 1, #900.
8. Scott Thill, "Superman Defies God, USA in *Action Comics*' Landmark 900th Issue," Wired.com, April 27, 2011. http://www.wired.com/underwire/2011/04/action-comics-900/.
9. See Pauline Kleingeld and Eric Brown, "Cosmopolitanism," *Stanford Encyclopedia of Philosophy*, http://plato.stanford.edu/entries/cosmopolitanism/, especially section 1.1 ("Greek and Roman Cosmopolitanism").

10. Kwame Anthony Appiah, *Cosmopolitanism: Ethics in a World of Strangers* (New York: W.W. Norton, 2006).
11. Adam Smith, *The Theory of Moral Sentiments* (London: A. Miller, 1759). Available at http://www.econlib.org/library/Smith/smMS.html.
12. Laura Hudson, "Superman Renounces U.S. Citizenship in *Action Comics* #900," April 27, 2011. http://www.comicsalliance.com/2011/04/27/superman-renounces-us-citizenship/.
13. As Mark D. White has pointed out (http://www.comicsprofessor.com/2011/04/on-supermans-renouncing-his-us-citizenship-in-action-comics-900.html), Superman's efforts to detach himself from the United States might also be intended to protect American citizens from retaliation for his actions.
14. If the renunciation was for our benefit, it wouldn't be the first time Superman did something that was largely symbolic for our benefit. In *Superman: Peace on Earth* (1998), Superman spends a day trying to feed the hungry around the world. He knows that his efforts alone can't eliminate hunger, but he hopes that his attempt to do so will inspire others to pay attention to the problem.

Part Three

THE WILL TO SUPERPOWER
NIETZSCHE, THE *ÜBERMENSCH*, AND EXISTENTIALISM

Chapter 8

Rediscovering Nietzsche's *Übermensch* in Superman as a Heroic Ideal

Arno Bogaerts

> *"Behold! I teach you the superman: he is this lightning, he is this madness!"*
>
> Friedrich Nietzsche, *Thus Spoke Zarathustra*

Very few philosophical concepts have been as closely linked to the superhero genre and the mythology of its greatest representative, Superman, as the *Übermensch*.[1] The influential German philosopher Friedrich Nietzsche (1844–1900) described this idea of a "superman," capable of feats far beyond those of mortal men (sound familiar?), in his seminal work *Thus Spoke Zarathustra*.[2] Since then, it has been interpreted by many writers, not least of whom is comic book writer Grant Morrison, who mentioned it in his recent superhero history-slash-autobiography *Supergods*, and who even gave Nietzsche a cameo in the comic book *All-Star Superman* #10 (May 2008).[3] In that book, we saw the nineteenth-century philosopher writing *Thus Spoke Zarathustra* in a series of panels portraying real-life events that eventually culminated in the creation of the Superman in the 1930s by Jerry Siegel and Joe Shuster.

Despite the name connection, however, most scholars see Siegel and Shuster's Superman and Nietzsche's *Übermensch* as nearly polar opposites. This stems mainly from a conflict in moral values that resulted from the changing ways both supermen have been interpreted over the years. The comic book hero Superman grew from a social

Superman and Philosophy: What Would the Man of Steel Do?, First Edition. Edited by Mark D. White.
© 2013 John Wiley & Sons, Inc. Published 2013 by John Wiley & Sons, Inc.

crusader and a "champion of the oppressed" in the 1930s, to a patri-
otic and paternalistic fighter for "Truth, Justice, and the American
way" in the 1940s and 1950s, to a compassionate Christ-like savior
in the latter part of the twentieth century—and always defending the
Judeo-Christian values upheld by the American majority. Nietzsche's
"superman," on the other hand, firmly rejects the very same values its
superhero namesake upholds.

Because of the *Übermensch*'s glorification of power, favoring the
strong over the weak, and its subsequent misuse by the Nazi regime
during World War II, the *Übermensch* pretty much went from a goal
that humanity should aspire toward, to a frightening, amoral creature
that humanity should try to avoid. While it has certainly been a
common trope in the superhero genre and popular culture in general
to characterize figures explicitly based on Nietzsche's *Übermensch* as
inhuman monsters, I will argue that Nietzsche's concept—originally a
heroic (if not super heroic!) ideal—can be reinstated through the
character of Superman himself.

Truth, Justice, and the Nietzschean Way

But first, let us find out just what Nietzsche meant by *Übermensch*
and the place of the concept in his overall philosophy. We find glimpses
of it looming throughout the philosopher's work, but it is in *Thus
Spoke Zarathustra* where Nietzsche—or rather, his mouthpiece, the
prophet Zarathustra—comes down from the mountain and metaphorically describes several characteristics of this revolutionary higher
form of humanity. The *Übermensch* remains quite an elusive figure,
however, for Zarathustra never precisely defines the term. Furthermore,
since Nietzsche had an extremely lyrical writing style, especially in
Zarathustra, the *Übermensch* is left open to interpretation.[4]

To understand Nietzsche is to understand his famous claim that
"God is dead." No, the Almighty wasn't slain by Doomsday or
anything. Rather, Nietzsche claimed that humanity's *belief* in a
personal, all-caring God as the foundation of our conventional,
objective moral values had become obsolete. The philosopher was
highly critical of values originating from moral or religious belief
systems that demand faith in other-worldly hopes and that promise
salvation for humanity in another life beyond this one (like Christianity

and Judaism). For Nietzsche, the promise that another, kinder life awaits us is a denouncement of this true earthly existence. Very little mattered more to Nietzsche than the value of human life. Christianity, as he saw it, filled life on earth with guilt, fear, and suffering.

He thus spoke of religion as one of the most unfortunate things ever to have befallen mankind, and as anti-life as, well, Darkseid's Anti-Life Equation.[5] Christianity thus made humanity "sick" by imposing its doctrine as the only way to live one's life. People and cultures that have been affected by Christian belief systems, according to Nietzsche, cling to a weak and mindless herd or "slave" morality based on guilt, resentment, and false hope. In order to free people from this moral tyranny, Nietzsche thus urged a "revaluation of all values." But with the death of God and the collapse of traditional moral values, the "sick" man could be in serious danger of succumbing to *nihilism*, the view that life essentially has no meaning (which would prove Darkseid right after all).

Enter the *Übermensch*! In *Zarathustra*, the prophet proclaims that "all living beings have created something beyond themselves," and that man, too, is something that "shall be overcome."[6] To the *Übermensch*, who is as different from man as man is from ape, man is "a laughing stock," a "painful embarrassment." Nietzsche sees mankind as but a "rope over an abyss." We are not an end unto ourselves, but just another bridge to be crossed on the road to the *Übermensch*. Placing himself "beyond good and evil," the *Übermensch* "breaks tablets and old values" and afterwards "writes new values on new tablets," thereby threatening both the ways of the bad and the good, who call him "lawbreaker" in return.[7] Furthermore, the life-affirming *Übermensch* lives in the here and now, independent from any higher being or promise of an otherworldly life, hereby giving "meaning to the earth." He understands the suffering that comes with this earthly existence and welcomes the "eternal recurrence of the same" (another important Nietzschean theme) as the ultimate affirmation of life![8]

Putting the *Über* into the *Übermensch*

To overcome the moral void of nihilism, the *Übermensch*, who is able to look into the abyss of meaninglessness without flinching, is positioned as an independent creator of new myths and entirely new values. These values must be without foundations, since they cannot be based on any pre-existing cultural, religious, or metaphysical conditions. But to create new values without foundations, as Nietzsche proposes here, seems like a near impossible task (or perhaps, a job for Superman). However, Nietzsche does imply that, before one can create new values, one must first create oneself. Overcoming nihilism therefore becomes a part of *self-overcoming*, of mastering one's deepest desires and emotions and creating a strong, harmonious, independent, and wholesome identity in the process.

This all-important creativity stems from another important aspect of Nietzsche's philosophy: *the will to power*. Nietzsche conceived the will to power as a response to "the will to live," proposed by another esteemed German philosopher, Arthur Schopenhauer (1788–1860), who influenced Nietzsche's early writings. Schopenhauer claimed that the will to live, which leads us to procreate and to avoid death, is the primordial driving force of every living thing in existence.[9] Nietzsche, however, responded that even the strongest creatures will risk their lives for more power. Thus, for Nietzsche, the will to power stands as "the unexhausted, procreative will of life."[10] As Nietzsche further describes the will to power,

> My idea is that every specific body strives to become master over all space and to extend its force (its will to power) and to thrust back all that resists its extension. But it continually encounters similar efforts on the part of other bodies and ends by coming to an arrangement ("union") with those of them that are sufficiently related to it: thus they then conspire together for power. And the process goes on ...[11]

Nietzsche's concept should not merely be understood as asserting power over others, but rather asserting power over oneself. The will to power is the fundamental driving force behind our self-mastery and self-creation, two important steps on the road toward becoming an *Übermensch* and a creator of new values.

Nietzsche describes the *Übermensch* as a heroic figure, the end goal for humanity. But others have interpreted Nietzsche in dark, self-serving ways. Adolf Hitler, for example, tragically abused Nietzsche's philosophy to justify his racist propaganda and his goals of creating a master Aryan race of superior *Übermenschen* through selective genetic breeding.[12] Nietzsche himself, though, made no connection between the *Übermensch* and race or genetics. Instead, the

Übermensch is a figure who becomes possible after the death of God. If and when this revolutionary figure should arrive, however, will we welcome it as a noble, inspiring, and elevating superhero, or rather as an amoral, dominating, and unimaginable supervillain? As always, our very own modern-day mythologies can provide the answer. First, though, let us see what the ultimate superhero has in common with the Nietzschean *Übermensch*.

The Nietzschean Superman

Most people find it is easy to dismiss the possibility of the Man of Steel as a Nietzschean *Übermensch* with a cape. I too found the world's premier superhero and the philosopher's concept an odd match at first. How could Superman represent the end goal for humanity if he's not even human in the first place? We all know the story, brilliantly formulated in the first pages of *All-Star Superman* #1 (January 2006) as a simple equation: "Doomed planet + Desperate Scientists + Last Hope + Kindly Couple = Superman." The details of the myth have changed several times throughout the years, but the core concept remains the same: Superman is not from this Earth and is constantly reminded of that fact. Likewise, no matter how hard we try, none of us can ever be Superman. Although Nietzsche said that there has yet to be an *Übermensch* in the history of mankind, he did suggest that the goal was attainable for human beings. It does not require a "strange visitor from another planet."

While the *Übermensch* has often been interpreted solely in Darwinian terms as the next step in human evolution, Nietzsche's concept should be understood as a moral concept and not a physical one. For Superman, it's his Kryptonian physiology that makes him super and distinctly non-human. On a moral level, however, Superman, both as the Man of Steel and as his alter ego Clark Kent, is as human as they come. He may even be a bit too human, as his friend and Justice League teammate Batman says: "It is a remarkable dichotomy. In many ways, Clark is the most human of us all. Then … he shoots fire from the skies and it is difficult not to think of him as a god. And how fortunate we all are that it does not occur to *him*."[13] Later, during the massive *Infinite Crisis* crossover, which temporarily saw DC's "Trinity" of Superman, Batman, and Wonder Woman at odds, the

Dark Knight accuses his friend of perhaps relating to humanity too much, thereby failing to provide the strong, confident, and inspirational leadership their fellow superheroes need.[14]

In any case, we can agree that, rather than his powers, it's primarily Superman's human side, forged and strengthened by his strong morals and Midwestern upbringing on a Smallville farm by Jonathan and Martha Kent, that makes him a hero. As Gary Engle states: "Superman's powers make the hero capable of saving humanity; Kent's total immersion in the American heartland make him want to do it."[15] In a recent two-page origin story, among Superman's impressive arsenal of powers and abilities, his greatest weapon is defined as "his honest, unwavering (and thus very much human!) heart."[16] If, as Nietzsche claims, the seeds of the *Übermensch* lie in mankind's potential for creativity, overcoming both the self and the moral void, and creating new moral values in their place, Superman is as good a candidate for the concept as anyone.

Superman vs. Clark Kent

Much has been made about which identity is the more authentic one, and which one is the disguise.[17] The truth is that they're equally important and very much constructed parts of his character. The real person, whether we call him Kal-El, Clark, or Superman, is the one who journeyed from Krypton to Earth, was raised on a Smallville farm, developed superpowers under a yellow sun, and later in life combined all his talents and facets of his personality into one harmonious whole. His two "identities" are really nothing more than roles he plays in life, just like the roles each of us plays every day. Yes, Clark Kent, especially the bumbling, meek version portrayed in the movies by the late Christopher Reeve, is a performance, but so is the seemingly invincible Superman, and neither can claim to be "more real" than the other.[18] In constructing his two main "performances," Superman (or Kal-El, or Clark) shows remarkable creativity, which Nietzsche considered an important part of his *Übermensch*.

Superman's self-mastery and ability to overcome tragedy put him firmly on the road toward becoming an *Übermensch*. While some may say that Superman has it easy compared to other superheroes—after all, he did grow up in a safe, stable family environment with almost godlike abilities—a further reading into the myth reveals that this is not so. Sure, Batman lost both his parents as a young boy and spent the rest of his youth training to become a superhero—but Superman lost his whole planet![19] He is (at least initially) the sole survivor of an entire civilization and therefore probably more alone in this world than anyone. Furthermore, his incredible superpowers developed over time, and he had to learn and master each one of them, and with the utmost self-restraint, since he can never truly lose control as long as he lives in our "world of cardboard."[20] Finally, Superman faced more than his share of tragedy and loss throughout his life, including the deaths of loved ones (the Kents, in many story-lines), the destruction of "New Krypton" and the loss of nearly 100,000 fellow Kryptonians, and even the end of existence in *Final Crisis* (an almost literal interpretation of Nietzsche's moral void or meaningless abyss of nihilism).[21] Yet, every time, Superman overcomes and perseveres as a beacon of hope, even if he occasionally succumbs to depression in the meantime—just one indication of his underlying humanity.[22]

S Is for Savior

Like Nietzsche's *Übermensch*, Superman is strong, creative, noble, independent, and life-affirming, but unlike him, Superman is compassionate and looks out for the little guy. In his very first appearances from the Golden Age of Comics in the 1930s, and in the first arc of the relaunched *Action Comics* (part of DC's "The New 52" that began in September 2011), Superman is portrayed as a social crusader and defender of the weak and oppressed. This Man of Steel is a bit more morally ambiguous and more proactive toward tackling social problems and exposing Metropolis's corrupt elite. He beats down "bullies," if you will, by becoming an even bigger one. In one of his first appearances in the relaunched DC Universe, he declares, "You know the deal Metropolis. Treat people right or expect a visit from me."[23] In these early appearances, Superman is often met with fear and hostility by those in power, which is another characteristic of Nietzsche's *Übermensch*, who challenges the status quo and is called a "lawbreaker" by both the unjust and the just.

Although this early Superman operated outside the law, his moral compass was still very much in tune with the values and ideals he was raised with (and which form the basis of most laws anyway). As a reporter, he always puts the ideal of truth first, and as a superhero, his mission is to ensure that justice is served to wrongdoers. This Superman may be called a "lawbreaker," but he nevertheless stays true to mainstream ideals and values. Rather than being a creator of new moral values, like Nietzsche's *Übermensch*, he reinforces old ones and essentially adheres to the morality created by "lesser" men. But as Superman moved into the Silver Age of Comics, his powers increased exponentially, and so did his love for humanity and adherence to truth, justice, and the American way. The social crusader of old was being domesticated, becoming a law-abiding defender of the status quo or, as some tend to call him, "a Big Blue Boy Scout." The cultural assimilation of the ultimate immigrant from beyond the stars was nearly complete. Gary Engle writes that "*Superman* raises the American immigrant experience to the level of religious myth," becoming a "patron saint" of America in the process.[24]

Speaking of saints, the religious subtext of the Superman myth has never been far from the surface. As has often been pointed out, Superman's creators both came from Jewish backgrounds, *El* is short for the Hebrew word for God, and his origin story certainly parallels that of Moses. In the first two Superman movies, the messianic theme is made explicit when Jor-El, a "heavenly father" from beyond the stars, sends his only son to Earth where he can serve as the light to show mankind the way to greatness. The interpretation of Superman as a redeeming and compassionate angel in a cape, or, as Grant Morrison called him, "American Christ,"[25] was continued throughout the film *Superman Returns* (2006) and, to a lesser extent, the *Smallville* television series (2001–2011).[26] As a result, this religious interpretation of Superman is likely the version of the character that non-comic book readers are most familiar with.[27]

In the portrayals of Superman as an otherworldly Christ-like savior, a beacon of hope and faith, or, as iconic comics writer Alan Moore called him, "a perfect man who came from the sky and did only good," great emphasis is placed on his compassion and willingness to suffer for humanity, which Nietzsche would see as a vice.[28] While this perhaps led to several of Superman's less strong and proud moments (the infamous "gay-bashing" scene from *Superman Returns* comes to mind), the Man of Steel's enormous affinity for his adopted planet and its inhabitants remains necessary to counterbalance the darker, corrupting effects that his more *Übermenschian* characteristics might lead to. But does this mean that Nietzsche's superior man is destined to life as a supervillain?

Kneel Before Zod!

In a story from the late 1980s, the Man of Steel visits the remains of his home planet. Exposed to massive amounts of lethal kryptonite radiation, he experiences a sort of fever dream, where a different account of his origin is given. Here, instead of just one small rocket ship, a whole fleet of Kryptonians—including his parents Jor-El and Lara—escape the destruction of their home planet, set course for Earth, and develop powers under its yellow sun. Eventually, they use their powers to reshape and conquer the planet, with Jor-El becoming this world's rebel "Superman" in defense of humanity. Seeing this experience as a "morality play" and a "lesson in human nature [and] the harsh truths of the abuse of power," Superman concludes that "a race of supermen cannot help but be a race of conquerors, even if they begin with the best intentions," and finally that "being a man is always more important than being a superman."[29]

Knowing this, Superman was perhaps a bit too trustworthy when he freed 100,000 Kryptonians from their confines in the bottled city of Kandor, which had been shrunken and stored in the ship of the intergalactic supervillain Brainiac before Krypton exploded.[30] The newly freed Kryptonians, including Kal-El's uncle Zor-El and aunt Alura (the parents of Supergirl), each develop similar abilities to Superman, but lack the moral upbringing he received from Ma and Pa Kent, or even the guidance he himself gave to Supergirl and Superboy.

In recent depictions of Superman's origin, much emphasis is placed on his struggle to earn the world's trust. He is, after all, one of mankind's first encounters with extraterrestrial life. Not only is he an alien, he's an alien with almost godlike abilities. And the only assurance we have that he'll use these powers for the betterment of mankind, as his mortal enemy Lex Luthor states, "is his word."[31] Imagine then, that suddenly there appear not one or two, but 100,000 beings on Earth with the same powers and abilities. Even though Superman

tried to establish a stable working relationship between his two
worlds, the fearful tensions of both civilizations reached a fever pitch
(helped by Luthor and Lois's father, General Sam Lane), and it all fell
apart. Eventually, Kandor was relocated to a planet on the other side
of the sun from Earth and rechristened New Krypton, but tensions
remained and eventually an all-out "War of the Supermen" broke out.

A central figure in this was General Zod, now a military leader on
New Krypton who was once imprisoned in the Phantom Zone by
Jor-El himself, and who offers a frightening take on a supervillain in
the Nietzschean mold. Just as the *Übermensch* is characterized as a
superior form of humanity looking down on the primitive, animalistic
man, General Zod describes humans as "Sub-Kryptonians": fragile
and inferior little creatures on a backwater planet (or, to use the words
of Nietzsche himself: "laughing stocks" and "painful embarrass-
ments").[32] In *Superman II* (1981) Zod defines Superman's care of
humanity as his principal weakness, and Ursa, a fellow Kryptonian
criminal (and Zod's wife in the comics), compares it to taking care of
"pets." But, for all his proclaimed superiority and his apparent shift to
becoming a heroic leader throughout the *New Krypton* saga, Zod
falls prey to a base human emotion: the need for revenge on Jor-El (or,
in this case, his heirs). Resentment and the need for revenge are
all-too-human shortcomings that Nietzsche condemns, and so General
Zod falls far short of being a true Nietzschean *Übermensch*.

Perhaps ... Lex Luthor?

Superman's fiercest arch-nemesis seems like a worthy contender for the
title of *Übermensch*. Luthor has no superpowers, but is a human being
who sets out to improve and re-create himself again and again. Following
his tremendous will to power, he seems as if he can accomplish anything
he sets his mind to, yet still strives to be better and gain even more
power. Throughout his life, Luthor's morally questionable actions show
that he certainly places himself "beyond good and evil." If Nietzsche
were to read Luthor's life story, he might proclaim that the age of the
Übermensch has truly arrived. A greedy, self-affirming man with an ego
the size of Rao would certainly create his own values and rise beyond
the all-too-human herd and their conceptions. The rise of Luthor in
Metropolis, where he's initially seen as a philanthropist and even a hero

by most people (save for some truth-seeking reporters for the *Daily Planet*), can be seen in this respect. Luthor becomes the most powerful man in Metropolis and might potentially even become the greatest man who ever lived—at least, until a certain alien swoops into town.

In the instant Luthor gets bumped to the number two spot in Metropolis everything changes: the expansion of his will to power and his personal self-creation comes to a halt. From this moment, Lex Luthor's every action is driven by his need to prove himself superior to Superman. Sure, he does gain more power from time to time—he even became president of the United States in 2001—but eventually his antagonism toward Superman, stemming from a wounded ego, gets the better of him.[33]

To his credit, Lex Luthor makes some interesting and potentially valid points about his archenemy, which could be interpreted as Nietzschean in nature. In Superman, Luthor sees a powerful alien invader, a myth made real, without any sense of real human emotion that signals the end for mankind's (read: his) personal growth. In the miniseries *Lex Luthor: Man of Steel* (2005) he expresses his feelings this way:

> All men are created equal. All men. You are not a man ... but they've made you their hero. They worship you. So tell me, what redemption do you offer them? Those red eyes. I'm sure they look right through me, like I am nothing more than a nuisance. But when I see you? I see something no man can ever be. I see the end. The end of our potential. The end of our achievements. The end of our dreams. You are my nightmare.[34]

After his passage, Luthor characterizes Superman as his own personal abyss, his own moral void of nihilism that he has to face and overcome for the good of mankind. In a later dinner conversation about Superman with Batman's alter ego Bruce Wayne, Luthor claims "I'm not interested in bringing him down ... but obsessed with bringing us up. All of us – everyone – deserve a chance at greatness. All that takes is the belief it exists. But his existence threatens not just that belief ... but our existence."[35]

Yet, for all Luthor's talk of elevating humanity to its true potential, he only cares about himself and his personal victory over Superman. When a dying Superman visits him in his cell in *All-Star Superman* #10, he challenges Luthor to deliver on his claims that, if it weren't for the existence of the Man of Steel, he would have elevated humanity (saving the world through his technology, curing cancer, and so forth) a long time ago. Luthor responds by spitting in Superman's face. In the conclusion of "The Black Ring" storyline in *Action Comics*, vol. 1, #900 (June 2011), Lex temporarily gains near-omnipotent powers and has the ability to establish peace and bliss throughout the universe (something even Superman could not do), if he would just give up his hatred for his mortal enemy. Naturally, Luthor tries to kill Superman, loses his newfound power, and is defeated. Finally, under the sway of Wonder Woman's truth-compelling lasso, he admits the truth: "I want to be Superman."[36] So we learn that Lex Luthor's "nobility" is just a ruse to justify his jealousy of the "alien invader" who, ironically, is more human than he'll ever be. Although Lex Luthor at first sight seems the closest approximation of Nietzsche's *Übermensch*, he nevertheless lacks the self-overcoming and original heroic ideal ingrained in the concept from the moment his own "never-ending battle" against Superman starts.

Nietzschean *Übermensch*, American Christ, or Both?

In his essay "The Real Truth about Superman: And the Rest of Us, Too," comics writer Mark Waid shines a new light on Superman's heroic selflessness. Driven by a "need to belong," Superman actually helps others "by acting in his own self-interest."[37] Superman does what he does, not for worship or power, nor out of fear, dominance, or pity, but simply because he chooses to do so as the fulfillment of the destiny he carved for himself—in other words, Nietzsche's will to power. Furthermore, while he certainly doesn't transcend society's values, create new ones, or live "beyond good and evil," he does create new myths for others to follow. After all, as the first and possibly still greatest superhero, Superman is not only a leading moral exemplar for humanity, but for other superheroes as well. While we can never truly be Superman, nor should we believe in him so much it turns to worship, we can strive to be more *like him*.

Unlike some religious figures, Superman isn't weighed down by his humanity nor is it presented as some sort of curse. Instead, he embraces it and thereby gains his greatest strength. Although he can show great compassion, and will always be around to "catch us if we fall," he does allow "mankind to climb to their own destiny" because of his unwavering belief in humanity's potential for the future.[38] In these respects, Superman can certainly be seen as giving "meaning to the earth." Waid probably said it best in his introduction to the collected *All-Star Superman* series: "Gods achieve their power by encouraging us to believe in them. Superman achieves his power by believing in us."[39] I think even Friedrich Nietzsche would agree to that.

Notes

1. Although the German word *Übermensch* was initially translated into the English language as "superman," there really is no universally accepted translation of the term. Other translations include "overman" or "overhuman," but to avoid confusion with the character Superman (and Overman, his Nazi counterpart from Earth-10), I shall leave the term in its original language.

2. My interpretation of Nietzsche's philosophy is heavily indebted to that of American philosopher Richard Schacht; see his chapter on Nietzsche in *The Blackwell Guide to Modern Philosophers*, ed. Steven M. Emmanuel (Malden, MA: Blackwell, 2001), 390–411.

3. Grant Morrison, *Supergods: What Masked Vigilantes, Miraculous Mutants, and a Sun God from Smallville Can Teach Us About Being Human* (New York: Spiegel & Grau, 2011).

4. *Thus Spoke Zarathustra* was written and published in several parts between 1883 and 1885, before finally being published in complete form in 1892. In this work, Nietzsche makes clever use of several aphorisms and lyrical prose to get his philosophical points across. The structure and writing style of the work very much—and quite ironically—resemble that of the Bible.

5. Nietzsche described his views on Judeo-Christian morality in *On the Genealogy of Morals* (1887), and later wrote a much heavier attack on Christianity in *The Antichrist*, originally published in 1895. Nietzsche's negative views on Christianity found a metaphor in the DC Universe with the Anti-Life Equation, a concept introduced in Jack Kirby's Fourth World saga, a mathematical equation that has the ability to completely take over one's mind and free will. In its first appearance in *Forever People* #5 (November, 1971), it is said that "if someone possesses absolute control over you—you're not really alive," paralleling Nietzsche's views on Christianity. One of Superman's deadliest enemies, Darkseid,

sought to obtain and harness the Anti-Life Equation, and finally did so in *Final Crisis* (2008–2009). I would write the full formula down here, but ... well, you know ...

6. *Thus Spoke Zarathustra*, available in *The Portable Nietzsche*, trans. Walter Kauffman (New York: Viking Penguin, 1968), 124–128. (Unless otherwise noted, all descriptions of the *Übermensch* presented here are taken from this version.)

7. *Thus Spoke Zarathustra*, 324–325. Incidentally, *Beyond Good and Evil* is the title of another work by Nietzsche, published in 1886.

8. Along with the *Übermensch*, the concept of "the eternal recurrence" is primarily discussed in *Zarathustra* but has also seen its interpretation differ throughout the years, from the historical to the cosmological. For our purposes here, the *Übermensch*'s acceptance of the eternal repetition of one's life, down to every last detail, over and over again, can be seen as the ultimate affirming of his love for his earthly existence and a celebration of life itself.

9. For more on Arthur Schopenhauer's will to live, see his seminal work *The World as Will and Representation*, first published in 1818.

10. *Thus Spoke Zarathustra*, 226. Again, as with the *Übermensch* and eternal recurrence, the will to power has known many interpretations over the years.

11. See Friedrich Nietzsche, *The Will to Power*, trans. Walter Kauffman (New York: Vintage, 1968). While not a finished work by Nietzsche, this collection includes several of the philosopher's unpublished notes.

12. Although Nietzsche's writings were rather easily transformed into Nazi propaganda—with more than a little help from his sister and keeper of his archives, Elisabeth Förster-Nietzsche (1846–1935)—the philosopher himself was firmly against all proto-fascist and Nazi thought. For more on Hitler and Nietzsche, see chapter 10 by Barkman in this volume.

13. *Superman/Batman* #3 (December 2003), reprinted in *Superman/Batman: Public Enemies* (2004).

14. *Infinite Crisis* #1 (December 2005), reprinted in *Infinite Crisis* (2008).

15. See Gary Engle, "What Makes Superman So Darned American?" in *Superman at Fifty: The Persistence of a Legend*, ed. Dennis Dooley and Gary D. Engle (Cleveland: Octavia, 1987), 79–87.

16. See "The Origin of Superman" in *DC Universe: Origins* (2010).

17. Early Superman stories placed Clark Kent as the disguise and Superman as the "real" personality. After the *Crisis on Infinite Earths* rebooted DC's continuity in 1985–1986, *The Man of Steel* miniseries reversed the Superman/Clark Kent dichotomy, showing a more confident, assertive, and not so mild-mannered reporter. Later retellings of Superman's

origin, including *Superman: Birthright* (2003), *Superman: Secret Origin* (2009–2010) and the re-launched *Action Comics*, vol. 2 (2011–), combine story and personality traits from both interpretations. For more on Superman and identity, see chapter 18 by Michaud in this volume.

18. But not a parody of humanity, nor as an explicit statement of the way Superman "sees us," as Bill, played by actor David Carradine, seems to believe in Quentin Tarantino's movie *Kill Bill, Volume 2* (2004).

19. For a strong argument for Batman, rather than Superman, as the true superhero descendant of Nietzsche's *Übermensch*, see C.K. Robertson's "The True *Übermensch*: Batman as Humanistic Myth," in *The Gospel According to Superheroes: Religion and Popular Culture*, ed. B.J. Oropeza (New York: Peter Lang, 2005), 49–65.

20. See Superman's speech about "cutting loose" in a fight against Darkseid in the final *Justice League Unlimited* episode (season 3, episode 13).

21. The two year-long *New Krypton* story-arc played out in pretty much all Superman-related titles from December, 2008, until May, 2010. Superman stared down non-existence in *Final Crisis* #7 (March 2009), reprinted in *Final Crisis* (2010).

22. See the storyline "Grounded" in *Superman* #700–714 (2010–2011), collected in *Superman: Grounded Vol. 1* and *Vol. 2* (2011); for more on this storyline, see chapter 1 by White in this volume.

23. *Action Comics*, vol. 2, #1 (November 2011).

24. Engle, "What Makes Superman So Darned American?", 86.

25. From an interview in *Wizard* #143 (August 2003).

26. Ironically, in *Smallville*, many references are also made to Friedrich Nietzsche's writings. Concepts like the *Übermensch* and the will to power are mentioned briefly throughout the course of the series, and an original copy of *Beyond Good and Evil* may be found within Lionel Luthor's safe.

27. For an overview of the cultural evolution of Superman and the "superman" character archetype in fiction, see Thomas Andrae, "From Menace to Messiah: The History and Historicity of Superman," in *American Media and Mass Culture: Left Perspectives*, ed. Donald Lazere (Berkeley: University of California Press, 1987), 125–138. For more on Superman as a messianic figure in particular, see Ken Schenk's chapter "Superman: A Popular Culture Messiah," in Oropeza, *The Gospel According to Superheroes*, 33–48, and chapter 10 by Barkman in this volume.

28. See Moore's classic tale, "Whatever Happened to the Man of Tomorrow?", originally published in *Superman*, vol. 1, #423 (September 1986) and *Action Comics*, vol. 1, #583 (September, 1986) and reprinted in *Superman: Whatever Happened to the Man of Tomorrow?* (2010).

Interestingly, starting from 2003's *Superman: Birthright*, Superman's famous S-shield doesn't just stand for the House of El, but is the Kryptonian symbol for "hope."

29. "Return to Krypton," in *Superman*, vol. 2, #18 (June 1988), reprinted in *Superman: The Greatest Stories Ever Told, Vol. 1* (2004).

30. See *Action Comics*, vol. 1, #866–870 (August–December 2008), reprinted in *Superman: Brainiac* (2009), which led to the *New Krypton* event.

31. *Lex Luthor: Man of Steel* #3 (July 2005), reprinted in *Luthor* (2010). This storyline is extensively discussed in chapter 11 by Donovan and Richardson in this volume.

32. *Action Comics*, vol. 1, #846 (February 2007), reprinted in *Superman: Last Son* (2010).

33. This, of course, is the more well-known modern depiction of Lex Luthor and his struggle with Superman for the heart of Metropolis. In his original more simplistic Silver Age origin story, his hatred of Superman (when he was just Superboy) stems from the childhood accident which blew up his laboratory and caused him the loss of a protoplasmic life form and his hair. This, for him, is enough to swear revenge on Superboy for all eternity. See *Adventure Comics* #271 (April 1960).

34. *Lex Luthor: Man of Steel* #1 (May 2005), reprinted in *Luthor*.

35. *Lex Luthor: Man of Steel* #3.

36. *Blackest Night* #7 (February 2010), reprinted in *Blackest Night* (2011).

37. See Mark Waid, "The Real Truth about Superman: And the Rest of Us Too," in *Superheroes and Philosophy: Truth, Justice, and the Socratic Way*, ed. Tom Morris and Matt Morris (Chicago: Open Court, 2005), 3–10.

38. See *JLA* #4 (April 1997), reprinted in *JLA: New World Order* (1997).

39. From his introduction to *All-Star Superman, Volume 2* (2009).

Chapter 9

Superman or Last Man
The Ethics of Superpower

David Gadon

Let's be honest, if it weren't for Superman, Lois Lane would have bit the dust long ago. Her fierce ambition for journalistic success has attracted the attention of the Grim Reaper so many times, one begins to wonder if maybe fate is trying to tell her something. Nevertheless, Superman is always there to pluck her faltering helicopter from the sky; Superman is always ready to deflect the bullet for her; Superman is always on hand precisely when he is needed. And why shouldn't he be? It's no great effort on his part to save her from the many calamities that she always seems inclined to seek out, and saving a human life is an inherently good deed, right?

On an individual level, it's hard to see anything wrong with the deeds Superman performs on a daily basis. Lois, alongside the countless thousands of would-be victims that Superman has rescued, would surely call this issue a no-brainer. They're happy to be alive and rightly so. But what about the impact that Superman's presence would have, if he existed in the real world, on society as a whole? Would the presence of this powerful, interstellar immigrant make our planet stronger or weaker in the long run? To put it most simply, would the Man of Steel really be good for us at all?

Superman and Philosophy: What Would the Man of Steel Do?, First Edition. Edited by Mark D. White.
© 2013 John Wiley & Sons, Inc. Published 2013 by John Wiley & Sons, Inc.

Survival of the Weakest

If you're a die-hard fan of the Big Blue Boy Scout, as I am, your knee-jerk reaction to this question is probably along the lines of, "of course he's good for us! Superman has nearly god-like powers but chooses to use them to save lives and help people, instead of simply helping himself. What could be a better, nobler use of such power?" But in philosophy we can't rely on simple knee-jerk reactions. What we're really asking is whether or not Superman *should* act the way he does, regardless of how his actions might make us feel in the short-term. Only by deciding that his behavior matches what one in his position *ought* to do can we decide that Superman is morally praiseworthy, and not all thinkers would look upon Superman as beneficial to humanity.

The German philosopher Friedrich Nietzsche (1844–1900), for instance, would have found Superman's actions very problematic indeed. In his richly challenging story *Thus Spoke Zarathustra*, Nietzsche outlines two possible end results for humanity—one that leads to the praiseworthy *Übermensch* or overman (sometimes translated as "superman") and one that leads to the reprehensible last man.[1]

For Nietzsche, mankind is an unfinished journey with one clear beginning and at least two possible ends. *Zarathustra* uses the metaphor of the tightrope walker struggling to reach the other side of a wide chasm.[2] At his back are the beasts from which mankind evolved, and at the opposite end of the rope is his final goal, the overman, the next stage in human progress, and that which provides meaning to the whole of human existence.[3] If man fails to cross this chasm, he slips into the meaningless existence of the last man who no longer cares about self-improvement and no longer even remembers the feeling of accomplishment. The last man is completely comfortable and content, wanting for nothing and striving for less. The last man sees that nothing he does ever matters and so stops trying to do anything at all. If we reach this despicable state, Nietzsche argues that we as a people will never strive to improve ourselves, never lift ourselves up to the heights of our fullest potential, and never again practice true creativity.

What does this have to do with Superman? Well, let's take a look back on the beginnings of Superman's career as a hero. In *The Man of*

Steel, John Byrne's 1986 relaunch of Superman's origin, we find a young Clark Kent single-handedly delivering his high school football team an easy victory, leaving his teammates disheartened and idle as they warm the bench.[4] Sure, they're pleased enough to have won the last game of the season, but it wasn't exactly the team that won: it was Clark. This realization leads Pa Kent to pull Clark aside and explain to him—for the first time—his extraterrestrial origins, as well as the responsibility that his superpowers bring with them. Realizing the negative side-effects of his powers, Clark decides to keep his entire heroic existence a secret, so that those he is helping (like his football teammates) won't come to feel useless and disheartened. With the help of his super-speed, Clark then spends his first three years of superheroism moving unseen, allowing those he saves to attribute their survival to simple good fortune.

Introducing Superman–Whether We Need Him or Not

This all changes when Clark witnesses the experimental space-plane begin to break apart in the skies over Metropolis. In plain view of everyone, he is forced to reveal his existence to the world, lest those astronauts (and Lois, of course) perish in the blast. Superman, thus outed, seems to cast aside his earlier secrecy by openly thwarting a series of petty crimes, such as a purse-snatching and a liquor store heist. While the space-plane rescue seems like the perfect job for Superman, it should be quite clear that these later thwarted crimes are incidents that we humans are capable of handling—with varying degrees of success—on our own.

This overreaching heroism is mirrored in *Superman: The Movie* (1978) when Lois's helicopter crashes, forcing Superman into the open to intervene in human affairs (something he was explicitly forbidden to do by his Kryptonian father Jor-El). He then spends the rest of the evening thwarting jewel thieves and bank robbers, conflicts that we as humans could fully address if we really wanted to. We're all pleased that these crimes have been resolved and catastrophes averted, of course. But by intervening in these minor conflicts, Superman is essentially turning the whole of humanity into a team of football players sitting on a bench.

Nietzsche would argue that people need conflict in order to be the best we can, so we can struggle and thereby cultivate creativity and power. We need a goal to strive toward, and the overman, a symbol of the greatest heights to which humanity can soar, is just that goal. By handling our struggles for us, Superman serves to deflate our motivation to strive toward the overman by squashing the conflict for us. Furthermore, compared to Superman, all men and women appear equal, like ants to a normal human.

Nietzsche's work, however, hinges on the idea that all men are inherently *unequal.*[5] Though we may be equal before the law or before God, if there is no God then the small differences among us become magnified. We must have conflict and difficulty in order for those who arc strongest and best to rise above the rest and lead the way, setting their own strength and power forward as an example to all others.

But isn't this what Superman is doing when he sets himself up as an example for us to follow, inspiring us to be better and "rise" above others? Despite his best intentions, the answer has to be no. Superman can't be a goal for the average man simply because he is so extremely un-average. No matter how hard people try, they will never possess the powers that come from Kryptonian DNA and the ability to draw nourishing energy from the yellow sun (other than Vitamin D). No matter how good Superman's deeds may be, they cannot help but take away mere humans' desire to fix things for themselves. The overman, on the other hand, shows just how powerful a "mere" human can be and encourages weaker humans to strive to overcome conflicts, just as the overman has.

Waiting for Superman

At the end of Geoff Johns and Richard Donner's storyline "Last Son" in *Action Comics,* there is an exchange between Superman and Lex Luthor that offers the perfect example of what Nietzsche himself might say on this matter.[6] In the story, General Zod has broken free from the Phantom Zone and brought an army of Kryptonian criminals with him. In little time, Metropolis is on its knees, crushed beneath the strength of the invading alien force. Realizing that only one man will have the know-how and technology to take down so many Kryptonians, Superman seeks out his arch-nemesis for help.

Lex scolds Superman, telling him that Metropolis was so easily overthrown by Zod's army because the citizens have for so long been coddled into complacency by constant rescue from Superman. They were not simply physically overpowered, he argues, they were psychologically overpowered even before the first blow landed. Having had Superman around for so long, the people of Metropolis had grown weak; used to always being saved, they forgot how to save themselves. Lex then takes it upon himself to save humanity, grudgingly with Superman's help, but with the goal of showing the world the great heights mankind can reach all on its own. Ironically, this episode eloquently reveals how Lex Luthor better embodies the characteristics of the overman, while Superman's presence on Earth actually leads humanity down the dark path toward the idle contentment of the last man.

It's important to note that, before their planet exploded, Kryptonians were a powerful race of beings evolved far beyond humanity, both technologically and biologically. Also, Krypton never had a version of Superman flying about the planet eliminating major conflict with little to no effort. Indeed, Kryptonians fended for themselves just as we had done before Kal-El's appearance on Earth. Prior to Superman, humanity evolved and overcame incredible odds with ingenuity, technology, creativity, and courage, just as all species must. Isn't that whole process now stunted? Doesn't Superman's involvement defeat the need for humanity to ultimately push *itself* up, up, and away into the future?

Nietzsche would argue that Superman's constant rescuing of mankind from problems that we could tackle on our own might cultivate weakness in the rescued. That is, by overprotecting the planet Superman runs the risk of infantilizing the human race. After all, does an overprotected child ever learn to pick herself up after a fall, or will she forever be looking for her mother? Won't we all forever be simply waiting for Superman?

Resignation Superman

If we believe Nietzsche, we might now think that Superman should really just leave us alone, let us stand on our own two feet, and learn from mistakes and tragedies in order to better ourselves. But think of what that means. Picture a young Clark Kent leaving his new job at the *Daily Planet* just after being shot down for a date by his attractive co-worker, Lois Lane. Glancing up, he sees that Lois's helicopter is suddenly incapacitated at the ledge of the *Planet* rooftop with Lois herself dangling precariously by the seatbelt strap.[7] Are we really saying that Superman makes the *right* choice if he decides to merely shake his head, stroll on home, and watch the evening news over the rising steam of a microwave TV dinner? Sure, Superman might be morally culpable for the infantilizing of the human race that his involvement produces, but isn't he also morally responsible for what he *doesn't* do? If Lois falls to her death on the cold sidewalks of Metropolis, shouldn't we blame Superman for *not* intervening when he was so thoroughly capable of doing so?

This brings us to the work of contemporary moral philosopher Peter Singer. Singer espouses a form of moral philosophy known as *utilitarianism*, in which judgments of right and wrong depend upon how much an action promotes happiness and prevents suffering.[8] Using that foundation, Singer argues in his famous article "Famine, Affluence, and Morality" that one can be held morally blameworthy if one refuses to assist those in need when doing so will not result in the sacrifice of anything morally important.[9] In other words, as long as there is no great risk or harm to a person, he or she is morally *required* to assist those in need to the full extent of his or her ability.

Singer's argument was meant to urge citizens of developed countries like the United States and the United Kingdom to expand their efforts to lessen starvation and famine in developing countries. The wealth that these more advanced nations have accumulated is immense when compared to the resources of the third world. We cannot consider ourselves ethically just if we live comfortable lives in material excess while our fellow human beings suffer and die needlessly from mere want of food and medicine. Singer argues that donating as much money as we can reasonably afford to give is the only truly ethical action to take in the face of human suffering.

Although famine is the core example in his argument, Singer uses an analogy that can be easily applied to many kinds of suffering. He argues that, if I come across a child face-down in a foot-deep pool, I am morally required to rescue her. Though I may muddy my clothing when wading in to rescue the child, my soiled clothes are morally inconsequential compared to the greater moral good that is served when I save the child from drowning.[10]

Singer vs. Nietzsche

For Singer, it makes no difference if I am only one among many who could potentially save the child in his analogy. The individual in question is always deemed praise- or blameworthy on the basis of what she does, *not* on what other people do not do. So say there are ten other people near the shallow pool. We all see the child drowning, but no one else chooses to go in for a rescue. The fact that these people *could* save the child but are not doing so has absolutely no bearing on my responsibility to do so.

In this way, Singer might argue, contrary to Nietzsche, that just because humanity *should* and ideally would be able to solve the problems that it faces, given enough time and advancement, this cannot absolve Superman of moral reprehensibility if he chooses to be a passive bystander as Lois falls to her death. After all, Superman risks next to nothing in his intervention in human problems, and the gain to be had by those who call out for help in the night is immeasurably high.

Nonetheless, imagine Superman does nothing to save Lois. Maybe, just maybe, some firemen will heroically break through the top-floor window and snatch her from certain death just in time, thus proving the ingenuity, compassion, and power of the human race. Or perhaps she will fall to the street below, and her death will force the helicopter manufacturer to iron out the faults in its shoddy workmanship. Maybe this will inspire us to improve flight technology entirely, making Lois a regrettable sacrifice yet thereby proving the human desire to push our technology and creativity to the fullest. To Singer, none of these possibilities can absolve Superman from the fact that he could have intervened at no real moral cost to himself or others. These other potential outcomes of Lois's endangerment are like additional people standing at the edge of the pond. Maybe they'll jump in and save the child before I do, maybe not. Regardless, my ethical correctness is still determined by whether or not *I* did everything I could to save that child. Superman, likewise, can always be held accountable for what he doesn't do just as much as he can for what he does.

By Singer's measure, then, Superman is the moral equivalent of the wealthy post-industrial nation, while individual humans—suffering their own cruel fates on the streets of Metropolis—are the equivalent of the starving peoples of poorer, developing nations. So it seems clear that we cannot call Superman a moral person if he turns a blind eye to the sufferings of mankind, especially when little or no real effort on his part would alleviate that suffering entirely. But then again, if Superman fails to save Lois, it is out of a broader concern for the future well-being of humanity—might this do more to alleviate suffering of mankind in the long run than saving Lois now?

It Ain't Easy Being Blue

Great Caesar's ghost—what's Superman supposed to do, then? What seemed like a non-question, an ethical no-brainer, now seems a great deal more puzzling. Those broad blue shoulders will have to carry this massive ethical burden for the rest of their days, because every moment of every day, Superman is forced to choose when, if, and just how much he should interfere with the troubles that face humanity.

When speaking of pity, Nietzsche once quipped that if you have a friend in pain your obligation is to provide him a bed in which to take comfort, but you should also make sure this is the least comfortable bed possible, like a cot or a foldout sofa-bed with an uncomfortable metal bracing beneath a thin mattress.[11] The idea here is that we are right to recognize and help alleviate the suffering of others, but we should always remain keenly aware that the only meaningful improvement is self-improvement. As long as our friend is completely comfortable in bed, he will never feel the inner calling to rise up again.

Perhaps this kind of thinking should drive Superman's interaction with humanity, and in fact, in J. Michael Straczynski's re-imagining of our hero's origin in *Superman: Earth One* (2010), the Man of Steel attempts to adopt just such a stance. In a suspiciously timely interview with mild-mannered reporter Clark Kent, Superman reveals that he will only intervene with human crises when the situation is such that *only* Superman could succeed. It's a noble sentiment, but as we've seen it's almost impossible to draw the line between situations that humanity can solve on its own (even if it takes time and great sacrifice) and those situations when it truly is a job for Superman. Recall also that this declaration means that incidents of petty crime and natural disaster will fall outside of Superman's jurisdiction, as these are events that we can and have been able to handle in the past. Furthermore, even with this moral stance, just because there may be others at Singer's allegorical pond capable of saving the drowning child, Superman is still answerable for the blood that is shed whenever he fails to intervene if there was any reason to expect that he actually was the only one who could help. (Nor should we forget that our favorite journalist-in-distress Lois Lane wouldn't last a single day if Superman actually held fast to such a creed!) Indeed, though Superman's intentions are commendable here, we have seen quite clearly just how morally complicated the consequences of any such stance would be.

Is He Worth It?

So, would Superman be good for us? Well, if we want moral simplicity from life, then we're forced to answer that he is probably more trouble than he's worth. If he wasn't around, after all, we wouldn't have to make such a cynical analysis by wondering whether or not the good of a handful of human lives can be pitted against the whole of humanity's development. What we find ourselves wishing is that Superman possessed the clarity to somehow foresee the long-term results of his actions, but sadly, seeing into the future is not among the many amazing Kryptonian powers.

Indeed Superman is as fallible and imperfect as the humans he struggles to protect. As such, his presence in the world necessitates that he constantly walk a delicate ethical tightrope between compassion and overprotection. A misstep to one side and Superman becomes the catalyst to the Nietzschean last man; a misstep to the other, and he falls into the atrocious position of the complacent bystander. It's a tough thing to do, but it's a choice he is forced to make every day. After all, Superman didn't ask to be sent here, nor did he ask to have these remarkable powers. He's simply doing the best he can day by day, and perhaps, in the end, that's all any of us can do, whether we're Super or not.

Notes

1. Friedrich Nietzsche, *Thus Spoke Zarathustra: A Book for None and All,* trans. Walter Kaufmann (New York: Penguin, 1978), especially pages 12–19.
2. Nietzsche, *Thus Spoke Zarathustra,* 14.
3. Ibid., 60.
4. *The Man of Steel* #1 (1986), reprinted in *Superman: The Man of Steel Volume 1* (1991).
5. Nietzsche, *Thus Spoke Zarathustra,* 101.
6. *Action Comics Annual* #11 (2008), reprinted in *Superman: Last Son* (2008).
7. Which is precisely where we found her in *Superman: The Movie.*
8. For a more in-depth discussion of utilitarianism and this "moral calculus," see Jeremy Bentham, *An Introduction to the Principles of Morals and Legislation* (Buffalo: Prometheus Books, 1789/1988).
9. Peter Singer, "Famine, Affluence, and Morality," reprinted in *Exploring Ethics,* ed. Steven M. Cahn (Oxford: Oxford University Press, 2009), 226–238.
10. Ibid., 228. For more on Singer and the drowning child example, see chapter 14 by Anton in this volume.
11. Nietzsche, *Thus Spoke Zarathustra,* 90.

Chapter 10

Superman
From Anti-Christ to Christ-Type

Adam Barkman

Although the Roman poet Lucian was probably the first to speak of a "superman" or *hyperanthropos*, the term was popularized and entered the English language from the writings of the German philosopher Friedrich Nietzsche (1844–1900), who wrote about an *Übermensch*. For Nietzsche, this word was a positive one, meaning a man whose ethics were "beyond good and evil," who had the "courage" to reject traditional morality in order to forge his own unrestricted destiny. Most Jews and Christians, who believed in a universal moral law, reacted negatively to the Nietzschean concept of a superman.

But something happened that rehabilitated the word "superman"—not reviving the Nietzschean meaning of the word but instead the opposite, Judeo-Christian sense. That event was the advent of the DC Comics hero Superman, a character who, I will argue, was created intentionally to subvert Nietzsche's *Übermensch*. What resulted over time, however, was far more than the original authors dreamt of. The superman in the works of Nietzsche and the first *Super-Man* short story is a literal anti-Christ, but gradually, over the years, he became nothing less than the ultimate Christ figure.

Superman and Philosophy: What Would the Man of Steel Do?, First Edition. Edited by Mark D. White.
© 2013 John Wiley & Sons, Inc. Published 2013 by John Wiley & Sons, Inc.

Übermensch as Anti-Christ

Nietzsche argued that God does not exist and thus there is no objective moral law. While this may at first be terrifying news, it makes possible a new, superior type of man: the *Übermensch* or superman. Because Nietzsche believed living in any kind of illusion is bad, he thought the superman needs an unwavering desire to be free from the myth of objective morality (in particular, Judeo-Christian morality). Furthermore, accepting that people desire happiness but insisting that happiness actually means "power," Nietzsche thought the superman— no less than a lesser, normal man—would have a "will to power." But the superman would distinguish himself from the lesser man by desiring power in a way that is free from all moral and social constraints. He wouldn't worry about what others say is "good" or "bad" but would construct, with his own genius and creativity, his own norms in order to create a persona of his choosing. The superman would thus revile such "weak" virtues as pity and mercy, since they would distract the superman from his own goals of self-actualization.

The superman thrives on conflict and challenge, but not, as the Judeo-Christian tradition has maintained, on the challenge of helping the weak. The sense of power that the superman would get from helping the weak is dependent on conforming to society's arbitrary and illusory moral standards. As a result, to most of society the superman will be a kind of "anti-Christ"—not because his primary goal is to hurt and deceive others (as the weak see him) but rather because he hurts others "without thinking," as a byproduct of his self-creation. As Nietzsche scholar Walter Kaufmann put it, "the truly powerful are not concerned with others but act out of fullness and an overflow."[1] We can see, then, that Jesus is far from Nietzsche's superman; even though Christ suffered under challenge, he lacked clarity about the proper purpose of such striving.

Lex Luthor: Super-Man?

During World War I, especially in the United States and the United Kingdom, "Nietzsche began to be considered the apostle of German ruthlessness and barbarism ... During those war years, the 'superman' began to be associated with the German nation."[2] This feeling in

America was intensified during World War II with "the advent of Hitler and the Nazis' brazen adaption of Nietzsche."[3] Even though Nietzsche himself was neither a proponent of German nationalism nor a racist (he called himself an "anti-anti-Semite"[4]), many in the English-speaking world, especially Americans, tended to see him as the unofficial philosopher of the Nazi Party.

In 1933, while Hitler—fueled by a misunderstanding of Nietzsche's superman—started to dream of world domination, two American Jewish cartoonists named Jerry Siegel and Joe Shuster wrote a short story for *Science Fiction* #3 called "The Reign of the Super-Man." The use of the word "Super-Man" was a clear allusion to Nietzsche, though it depicted Nietzsche's superman as a bald megalomaniac bent on global conquest. You guessed it: Super-Man started out as a proto-Lex Luthor, and Lex Luthor was what Siegel and Shuster thought Nietzsche and Hitler were all about. Indeed, by making their Super-Man a villain, Siegel and Shuster clearly intended to subvert Nietzsche's concept.

This understanding only gets Nietzsche partially right, however. Even though Nietzsche's superman does crave power and is willing to sacrifice whatever it takes to achieve it, he craves power more for self-actualization and absolute freedom of will than for world domination (even if world domination could arguably be an expression or entailment of his true goals). Nietzsche's superman, in other words, is more nuanced than Hitler's version or Siegel and Shuster's early Super-Man, yet all three share the same hatred for Judeo-Christian morality, especially its promotion of pity, mercy, and self-sacrificial love.

Jesus Without the Christ

Five years after his debut, the Super-Man lost the hyphen and the lust for power, becoming Superman. In *Action Comics* #1 (June 1938), Siegel and Shuster reinvented Superman as nearly the opposite of their early, Nietzschean Super-Man. Rather than let a perfectly good word like "superman" be associated with the likes of Nietzsche and Hitler, they redeemed it, although it remained subversive. While still strong and determined like the Nietzschean ideal, this new Superman became a hero of the Judeo-Christian variety: he accepted the principles of the universal moral law, especially love for the weak.

Moreover, even if Siegel and Shuster based some of their new character on Moses—for instance, both were sent away from their parents only to become great heroes[5]—the parallels between Superman and a more famous Jew are much more striking.[6]

Jesus was, at least on the level of myth and morality, the figure behind the creation of Superman. Some of this was very intentional and explicit. For instance, in *Superman* #1 (Summer 1939), the Man of Steel's adoptive mother, Martha Kent, was originally named Mary, and his adoptive father, named in a later issue, is Jonathan Joseph Kent. Though this allusion would later become obscured by changing "Mary" to "Martha," it reappears in the debut episode of the television series *Smallville*, when Martha, reworking St. John's "not that we loved God but that He loved us,"[7] says of young Kal-El, "We didn't find him; he found us."[8]

However, some of the connections between Superman and Jesus were only loosely made. "Clark" is an Old English name meaning "cleric" or "priest," and "Kent" is a form of the Hebrew word *kana*, which, in its *k-n-t* form, appears in the Bible, meaning "I have found a son." Thus, "Clark Kent" means, roughly, "I have found a son, a priest," which may be an allusion to Jesus, who is called the True Priest. *Kana* can also be connected to the Greek word *krista* or our English word "Christ." Those who think this is a stretch—I did too, at first—should keep in mind that the word "Krypton" comes from the Greek word *kryptos* or "hidden," meaning that Superman's home planet was forever "hidden" from him due to its destruction.

Superman's real name was revealed later to be Kal-El, of the family El (his father, of course, was Jor-El). *El* is the Hebrew word meaning "(of) God," suggesting a strong connection, both mythically and morally, between God and Superman. Indeed, even when the Hebrew word *el* is explained (in the comics) to be actually a Kryptonian word, the divine connotations aren't completely lost. If the Kryptonian "El" means "child" and "Kal" means "star," then Kal-El is a "starchild" like Jesus, whose birth was heralded by the Star of Bethlehem.[9]

We should note, though, that the Hebrew *el* doesn't necessarily imply identity with God, but could simply suggest service to God and His righteousness (as in the helper angel Gabri*el*). Moreover, Superman was initially shown performing local acts of justice, such as stopping wife beaters and gangsters—often in a very rough, non-idealized way. This suggests that at this stage Superman was more like an angel, or

Jesus the healer and priest, than a cosmic Christ figure. Thus, though both Jesus's and Superman's local acts of healing and heroics should be seen as representative of their pure hearts and devotion to even the lowliest, such acts, at least by themselves, aren't the acts of a truly mythical hero.[10] Although a direct challenge to Nietzsche's ideal, Superman was starting on the road to being a full Christ figure when he was re-imagined in the 1930s.

Moral Illumination

A short while later two new elements were added to the Superman mythology that further distinguished him as a Christ-type. The first has to do with Superman's powers. Although Superman's powers were first said to be the result of advanced Kryptonian evolution, this story was revised later to make his powers due to the Earth's yellow sun (and the lesser gravity of Earth). This had nothing to do with the evolution vs. creationism debates of the time, but rather with substituting a poor myth for a more potent one. Superman's reliance on the yellow sun had nuances of Christ's reliance on God the Father, who is metaphorically, and cross-religiously, spoken of as the sun. Indeed, there aren't many better metaphors for Truth and Justice than the sun, which means that the Superman myth, here, takes a sharp turn upward toward a profound, irreducible, timeless fact about Reality. Plato, Carl Jung, Joseph Campbell and C.S. Lewis would all applaud.

The second new element deals with Superman's near-absolute code against killing. Usually his powers allow him to resolve dilemmas without killing, but occasionally he faces a tough moral dilemma. For example, after Superman executed some homicidal criminals from the Phantom Zone, he quickly repented, saying that because he had the strength not to kill them, he was wrong for doing so.[11] In the animated series *Justice League*, Superman has to choose whether to kill Mongul's henchman Prega or keep his chains on and be beaten to a pulp. Superman chooses to remain prisoner and be beaten until the fight is declared over, at which point he easily breaks the chains. When Prega asks why he didn't break the chains earlier, Superman quotes Jesus: "It's called 'turning the other cheek.'"[12]

Considered as a strict philosophical position, an absolute code against killing is hard to maintain, given the wide array of circumstances that have at least a chance of justifying killing. But Superman's inflexibility came to be seen, more generally, as a symbol of moral integrity, a sign that Superman is willing to do whatever he can to respect all his moral principles simultaneously rather than weigh one against another. Because of this, he became a kind of perfect moral ideal—as Christ was and is. It isn't his actual belief that killing is wrong that made him a Christ-type, but rather his unshakable moral convictions and refusal to compromise what he believes is right.

Superman's absolute devotion to the universal moral law and Judeo-Christian morality stands in stark contrast to Nietzsche's morality of power. Where Nietzsche sees sacrificial love as a weakness because it conforms to social standards, Superman sees sacrificial love as strength insofar as it conforms to the Highest Law. Consider, for example, the time when he offers up his very soul to the demon Satanus in exchange for the souls of the citizens of Metropolis.[13] Nietzsche's superman thinks himself brave for rejecting notions like pity, but ends up aligned with Lex Luthor, who, according to Superman, "doesn't have the *courage* to change."[14] Nietzsche might agree with *The Essential Superman Encyclopedia* when it says that "enemies preyed upon [Superman's] moral code, turning it into a weakness."[15] Love is only a weakness, however, if one thinks that true strength or happiness means, as Nietzsche would have it, caring only about oneself.

Trinitarian Movie Mythos

While the Superman comics during the 1950s, 1960s, and 1970s often had little in the way of mythical or moral *gravitas*, the first two Superman movies, *Superman: The Movie* (1978) and *Superman II* (1981), played important roles in furthering the Man of Tomorrow's role as a Christ-type. For instance, in *Superman: The Movie*, Jor-El is portrayed as a God-figure sending his only son to become the savior of a world. "Even though you've been raised as a human being, you're not one of them," he tells his son. "They can be great people, Kal-El, if they wish to be. They only lack the light to show the way. For this reason, above all, their capacity for good, I have sent them you, my only son."

The connections in the movie between Jesus and Superman don't stop there. Each was raised incognito on Earth, each began his mission at the age of 30, each tries (at least for a while) to hide his identity, each assumes self-imposed servitude—just to name a few.[16] In *Superman II*, when Jor-El restores Superman's powers (exhausting his own in the process), we are told that "the Kryptonian prophecy will at last be fulfilled: the son becomes the father and the father becomes the son." Superman embraces the vision of his father, and in turn his father fills his son with the power to achieve his vision. This is but one example of Trinitarian symbolism in the Superman myth.

In the 2006 movie *Superman Returns*, the Man of Steel becomes, in the words of its director Bryan Singer, "the Jesus Christ of Superheroes."[17] Parallels between Superman and Christ are everywhere, though several in particular are worth mentioning here. From high above the world, Superman tells a disenchanted Lois Lane, who denies hearing anything from up there, "I hear everything. You wrote that the world doesn't need a savior, but every day I hear people crying out for one." Later, Superman lands on a kryptonite-poisoned landmass, whereupon he is beaten, scourged, humiliated, and then stabbed in the manner of the impassioned Jesus. After that, he is pushed into the water—a typical symbol of passage to the underworld—only to emerge, revitalize (thanks to the sun), and then return to destroy the landmass. Finally, after heaving the landmass into space, Superman falls from the sky to Earth in a crucifixion position, flatlines in a hospital, and then returns from the dead.

The movies weren't the only places that these biblical parallels could be seen, of course; more recent comics and television series also showcased them. In the mini-series *Kingdom Come* (1996), showing a possible future of the DC Universe, Superman is depicted as departing the world of man—and taking hope with him—only to return in a "second coming" to restore justice and order. Indeed, in a follow-up story, the Man of Steel even asks the Reverend Norman McCay, "Couldn't you tell me how you see my journey fulfilling biblical prophecy? Could I be part of Revelation?"[18] In *Superman: For Tomorrow* (2004–2005), Superman's priest, friend, and pseudo-confessor, Father Daniel Leone, is transformed into the monster Pilate, who then opposes Superman the Christ-type.[19] In *Smallville*, Clark Kent is shown in a crucifix position in a cornfield, spoken of as a "savior," and would be pitted against Doomsday, a biblically-named villain representing the final enemy.[20]

The character of Doomsday was taken from an even earlier stage in Superman's history. In 1992, in an event that sold more than six million comics, DC Comics had Superman die at the hands of the monster Doomsday. Reminiscent of Michelangelo's *Pietà*, Lois (Mary) holds the dying Superman (Jesus) in her arms and says, "You stopped him. You saved us all!"[21] In keeping with the Christ story, which talks about countless anti-Christs rising in Jesus's absence, Superman's death makes room for a number of Superman-pretenders to claim his identity, some of whom committed evil in his good name. In the end, Superman comes back to life in time to defeat the worst of the pretenders and restore hope to the world once again.

Is Superman Christ or a Christ-Type?

Nowadays the Man of Tomorrow has become such a Christ-type that Superman literature, movies, and television shows regularly make allusions, both comical and serious, to Superman being a god. It's not surprising, then, that some people have confused Superman as a Christ-type with Superman as an idol, or even, in a strange twist, Superman as an anti-Christ. When *Superman: The Movie* first came out, Richard Donner, the director, said that he received numerous threats (presumably from devout Christians) for making connections between Superman and Jesus.[22] Christians may have been concerned— legitimately—that Superman was being represented as a secular *replacement* for Christ.[23] But they would not have been so concerned if they had looked at it as Superman living up to Christ's example; the more Superman becomes like Christ, the more Christ is revealed.

And Superman himself agrees. While Gog says, "worship me," and Lex Luthor asserts, "they will worship me as a god,"[24] Superman constantly denies his "godness," breaking up cults dedicated to his worship, wrestling with his own inner demons (in *Superman* #666, no less), and stating plainly: "I'm not God ... I'm just a man."[25] Indeed, Superman would even agree with Nietzsche that people shouldn't put "blind faith" in him because it weakens individual dignity and resolve.[26] Perhaps the right balance between seeing Superman as a Christ-type that enables, rather than a god-tyrant that stifles, is in *Superman: Peace on Earth* (1998), which powerfully depicts Superman side-by-side with the Christ the Redeemer statue in Rio de Janeiro. The book makes it clear that Superman's mission is not to usurp Christ but to be a Christ-like inspiration to people, saying of world hunger that "it's not my place to dictate policy for humankind. But perhaps the sight of me fighting hunger on a global scale would inspire others to take action in their own way."

Seduction of the Innocent?

In 1954, Fredric Wertham's *The Seduction of the Innocent: The Influence of Comic Books on Today's Youth* argued that comic books and superheroes are unhealthy and dangerous (and resulted in the industry establishing the Comics Code Authority to regulate its own content). In his own way, Nietzsche would agree with Wertham: since he thought Judeo-Christian morality was toxic, and since comic books, especially Superman comics, are permeated with this morality, superhero comics would be toxic and dangerous as well. But it was this negative attitude toward Judeo-Christian morality that prompted such a strong response from Jerry Siegel and Joe Shuster, who set out to subvert Nietzsche's anti-Christ superman, by making Super-Man a villain and then a Judeo-Christian hero of the first order. Could they have imagined where creators would take Superman over the next 75 years? God only knows …

Notes

1. Walter Kaufmann, *Nietzsche: Philosopher, Psychologist, Antichrist*, 4th ed. (Princeton: Princeton University Press, 1974), 194.
2. Kaufmann, *Nietzsche*, 8.
3. Ibid., 9.
4. Friedrich Nietzsche, Letter #430, in Kaufmann, *Nietzsche*, 44.
5. Simcha Weinstein, *Up, Up, and Oy Vey: How Jewish History, Culture, and Values Shaped the Comic Book Superhero* (Baltimore: Leviathan Press, 2006), chapter 1 ("Superman: From Cleveland to Krypton").
6. In addition to Weinstein's book, see Stephen Skelton, *The Gospel According to the World's Greatest Hero* (Eugene, OR: Harvest House, 2006), and John Wesley White, *The Man from Krypton: The Gospel According to Superman* (Minneapolis, MN: Bethany Fellowship, 1978).
7. 1 John 4:10.
8. *Smallville*, season 1, episode 1.
9. *Superman's Pal, Jimmy Olson* #121 (July 1969).

10. In this sense, contemporary philosopher Umberto Eco was wrong to think these acts are a "waste of means" ("The Myth of Superman," in *The Role of the Reader: Explorations in the Semiotics of Text*, n.p.: First Midland, 1984, 123).

11. *Superman*, vol. 2, #28 (February 1989).

12. *Justice League*, season 1, episode 12.

13. *Action Comics*, vol. 1, #832 (October 2005).

14. *Action Comics*, vol. 1, #900 (June 2011).

15. Robert Greenberger and Martin Pasko, *The Essential Superman Encyclopedia* (New York: Del Rey, 2010), 405.

16. See Anton Kozlovic, "Superman as Christ-Figure: The American Pop Culture Movie Messiah," *Journal of Religion and Film* 6(1) (April 2002), available at http://www.unomaha.edu/jrf/superman.htm.

17. Quoted in "The Spiritual Side of *Superman Returns*," *SuperHeroHype.com*, December 4, 2006, available at http://www.superherohype.com/news/featuresnews.php?id=4972.

18. *JSA Kingdom Come Special: Superman* #1 (January 2009).

19. *Superman: For Tomorrow* (published in two trade paperbacks in 2005 and an Absolute hardcover in 2009) collects *Superman*, vol. 1, #204–215 (June 2004–May 2005).

20. *Smallville*, season 1, episode 1; season 9, episode 11; and season 8, episode 18.

21. Roger Stern, *The Death and Life of Superman: A Novel* (New York: Bantam, 1993), 130.

22. *The Making of Superman: The Movie and Superman II*, available on many DVD releases of *Superman II*.

23. John Lawrence sees Superman and other superheroes as "secular counterparts of religious leaders" ("The Mythology of Superman," *You Will Believe: The Cinematic Saga of Superman*, Warner Brothers DVD, 2006). Also, Christopher Knowles believes that "superheroes have come to *fill* the role in our modern society that the gods and demigods provided to the ancients" (*Our Gods Wear Spandex: The Secret History of Comic Book Heroes*, San Francisco: Weiser Books, 2007, xv).

24. *JSA Kingdom Come Special: The Kingdom* #1 (January 2009); *Action Comics*, vol. 1, #900.

25. *Superman/Batman: Worship* (2011); *Superman*, vol. 1, #666 (October 2007); *Superman: Godfall* (2004).

26. *Superman: The Last Family of Krypton* #3 (December 2010).

Chapter 11

Superman Must Be Destroyed!
Lex Luthor as Existentialist Anti-Hero

Sarah K. Donovan and Nicholas Richardson

Lex Luthor despises Superman. He obsesses about Superman. He tries to kill Superman. At first glance, Luthor seems like a one-dimensional character: a demented criminal mastermind. What else would explain his profound hatred of the "perfect boy scout?" (We'll ignore the issue of hair loss.) But a closer look through the lens of *existentialism* can help us to see that Luthor is actually a complex, self-determined person who grapples with legitimate concerns regarding Superman. Luthor takes existentialism to the extreme, though, rejecting ethics and becoming an anti-hero.

A Man Who Writes His Own Script

There is great variety among the philosophers who are labeled as existentialists, but all of them believe that we should concern ourselves with living *authentically*, and that this requires facing some hard truths about the world we live in. These truths can include admitting that there is no God, that there is no greater purpose to our lives—except what we make of it—and that many of the people around us are leading shallow and silly lives because they fail to take true responsibility for their own actions. Existentialism is not a philosophy for the faint of heart. It stresses independence, autonomy,

Superman and Philosophy: What Would the Man of Steel Do?, First Edition. Edited by Mark D. White.
© 2013 John Wiley & Sons, Inc. Published 2013 by John Wiley & Sons, Inc.

and courage to go against norms. Some existentialists are suspected of doing away with ethical norms (for example, no God means we get no morals from God), although most try to avoid this.

Many storylines in the comics depict Lex Luthor as fitting with existentialism by rejecting societal ideals and being autonomous and self-directed. In particular, we see his rejection of ideals and his independent nature in *Superman: Secret Origin* (2009–2010), *All-Star Superman* (2006–2008), and *Lex Luthor: Man of Steel* (2005). In *Superman: Secret Origin*, a young Luthor is working in his home science lab when he receives a call from the police telling him that his father miraculously survived an "accidental" car crash. Luthor's thought to himself is pure skepticism: "A 'miracle'? Miracles don't exist."[1] Luthor considers himself a man of science and believes everything is explicable through science. He doesn't readily accept the judgments of authorities unless he can independently verify their accounts, including the police—and, of course, the church. In *All-Star Superman*, Luthor is strapped into the electric chair when a priest is brought in to give him his last rites. True to form, Luthor professes his atheism when he says, "Now can someone tell the Padre to get out of my olfactory range. He stinks of the irrational."[2]

Turning from the sacred to the secular, in *Lex Luthor: Man of Steel*, Luthor claims that the American public has been sucked in by a false belief that Superman represents "truth, justice, and the American way." But it's not just Superman that he distrusts; it's the ideals he claims to represent.

> Truth? That's in the teller. Just calmly messaged words that very well may be nothing but carefully finessed lies. Justice? Belongs to the judge, who sits above those who put him there because they can't trust themselves. And the American way? It constantly evolves out of something that proves to be true and a lie, just and more ... all men are created equal.[3]

Luthor thinks the appeal of Superman comes from his promise to take care of us so that we don't need to take care of ourselves, offering us a kind of "redemption" from responsibility. In existentialist form, Luthor refuses this redemption.

In *Superman: Secret Origin*, Luthor is presented as self-directed from an early age. When young Clark Kent and Luthor meet in the library, Luthor tells Kent that he is planning to move to Metropolis. When Kent asks why, Luthor replies,

> Society has been led by a handful of those brave, strong and smart enough to shape its history, Clark ... Metropolis is called the city of tomorrow, Clark. It is the city where those who hope to turn their greatest postulations and infinite imaginations into reality venture. If you want to change the world, there's no other place on earth to be than Metropolis![4]

The young Luthor has already decided that he will change the world, and that it is possible.

Unfortunately, Luthor's self-directed rejection of societal ideals leads him down dark paths that most existentialists try to avoid. For example, in *Lex Luthor: Man of Steel* he is willing to have innocent children killed in an elaborate plan to cast Superman in a poor light. In *Superman: Secret Origin*, Luthor's alcoholic father dies, and it is implied that Luthor had something to do with it. The police tell Luthor his father is dead, and say that they assumed it would have been from drunk driving. Luthor replies that his father had a weak heart, but the police say nothing in his father's medical record indicated this. When we see Luthor alone, he is smiling with elation and talking about moving to Metropolis, with a copy of his father's insurance policy next to his map.

An Iconoclast

While Luthor clearly demonstrates affinity with the general existentialist agenda, he becomes more interesting when we determine which specific strain of existentialist thought best matches his own (although his lack of ethics always lurks as a problem). German existentialist philosopher Friedrich Nietzsche (1844–1900) is famous for proclaiming "God is dead"[5] and explaining how to "philosophize with a hammer."[6] So Nietzsche can help us understand Luthor as an iconoclast, literally one who breaks sacred images.

Nietzsche was a sarcastic and witty writer who took every opportunity to critique the branch of philosophy known as *metaphysics*. Metaphysics investigates things that are beyond the physical, such as God and the soul. Nietzsche rejects metaphysical explanations of life (such as saying that things happen as the result of God's will) and instead suggests we try to understand the world in terms of power relationships. This is what marks him as an existentialist: he believes your fate is your own. There is no grand plan, no fate, no karma. There is only power and the people wielding it—history is determined by who has power and who doesn't. For example, in *On the Genealogy of Morals*, he suggests that the rise of Christianity is about power, not God, and that Christian metaphysics is used only to trick people into becoming followers.[7]

Luthor similarly attacks Superman's image because Luthor believes that Superman has gained a dangerous and false metaphysical or god-like status. In the "Last Son" storyline, Earth is infiltrated by hostile Kryptonians who have escaped from the Phantom Zone.[8] Superman has to ask Luthor for help in defeating the Kryptonians, but Luthor accuses Superman of teaching the people of Earth to be submissive. "You've taught humanity to rely on you and not fight for themselves. That's why General Zod and his army were able to take control."[9] Luthor continues to say that humans need to be inspired by other humans, not aliens they have made into gods. Like Nietzsche, Luthor is focused on who gains power when someone or something is set up as a god.

Nietzsche believed that there is nothing greater than ourselves to believe in. Life is a combination of joy and suffering. We must accept that the world is a highly imperfect place and there are no scales of justice balancing out what happens. Nietzsche urges us to see life for what it is and love it anyway. The Nietzschean ideal is to love both the joy and suffering so much that we accept and affirm every single thing that has happened to us *as if* we willed it ourselves. It is up to us to make works of art of our own lives, growing in strength and letting go of negativity.

Luthor is presented as a creative genius (albeit villainous) in many storylines. In *Superman: Secret Origin*, Luthor becomes the most powerful man in Metropolis. He runs his successful company Lexcorp, manipulates the people of Metropolis with a daily lottery that promises to change one lucky person's life, and has connections with the American military—whom he convinces to help him terminate Superman. Luthor has used his intelligence, will, and creativity to build an empire. In fact, he has done exactly what Nietzsche accuses Christianity of: he has set himself up as a God among men who is to be worshipped and feared.

Luthor's plan goes well until Superman shows up. When the public asks Superman what he wants of them, he says, "I want you to stop looking for a great savior. Lex Luthor isn't it. I'm not it. You are. All of you."[10] Superman is trying to tell the people of Metropolis that the emperor has no clothes, and Luthor does not appreciate this unveiling.

One Man Is an Island

French existentialist philosopher Jean-Paul Sartre (1905–1980) can help us explore the depths of Luthor's commitment to self-determination.[11] Sartre argues that "existence precedes essence," which means that we exist before we know what we will become. People are responsible for who they are because life is a series of choices. While you are limited by your circumstances, everyone still has choices to make every day.[12] We cannot truly claim that life happens to us because even when we do not choose, we still have made a choice by default. Sartre thinks we all need to understand the role we play in our own "fate" (which, of course, doesn't exist—it's all up to you).

Sartre's philosophy is one of radical responsibility, but it can also cause anxiety, dread, and fear. It is daunting to truly believe that your life has no meaning beyond what you choose for it. *Authenticity* means living in the face of that belief and embracing the challenge of giving one's own life meaning at every moment. Whether we like Luthor or not, we have to give him credit for being a person who takes responsibility for his actions, and sees himself as the sole protagonist in his own life. In *Lex Luthor: Man of Steel*, Luthor's reflections on the existentialist ideals that guide him include the following frank approach to reality, of which Sartre would approve:

> More often than not, when choosing a path, it's the easy road that's taken. The reasons are obvious, understandable ... but ultimately, undefendable. Because we were created to create ourselves ... it's the greatest gift our creator gave to us ... Destiny is something we hold in our hands.[13]

Luthor also explains why he is so obsessed with bringing down Superman. Part of his hatred for Superman is Sartrean: Superman has been viewed as a god among men, which interferes with people determining their lives for themselves:

> I believe there's something inherently dangerous when something real becomes mythic. I believe when that happens, we lose the part of ourselves that yearns to be great. Because when faced with a myth? We can't win. So the mythic must be exposed for what it is. So we can believe in ourselves.[14]

Luthor thinks that Superman interferes with people viewing their lives as an existential project. With Superman as their hero and protector, people don't have to think for themselves or accept responsibility for their lives. Superman wants to represent hope and a dream of something greater, but Luthor wants to show that this is a myth and that a life lived under these terms will be inauthentic and misguided. Luthor sees himself as giving people back their existential freedom, but ironically, Luthor tries to set himself up in a similarly mythic position!

Luthor is so convinced of his beliefs that he is prepared to perform acts that most people would find morally repugnant. It is here that Luthor slides from the position of existentialist hero to its photo negative: the anti-hero. In *Lex Luthor: Man of Steel*, Luthor has a team of scientists create his own superhero, Hope, and then orchestrates a horrible disaster that will turn people against Superman. He hires a convicted pedophile, Winslow Schott, to build a bomb on the pretext that it will be used to rob a jewelry store. But Luthor has his men blow the bomb up next to a daycare center, killing a number of children, and then frames Schott for it. Hope hunts down Schott and, with the eyes of the public watching, flies him up into the sky so that she can drop him to his death (which is the kind of raw justice the public yearns for). But as Schott plummets toward the ground, Superman saves him. Luthor wants the public to see Superman saving a convicted pedophile and accused mass murderer of children so that they will find him as disgusting as the man he saved.

It would be difficult to find an existentialist who would condone these acts, much less regard them as justified by existentialism. Freedom is widely seen by existentialists as a good, of course, and many reject God, but all try to guard against sanctioning hideous acts such as Luthor's even if his goals are admirable. Sartre was aware that ethics was a problem in his theory, and he sought to correct that in his later writings. In fact, his intellectual and life partner, Simone de Beauvoir (1908–1986), wrote a book entitled *The Ethics of Ambiguity*, which tackles this problem.[15] Critics have argued that when existentialists claim that radical freedom and ethics can co-exist, they are trying to have their cake and eat it too. It is a messy debate, and Luthor stands as an example of why the stakes are so high.

The Anti-Hero of Faith

Danish philosopher Søren Kierkegaard (1813–1855) was an early existentialist who affirmed that we have to follow our own, self-directed path (albeit toward God), which is a solitary, anxiety-provoking experience. Unlike other famous existentialists, he is a man of faith; in fact, it is his belief in God and his disgust for organized religion that led him to emphasize the distinction between the moral norms of society and those of God.

The biblical story of Abraham and Isaac is a quintessential example of this difference. In *Fear and Trembling*, Kierkegaard writes that preachers talk about Abraham's bravery and devotion to God without discussing the stark and unpleasant reality of his situation.[16] Not only has Abraham been ordered to kill his beloved son, Isaac, but he must travel to a faraway location to make the sacrifice. Kierkegaard describes the journey as riddled with anxiety and doubt. God has asked Abraham to sacrifice something dear to him, but according to human law, this would be a father murdering his own son, not serving his God. Because God told Abraham what to do but did not tell everyone else that he told Abraham to do it, Abraham stands alone. This, according to Kierkegaard, is indicative of the anxiety and doubt that accompany true faith.

Kierkegaard focuses on this story because it underscores what he calls in *Fear and Trembling* "the teleological suspension of the ethical." For Abraham to do what God is asking him to do, he must step outside of the realm of human morality, and believe that he is nonetheless doing the right thing. Kierkegaard stresses that this happens within an intensely personal relationship with God that only Abraham can understand. In the teleological suspension of the ethical, Abraham becomes incomprehensible to other people. He seems unethical according to human standards, but he is obeying divine commands—and is profoundly alone in his convictions.

We won't argue that Luthor is somehow a man of faith, ordered by God to kill Superman for the good of humanity. Luthor is an anti-hero, but the characteristics that define Abraham's dilemma—solitariness and having to ignore ethical norms for a higher purpose intelligible only to himself—apply to Luthor's vendetta as well. The general public cannot understand what motivates Luthor. Like Abraham, Luthor is alone in his belief about what must be done. As he repeatedly reminds us, Superman is not human, which fuels Luthor's perennial question: "What would happen if Superman turned against humans?"

All-Star Superman explores this theme from two different angles. First, Jimmy Olsen gets a new gig as the star of the "for a day" column in which he assumes someone else's role. When he is acting as eccentric billionaire scientist Mister Quintum, he almost falls into a pit that contains the foundations of reality. (Seriously.) Superman pulls Olsen out (of course), but also pulls out an unknown material that turns out to be black kryptonite. Superman is radically, negatively affected by the black kryptonite and turns against humans, saying, "Earth! Look at them! Swarming like futile bugs in the sun. Who's going to stop me from doing anything I want?"[17] Superman is transformed from the alien who loves humankind to Luthor's nightmare of the alien who will destroy us all.

Later in the series, Superman becomes trapped in the "underverse." Quintum fears that Superman will not be able to return, so he replaces Superman with Ber-El and Lilo, Kryptonians who have been lost in space. Unfortunately, they disdain humanity and dream of turning Earth into the new Krypton. When Superman returns (of course), he tells Ber-El and Lilo, "I'd hoped maybe you could replace me if … if anything happened to me … But I don't think you have the best interests of this planet at heart, do you?" They answer, "You betrayed your heritage. You went native," and then attack Superman.[18] Again, Ber-El and Lilo represent the dangerous possibility that Superman could also turn on humanity.

In both scenarios, we face the possibility that Superman, or another Kryptonian, could destroy life as we know it. Of course, we will never know if the threat is real unless (or until) Superman betrays us—and Superman seems to have more faith in humanity than perhaps we deserve. So it seems Luthor is misguided in pursuing his vendetta.

Perhaps Luthor is simply jealous that Superman thwarts Luthor's own plans to control humankind.

Existentialists Gone Wild!

Lex Luthor underscores the complexities of existentialist philosophy. While he is creative, self-determined, and autonomous, he is also completely immoral. His willingness to sacrifice anything or anyone takes existentialism to an extreme that Nietzsche, Sartre, and Kierkegaard would reject.

And so, we are left to wonder: is Lex Luthor an evil genius and an abomination to existentialism, or might he be a true evolution of what existentialism can become (against existentialists' own wishes)? This is the question that makes Luthor one of the more compelling characters in the Superman mythology, forcing us to ask ourselves where the moral lines are (if there are any) with regard to self-determination and freedom. If Luthor is wrong, we are the moral heroes. But if Luthor is right, he would challenge our most basic moral beliefs, and the world would become a very scary place to live indeed.

Notes

1. *Superman: Secret Origin* #2 (December 2009), reprinted in *Superman: Secret Origin* (2010).
2. *All-Star Superman* #11 (July 2008), reprinted in *All-Star Superman, Volume 2* (2009).
3. *Lex Luthor: Man of Steel* #1 (May 2005), reprinted in *Luthor* (2010).
4. *Superman: Secret Origin* #2 (December 2009), reprinted in *Superman: Secret Origin*.
5. See Nietzsche, *The Gay Science*, trans. Walter Kaufmann (New York: Random House, 1974), and *Thus Spoke Zarathustra*, trans. Walter Kaufmann (New York: Penguin, 1978). Kaufmann is an excellent translator of Nietzsche's work, and has written extensively on Nietzsche as well. *The Portable Nietzsche* (trans. Walter Kaufmann, New York: Penguin, 1976) is a great introduction to a variety of Nietzsche's texts.
6. See Nietzsche's *Twilight of the Idols* in *The Portable Nietzsche*.
7. Friedrich Nietzsche, *On the Genealogy of Morals*, trans. Walter Kaufmann (New York: Random House, 1967).

8. *Action Comics*, vol. 1, #844–846, #851, and *Action Comics Annual* #11 (published across 2006–2008), reprinted as *Superman: Last Son* (2008).

9. *Action Comics Annual* #11 (July 2008).

10. *Superman: Secret Origin* #6 (October 2010), reprinted in *Superman: Secret Origin*.

11. Sartre wrote a short book titled *Existentialism and Human Emotions*, trans. Bernard Frechtman (New York: Kensington Publishing, 2000), which is a clear introduction to his work.

12. See Sartre's *Being and Nothingness*, trans. Hazel Barnes (New York: Washington Square Press, 1993).

13. *Lex Luthor: Man of Steel* #3 (July 2005), reprinted in *Luthor*.

14. Ibid.

15. Simone de Beauvoir, *The Ethics of Ambiguity*, trans. Bernard Frechtman (New York: Citadel Press, 1996).

16. Søren Kierkegaard, *Fear and Trembling/Repetition*, trans. Howard V. Hong and Edna H. Hong (Princeton: Princeton University Press, 1983).

17. *All-Star Superman* #4 (July 2006), reprinted in *All-Star Superman, Volume 1* (2007).

18. *All-Star Superman* #9 (December 2007), reprinted in *All-Star Superman, Volume 2*.

Part Four

THE ULTIMATE HERO
WHAT DO WE EXPECT FROM SUPERMAN?

Chapter 12

Superman's Revelation
The Problem of Violence in *Kingdom Come*

David Hatfield

Stop me if you've heard this one before: a powerful menace beyond the abilities of normal humankind threatens to destroy or enslave us. A hero rises to confront this challenge, and after a series of tests of will, strength, and wits, a climactic battle ensues. The hero, through the use of force and violence, ultimately prevails, alleviating the threat, and then things return to normal. Of course, you'd have stopped me long before I finished, because you recognize this story not only from classical mythology, but also as the iconic superhero story. Indeed, the modern superhero story *is* our own modern mythology, and Superman our own iconic, mythic hero.

But if Superman is so super, if he has fought so much and so often and so hard for the peace, why is he still fighting? Is Superman somehow destined to play out this story of violence, over and over? Or have all these years and all these conflicts taught Superman something about the nature of violence? And, more importantly, what can Superman teach us about it, especially in the context of the classic alternate-future storyline, *Kingdom Come*?

The Never-Ending Battle

Contemporary philosopher René Girard might indeed argue that Superman is locked into endless violent conflict. Girard writes in the field of *philosophical anthropology*, which deals with human nature,

Superman and Philosophy: What Would the Man of Steel Do?, First Edition. Edited by Mark D. White.
© 2013 John Wiley & Sons, Inc. Published 2013 by John Wiley & Sons, Inc.

its role in human interaction, and the resulting values and behaviors that shape human culture. In particular, Girard examines the role of violence in maintaining social cohesion and the ways that cultural mythology hides and thus allows such violence to continue.[1] According to Girard, humans have a unique ability to imitate, which early in the development of human culture enabled our ancestors to learn behaviors that allowed us to flourish, use tools, and adapt. But there's also a dangerous side to this ability to imitate, because we also come to imitate others' desires. This imitative, or *mimetic*, desire has the potential to cause great harm.

Girard's secret formula goes something like this: first, we imitate another's desire (for anything, whether a yummy piece of fruit, an attractive mate, or a hut that doesn't flood when it rains), then we fight over the shared object of desire. Next, we tend to lose sight of the object of desire and begin to imitate others' desire for violence itself. As this scenario plays out, violence has a propensity to go viral. Individuals enact plans of vengeance and retribution, then, friends get involved, and next, families become embroiled in the aggression. Eventually, we have all the clansfolk involved. The violence begins to spiral out of control, and if left unchecked, would result in genocide, the worst possible result. So, some cultural mechanism must come into play before we reach the genocide stage. Oddly enough, that mechanism is ... wait for it ... more violence.

But this violence can't be ordinary violence. It has to be super-violence, an act of violence so significant that it can satisfy the blood lust of a culture already awash in it. Girard observes that cultures tend not only to sanction but also to sanctify such super-violence—and from it, we have the beginnings of religion.

Things Hidden Since the Foundation of the World[2]

Now, why did I label Girard's formula a "secret"? A headline such as this would hardly stop the presses at the *Daily Planet*: SUPERMAN RESORTS TO VIOLENCE IN LATEST ATTEMPT AT CONFLICT RESOLUTION. We expect violence from our superheroes. For example, when new comics fans hear of the Charlton/DC Comics superhero the Peacemaker, they can safely (and correctly) assume that his name carries a certain amount of irony. And we expect violence from even our most super of super-heroes: our first ever glimpse of Superman from the cover of *Action Comics* #1 (June 1938) shows him smashing a car and men cowering and fleeing in fear. We likewise cheer when he gives a wife beater—one of Superman's first "villains"—a taste of his own medicine in that same issue. Superman, an enforcer of mythic proportions, is in the business of meeting violence with violence, of using violence as a way to—oddly enough—enforce the peace, to maintain order, and to fight for the status quo.

But why are we thrilled by the *Action Comics* cover instead of shocked? And why do we cheer about the wife beater? Why aren't we troubled? These reactions are, in fact, something that Girard would predict—and it's what makes his formula secret. Our imitative desires—whether for fruit, or mate, or hut, or violence—appear to come from within us, and because of that they seem inevitable, and perhaps even just. In order to sleep at night and feel okay about ourselves and our desires, we create grand master-narratives—such as Superman's—to hide from us our proclivity to violence and to make it seem natural. Clark Kent may be Superman's secret identity, but Superman is the secret identity of our own cultural inclination to violence.

Superman is a part of our mythology, and Girard in particular argues that myth performs a specific function in regard to violence. Our mythology transforms our violent nature into socially tolerable forms that are sanctioned, often sacred, and at times—though only momentarily—comforting. Because of the role of myth in our culture, though, the concept of "enforcing the peace" or using violence to stop violence does not seem odd or unusual to us. We're not invited to interrogate or question our mythology. Girard argues that mythology actually hides things from us.

This violence that hides in our mythology, however, presents a problem. Girard argues that as long as this mythology remains hidden to us, as long as it seems normal or natural, as long as we don't see it for what it is or question it, we are destined to repeat it. But haven't we come a long way in this modern day and age? For example, we really don't think "mythology" is real. We really don't believe we have to offer human sacrifices to appease displeased gods. And we know the story of Superman vs. Doomsday is just a story. Right?

Well—maybe so, at least on the literal level. But on the mythologi-cal level, we run into trouble. There, our violence is at the same time hidden and sanctioned, and in our cultural stories we not only expect it, but we also cheer it, and oftentimes require it. In this way, we're locked into a cycle of violence. To break this cycle, somebody will have to reveal to us what we've hidden about ourselves. And who would be better suited to this super-human task than our most super of superheroes?

Kingdom Come

Such a challenge requires not only an epic hero, but also an epic tale. The story of Superman in *Kingdom Come* (1996) fills the bill. The tale is set in an unnamed future in which the heroes of old—among them Superman, Wonder Woman, and Batman—have been retired for ten years. Instead of these familiar heroes, the world is now filled with the "children and grandchildren" of these heroes, and they number "in the nameless thousands." By now, they have "all but eliminated the super-villains of yesteryear." But there seems to be a problem: these younger metahumans are "inspired by the legends of those who came before." And as Girard's formula predicts, this inspiration leads to imitation: they do battle. But since there are no more villains, they "no longer fight for right. They fight simply to fight, their only foes each other."[3] Metahuman aggression escalates, until during one battle they level the entire state of Kansas.

This looks like a job for Superman, who returns to battle in a "blur of motion" during a dangerous metahuman clash, "bending the steel of their weapons" and even "changing the course of the mighty river below" to save innocent bystanders.[4] Power of such mythic proportions cannot be resisted, and the fight ends quickly with Superman gliding down to earth, fists full of unconscious reprobates. The hope and faith of the normal people of Earth are fulfilled, as is the mythological formula: Superman returns to meet the imitative violence that is threatening to spiral out of control with violence of his own. And just as the humans in the story are rewarded, so are we as readers, the con-sumers and creators of our own mythology. After all, who can be disappointed when Big Blue swoops in from nowhere, beats up the bad guys, and saves the day?

Superman even reveals his intentions soon after his momentous arrival while speaking outside the United Nations. He explains that he has returned, with other heroes, to teach the violent metahumans—who are "unwilling to preserve life or defend the defenseless" and who have "perverted their great powers"—the "true meaning of truth and justice," to "guide them with wisdom ... and if necessary, with force. Above all we will restore order."[5] And there it is, straight from the Superman's mouth. He's back to restore order, to guide with wisdom, but he's ready to do what's necessary if wisdom doesn't work. Paradoxically, he's ready to enforce the peace.

Superman's Dilemma

As promised, Superman confronts the metahuman problem, gathering to his side those who honor his principles while fighting against those who refuse to fall in line. But we should begin to suspect that things won't go easily for the Man of Steel, especially keeping in mind the mechanisms at play in this mythological tale. Already, he's entered a setting in which imitative violence is running high—the metahumans emulate the heroes of legend, and so, they fight, even in the absence of super-villains. And now Superman has entered the fray, appealing to reason to win converts to his side. But he's also acting as he has always acted, as he is expected to act, and to some extent, in ways only he can act. Superman's own violence becomes a basis for imitation, a fuel for a fire already lit. Fewer and fewer metahumans join his ranks, more and more choose to rebel, and the violence escalates. The harder Superman fights, the less success he has, and the more violent things become.

The dilemma is not lost on the not-so-simple farm boy from Krypton. "It's not supposed to be this way," he says. "We shouldn't have to fight this hard ... We're coming up with more captives than converts."[6] What Superman says is fascinating for two reasons. First, "it" actually *is* supposed to be this way, because we're reading a comic book about the greatest superhero. There's supposed to be a threat, there's supposed to be fighting and violence, and Superman is supposed to use force when wisdom falls short. Second, it's highly significant that Superman actually realizes that he has to fight so hard. It's a moment of rare, if not unique, insight on his part. He's not saying that his foes are so mighty or ingenious that he's having a difficult time handling them—that's what drives any Superman story. If the villains were easy, we wouldn't need Superman. What Superman begins to realize is that by fighting, he has to fight harder; and the harder he fights, the harder his job becomes. His red-sun-gravitas is not enough to quench the desire for violence, and his own violence only adds to that desire.

What's different is that this time, Superman faces an adversary that is neither the metahumans nor his own shortcomings. Despite retaining all his powers granted by his Kryptonian heritage, Superman is rendered impotent by his most challenging foe to date, namely the cultural mythology in which he participates. His story is one of violence, and Girard would argue that's why we created him: so we could put a heroic face on our own violent inclinations, so we could have an acceptable outlet for that inclination, and so we could find some comfort in tales of violence in which the outcomes are what we could consider good. But this time the violence isn't working, and Superman finds himself at an impasse. Caught up in the quandary of his own mythology, what's a Superman to do?

Good Violence vs. Bad Violence

One thing Superman could do is simply to kill those who don't join him. Based on what we've seen, however, this probably would not be the best course. If Superman's beating up the metahumans has made things worse because they imitate the violence, killing them ... well, you get the idea by now. Besides, killing is a line that Superman will not cross—partly because of his own morals, but keep in mind that Superman's morals are part of the mythology we have created about him. As a culture, there are certain forms of violence that we authorize or sanction, and certain forms we do not. Superman killing uncooperative metahumans would be a form we do not.

Superman has always operated in the realm of "good" violence, the type that helps to maintain the peace. The problem he faces is that peace-maintaining violence is no longer enough. It has lost its ability to restore order, and that's part of the paradoxical nature of the notion of "enforcing the peace." But the culture Superman finds himself in has already taken the first slip down that slope of "bad" violence, and that explains why Superman had taken his leave for ten years.

A metahuman anti-hero named Magog killed the Joker while the Clown Prince of Crime was in custody for gassing the *Daily Planet* and killing 93 people, including Lois Lane. Although Magog justified the action by arguing that he had actually saved lives, Superman arrests Magog for murder and he stands trial— only to be acquitted. "Justice Done" reads the headline on the *Daily Planet*.[7] The culture shifted the line of sanctioned violence to one that Superman would neither push nor cross, so he chose to isolate himself from an increasingly violent society. Furthermore, good violence was making a transition into bad violence as killing—the quintessential violent act—was becoming an acceptable means of enforcing the peace. Once this happened, the distinction between violence that restores order and that which destroys it became blurred, and things began to spiral even further out of control.

Magog's story helps us understand the situation that Superman must puzzle out. Not only is his use of force ineffectual, but he also cannot persuade the culture to turn away from the order-destroying violence that is washing over it. Neither can he participate in the kind of violence that the culture now demands, without crossing a line that he cannot cross. It may be OK for Magog to kill in the name of keeping the peace, but it's not OK for Superman. Our mythology of him won't allow that, because we hold totally different expectations for him: we expect Superman to save us from ourselves.

His next solution, then, is to try to contain the violence through passive means. In an admittedly desperate attempt, Superman builds a massive gulag in the heart of the Kansas wasteland. This "stronghold of justice" is meant to "imprison the deadliest and most uncontrollable of the superhumans."[8] But recalling Girard's formula, we know that this level and kind of violence cannot be contained, and that the mechanisms that Superman struggles against will again win out. The prisoners breach the gulag walls, and our superhero story will have its climactic battle. A massive conflict begins, and just as Girard would predict, it "isn't a fight that will eventually die down," but rather is a "war that may well end the world."[9] There is a mechanism, however, that will satisfy the blood lust and stop the rampant violence. When things are so very violent for so very long, someone has to die.

Sacred Violence

Girard describes human history as "a relentless chronicle of violence because when cultures fall apart, they fall into violence, and when they revive themselves, they do so violently."[10] So, what's the difference between the violence that leads to falling apart and the violence that revives? Though both involve killing, it's the meaning of the violence that's essential.

The killing cannot happen in the course of the conflict itself; that's part of the order-destroying violence that leads to crisis. Instead, the killing must be charged with super-significance, and primitive cultures did this by making the killing sacred. For Girard, this process explains the origins of religion and why ancient cultures practiced human sacrifice to curry favor from or to appease the gods—and to keep check on order-destroying violence. Once an act of violence has been raised to the status of the sacred, it has the power to diffuse uncontrolled violence. But as we observed before, our own mythology, our superhero mythology, is much too sophisticated to require human sacrifice—isn't it?

Though *Kingdom Come* follows the superhero-story outline, there are two ways it's very different from most. First, Superman doesn't win like he's supposed to. At the heart of this story there's an opponent that is bigger than him. He's trapped inside, and by, the elements of the story itself. Every decision he's made has led to this moment of crisis, not of resolution or victory. Second, something very unusual happens at the final battle at the gulag that transforms not only the fight, but also Superman. We know already that this "something" must be a death, and that it must hold religious, sacred importance.

As its title suggests, *Kingdom Come* makes heavy use of religious themes. For example, the first image we see of Superman clearly establishes him as a Christ figure. He's in his Kryptonian identity of Kal-El (the name references the Hebrew words for "vessel" or "voice of God"); he's doing carpentry; he wears the long hair and beard associated with the Western iconic image of Christ; he's carrying a heavy timber across his shoulders reminiscent of the cross beam carried by Christ; and tucked into the back pocket of his overalls are three very distinctive spikes.[11]

When Superman learns of the battle near the end of the story, he streaks there in a last desperate attempt. Given that we know who the Christ figure is, and given that we know a sacrifice must take place to save the day, it seems obvious what's in store for Superman. But as Superman reaches the battle, he's knocked from the sky by Captain Marvel, who has been brainwashed to fight for the rebellious metahumans. Marvel pummels Superman with magical lightning bolts; with each shout of "Shazam!" Marvel leaps away and the bolts pound Superman with devastating effect. Bloodied and battered, he is unable to join the fight. In the meantime, Wonder Woman strikes down one of the metahumans, killing him, and unleashes the full fury of war.

Humankind itself is now jeopardized by the ferocity of the conflict, but the humans have been paying careful attention to the metahuman threat from the beginning. Seeing their own existence at risk, they react to the violent threat in the only way they can conceive: with violence. They launch bombs toward Kansas, specifically designed to destroy the metahumans. Even in the heat of battle, Superman detects the missiles, and with a glance, "confirms the bomb's potency" and calculates that he has seconds to act. Leaping forward, he traps Marvel in a lightning blast, transforming him to his mortal state as Billy Batson.[12]

Superman begins to understand all the forces at work, and with his mighty hand gripping Batson's mouth shut, he explains,

> I don't know what to do! You can see that, can't you? Every choice I've made so far has brought us here—has been wrong! So listen to me, Billy. Listen harder than you ever have before … There's a bomb falling. Either it kills us—or we run rampant across the globe. I can still stop the bomb, Bill. That much I'm sure of. What I don't know is whether I should be allowed to. Superhumans or mankind … one will pay the ultimate price. And that decision … is not for me to make. I'm not a god … I'm not a man. But you, Billy … you're both. More than anyone who ever existed, you know what it's like to live in both worlds. Only you can weigh their worth equally … You can let me go … or with a word … you can stop me. Do you understand the choice that can be made by you alone? Then decide. Decide the world.[13]

Superman releases his grip and leaps skyward to stop the bomb. But at that moment, Batson whispers "Shazam," transforming into Captain Marvel. He too leaps skyward and hurls Superman back to earth. Marvel flies onward, upward to the bomb, and shouts "Shazam!", calling down the lightning that detonates the bomb. But in doing so, he changes back to his mortal form, and he is destroyed by the horrific blast. By his act of sacrifice, the battle is ended.

Caution: Mythology at Work

So, what has happened? At first glance, it appears that humanity is threatened by a power beyond its ability to handle; Superman appears and confronts the threat; Superman is put through a series of challenges of will and might; and in the end, he is key to a heroic act of sacrifice that saves the world. But the truth of the matter is not so simple, and is cleverly hidden.

First, it's important to note that even though Superman is the obvious Christ figure, just before the moment of sacrifice, Superman identifies Marvel as the one who is both god and man—a man who is thus endowed with sacred significance. The mythology we've established around Superman determines that he could not have been killed by the nuclear blast, and therefore could not have served as a sacrifice. The mythology requires a sacred death and puts Marvel on the altar. In this way, the mythological demands are met, as the tale weaves together ancient mechanisms, modern superhero mythology, and the powerful Christian tradition of sacrifice. It's important to note that the mushroom cloud is even depicted in the shape of a cross.

Second, there's Captain Marvel's sacrifice itself. We've come to expect that a superhero who "managed with his dying breath" to end a war, save the world from catastrophic violence, and prevent genocide, has succeeded. But the complex mythology at work complicates even this seemingly obvious interpretation. It turns out that Marvel detonated the bomb high enough above the ground for some metahumans to live. "Survivors?" asks an astonished Superman. "How many?" Leave it to Batman, also present at the battle, to rain on what looks like a perfectly good sacrifice: "Enough to leave us with the same problems as before. The same impasse. The same dangers. The same distrust. The same everything."[14] It is easy enough to dismiss this assessment as overly bleak and predictable, coming from Batman. Are things really that bad? Hasn't the sacrifice averted a major crisis? Didn't a hero just give his life in the name of goodness? And aren't these good things? How can something have gone wrong if things have worked out so well? And if something has gone wrong, what is it?

Only Superman realizes the truth: nothing went wrong. And that's the problem. Remember when Superman said at the United Nations that he was going to teach the metahumans "the meaning of truth and justice"? Superman had to learn that for himself first. He knows that things played out just as they had to. There remains a danger, but it's not the surviving metahumans, as Batman and the others think. It's the surviving cultural forces that started the whole matter and that are still around. Superman has his first glimmer of insight when he realizes that he "shouldn't have to fight this hard," because his foe was not the metahumans, it was the cultural mechanism of violence that required him to fight in the first place. And he now understands the meaning of Marvel's sacrifice: though the act won the peace, the cycle of violence is not broken by Captain Marvel's death. His death is *part* of the cycle. As Girard would argue, it actually participates in the "relentless chronicle of violence."

The Truth About Truth and Justice

Superman comes full circle, returning to the United Nations to teach us all the meaning of truth and justice. Flying Captain Marvel's cape high atop a flagpole, Superman tells us that Marvel "made the only choice that ever matters. He chose life."[15] That's a puzzling remark about someone who has just sacrificed himself—but only to those who have misunderstood. The true meaning of Marvel's sacrifice is not that he gave his life to save others. The truth is that as a violent culture, we required him to do so. Superman's hanging of the cape and his revelation about Marvel reminds us of and draws attention to the cycles of violence in our mythology and our history—and that we don't have to hang someone on the cross of a mushroom cloud to achieve peace. He has revealed to us what we have hidden about ourselves. And accomplishing all this has required a Superman, indeed.

Notes

1. René Girard, *Violence and the Sacred* (Baltimore: Johns Hopkins University Press, 1979).
2. This heading title is both the title of Girard's 1987 book (Stanford, CA: Stanford University Press) and is a quote from Matthew 13:35 (English Standard Version): "This was to fulfill what was spoken by the prophet: 'I will open my mouth in parables; I will utter what has been hidden since the foundation of the world.'"

3. *Kingdom Come* #1 (May 1996), reprinted with the rest of the mini-series in *Kingdom Come* (1997).
4. Ibid.
5. *Kingdom Come* #2 (June 1996).
6. Ibid.
7. Ibid.
8. *Kingdom Come* #3 (July 1996).
9. *Kingdom Come* #4 (August 1996).
10. Gil Bailie offers this concise but insightful summary of Girard's complicated notion of human history in *Violence Unveiled: Humanity at the Crossroads* (New York: The Crossroad Publishing Company, 1997), 6.
11. *Kingdom Come* #1. There are numerous other Superman-as-Christ Easter eggs scattered throughout and that are fun to search for. For more on the parallels between Superman and Christ, see chapter 10 by Barkman in this volume.
12. *Kingdom Come* #4. The humans actually launched three bombs; Batman and Wonder Woman chance across them and disable two, but the third makes its way into the arena of war.
13. Ibid.
14. Ibid.
15. Ibid.

Chapter 13

A World Without a Clark Kent?

Randall M. Jensen

A tornado hits Smallville. Almost by accident, a young Clark Kent saves a man's life. Afterwards, he confesses to Pa Kent, "I could have done more ..." He later asks his pastor a question that haunts him, "What if one man—just one man—could've stopped all this destruction? And he didn't ..." This question ultimately forces him to leave his town, his girl, and his parents behind to become the world's greatest superhero, determined "to help as many people as possible."[1] Some superheroes are spurred on by the past, fueled by the desire for retribution. Superman's gaze is fixed on the future. "As always, one thought drives me onward. Compels both my crusade and masquerade. The idea that disaster can be averted."[2] In more than one way, then, Superman is the Man of Tomorrow.

Yet the ordinary guy does not disappear with the advent of the extraordinary superhero. One man assumes two identities. Why does he continue to live the life of Clark Kent? Why does he spend so much time on the ground wearing a suit and spectacles when he could be in the air wearing a cape? Is it selfish for Clark to type a story or chat with Perry and Jimmy or enjoy a romantic dinner with Lois when he could be out saving the world? If Superman's overriding goal is to save as many people as he can, it looks an awful lot like Clark Kent is in the way. Should Superman say goodbye to Clark Kent? If so, does that have any implications for our own lives?

Superman and Philosophy: What Would the Man of Steel Do?, First Edition. Edited by Mark D. White.
© 2013 John Wiley & Sons, Inc. Published 2013 by John Wiley & Sons, Inc.

Goodbye, Clark?

Superheroes aren't the only ones who can be charged with selfishness. You and I can't battle Brainiac or Darkseid, but we are often in a position to help someone who's in trouble. In fact, we know that many people around the world suffer and die every single day because they lack life's basic necessities: food, drinkable water, shelter, medical care. Our world is faced with a truly superhero-sized problem.

The contemporary philosopher Peter Singer has proposed a "solution" to this problem. His solution is based on a deceptively plausible moral principle: "If it is in our power to prevent something bad from happening, without thereby sacrificing anything of comparable moral importance, we ought, morally, to do it."[3] This principle—call it "the S-Principle," both for Singer and for Superman—will remind some of you of *utilitarianism*, the moral theory which states that the right thing to do is whatever will bring about the greatest happiness of the greatest number of people. However, while Peter Singer is in fact a utilitarian, the S-principle itself is limited to the prevention of bad and remains silent about the promotion of good, and therefore is weaker than a full-blown utilitarianism. Still, as we'll see, it has a big bite.

Let's start with one of Singer's favorite examples. Imagine that you are walking by a shallow pond and you notice that a small child has somehow fallen into the pond and is starting to go under. You're the only one around. You can easily save the child, but it'll take some of your time and probably ruin some of your clothes. If Superman rushes to save a bratty kid who's fallen over the railing at Niagara Falls in the 1980 movie *Superman II*, surely you wouldn't hesitate to save this small child. In fact, Singer would say that you are morally *required* to do it. The death of a child is a bad thing and you can prevent it with only a small sacrifice of time and money. If you save the child, you're not an amazing hero, since you are only doing what anyone would do. But if you leave the child to drown, you are a low-down and dirty villain. While some philosophical examples leave us mystified, this one seems pretty darn straightforward.

The consequences are striking. There are children—and adults—"drowning" all around the world, and while we lack superpowers, we have modern technology to assist us in their salvation. With a few keystrokes we can use our monetary powers to equip organizations to provide relief and development to those in peril. Singer's view, then, is that those who have a lot must give a lot in order to save those in dire need. In a world where terrible things are happening to people, being a hero isn't an option but an imperative. Whether you have super-powers or only ordinary abilities and a bank account, this moral obligation to save others is staring you in the face. If you turn away, Singer says, you're rather like the awful person who walked by and left the child in the pond to drown.

The problem is that the S-Principle seems to demand that we give *so much*. We are required to sacrifice as long as we could help those in need without reducing ourselves to the level of need. And there are many things we enjoy that are important to us but just not *that* important. The reason so much is asked of us, of course, is that so many bad things are happening in our world. For Superman, perhaps this means a permanent exit for Clark Kent. Sure, he enjoys the chance to lead a normal life sometimes, but does that really matter when lives are at stake? You and I do not have a secret identity to sacrifice, but we are most likely engaged in various projects and relationships that might also have to give way in the face of people crying out for help. Can morality really demand so much of Superman, or of us?[4]

Golden Age Limits

In the early days, before his full array of superpowers "developed," Clark Kent's reporter persona was necessary for gathering information. Although he was pretty tough and fast, Superman didn't yet have the flight, the super-hearing, the super-vision, or the super-intelligence that he would later have. Tom De Haven's novel of the Golden Age, *It's Superman!*, even portrays Clark as a something of a blockhead in serious need of guidance.[5] The 1940s film shorts frequently showed Clark reading about some emergency on the teletype in the *Daily Planet* office and then sneaking off to be of service. This suggests a potential reason to keep Clark around: in order to further Superman's mission. Without Clark, Superman wouldn't know who needs help where and when. We don't have to say goodbye to Clark after all, because he is a necessary means to the end of saving others. We can accept the S-Principle and make room for Clark. Of course, if

Superman were to spend *too much* time lounging around as Clark when there are people in need, the S-Principle would indict him for it.

Likewise, our capacities to help others are limited. I cannot send a charitable donation if I have no money. A job that pays enough so that I can help others typically requires a quality education, a decent wardrobe, transportation, and other things. So, just as the Golden Age Superman needs to invest in the Clark Kent identity, I may need to invest in my education and my career. Furthermore, if other people are to be of help I may need to invest in them, too, whether they are my students, my employees, or my own children. Many things that might be seen as distractions may instead be seen as playing an instrumental role in the ongoing effort to save the world. Perhaps the S-Principle isn't quite as demanding as we feared. I don't have to abandon all my goals and instead take up the single goal of helping others, but I should structure my goals so they fit under the larger goal of helping others.

We also have physical and psychological limits. We need sleep, relaxation, and recreation. Human beings who overdo it become burned out and may be of little use to anyone. We also do not function well without meaningful social interaction. The S-Principle tells us to prevent bad things from happening when it is in our power, but sometimes it is not in our power to help someone, and morality doesn't ask us to do something that we literally cannot do.[6] No doubt this may often serve as a bad excuse—"But I just can't do that! It's too much to ask!"—but human beings can be quite frail and fragile, and these weaknesses moderate the ever-present demands of the S-principle.

The trouble for Superman is that he is not a human being, even in his relatively weak Golden Age incarnation. Although his powers wax and wane over the years, he clearly lacks most of our physical limitations. Does he grow tired? Does he have the same psychological frailties that human beings do? Does he experience strain when working too hard? The various writers of Superman don't often grapple with the psychological implications of his Kryptonian biology; he looks exactly like a human, so we are led to assume he thinks and feels like a human, too.[7] An exception to this rule is *Superman: Red Son* (2003), which imagines an alternate universe in which the young Kal-El fell to earth in the Soviet Union rather than America. As Kal-El comes into his vast and fully developed powers in this world, he seems to become more and more inhuman. At one point, he admits that, "If I was being honest with myself, I would admit that I was growing bored with human conversation."[8] This is a Superman who is able to create a Communist utopia of "almost six billion citizens and hardly anyone complained. Even in private."[9] (And with those ears he would know!) However, it might be a more psychologically realistic portrait of a being whose power, senses, and intellect so far exceed our own—a being who will not evade the S-Principle's pull by appealing to his own limits.

Even the Superman we know is in no need of the services of the *Planet*'s teletype machine. He can see and hear for miles and miles. He can be anywhere on the planet in seconds. Whereas the Golden Age Superman is a local Metropolis hero, the new and much more powerful Superman of the Silver Age and today is truly a global superhero. Why would *he* need Clark Kent to get the job done? The strategies that explain why a mere mortal or even a Golden Age Superman might not be up to meeting the demands of the S-principle full time just won't apply to today's Superman. We may face a choice: either we say goodbye to Clark or we abandon the S-Principle.

The Humanity of Martha Kent

In the alternate reality shown in the graphic novel *Superman: Earth One* (2010), a young Clark Kent has just moved to Metropolis. He has decided not to become a superhero. He has decided, in fact, to have a life. He wants to fit in, to be an ordinary person and to be accepted by others, something that turns out to be a common theme in recent Superman stories. (Anyone watch *Smallville*?) As a talented newcomer to the city, Clark's options are wide open, from doing cutting edge scientific research to playing pro sports. But he's worried about leaving his Ma behind and about what his late Pa would have thought of his decision. Ma offers the following motherly advice:

MARTHA KENT: When you raise a son up tall and strong, hearing, "This is what I'd like to give you," well, that's nice, but what you really want to hear is, "This is what I want. For me. To live the life and dream the dreams I've always longed for."

CLARK: But isn't that being selfish?

MARTHA: Oh, Clark, that's not selfish. That's how futures get built ...[10]

More than anything, Martha wants Clark to be happy. And she makes a key claim here: it isn't selfish to build a life and a future for oneself. More generally, it isn't necessarily selfish to act in one's own interests. Nobody says that I am selfish because I get out of the way of the truck that's headed right for me or because I go to a dentist appointment, yet I take these actions for my own sake. Selfishness is better understood as *excessive* concern with one's own interests. What Martha is saying is that it isn't excessively self-involved to see oneself as the subject of a life and to wonder what shape that life should take.

Since the S-Principle seems to ignore this aspect of the human situation, perhaps we should rethink our allegiance to it. We do not deliberate about what to do *sub specie aeternitatis* (a Latin phrase which means "under the aspect of eternity"), like Superman floating above Earth taking in everything that is happening on the planet. The S-Principle asks me to trade off goods in my own life against any bads that might be happening anywhere in the world. If I attempt to place any special weight on my own life, I am accused of being selfish. Martha's implicit point is that this utterly impersonal frame of reference isn't the only possible one. What if the starting point for ethical deliberation simply *is* my own life? Notice the point here is not that I am justified in caring about my own life because doing so helps me to promote some further cosmic value, nor is it that I am excused for caring about my own life because I am weak. Rather, the idea is that all of our thinking, weighing, evaluating, and deciding only makes sense in the context of a life.

Philosophers sometimes call this an *agent-relative perspective*.[11] This isn't a selfish perspective, necessarily, because much of what matters to someone might involve other people. We all want to live good lives rather than bad ones, and that will no doubt involve thinking about the place of compassion and generosity in the good life. Very few of us find the life of a supervillain attractive. Still, to ask what it would be for me to display compassion in the context of my own life is different from demanding that I prevent bad things wherever possible. And even though Superman's view of the world is more expansive than ours, since he really can look at the planet from space, he too has his own life to live.

Jor-El's Higher Calling

In the movie *Superman II*, Clark famously decides to give up his powers so he can marry Lois. Predictably, his Kryptonian parents aren't too happy about this, and of course it will turn out to be a tragic mistake. There are two versions of the momentous conversation, one shown in the original theatrical release and the other available in the more recently released Richard Donner cut of the film. In the former, Clark's mother Lara seems mostly concerned to know that he and Lois truly love each other and that Clark is sure this is what he wants. She sounds like the stereotypically worried but loving mother. However, in the Donner cut, the conversation, this time between Clark and his father Jor-El, takes a different and more interesting turn:

JOR-EL:	My son, I have tried to anticipate your every question. This is one I had hoped you would not ask ... You cannot serve humanity by investing your time and emotion in one human being at the expense of the rest. The concepts are mutually exclusive.
SUPERMAN:	And if I no longer wish to serve humanity?
JOR-EL:	Is this how you repay their gratitude? By abandoning the weak, the defenseless, the needy, for the sake of your selfish pursuits?
SUPERMAN:	Selfish! After all I've done for them? Will there ever come a time when I've served enough? At least they get a chance for happiness! I only ask as much, no more.
JOR-EL:	Yours is a higher happiness! The fulfillment of your mission! The inspiration! ... You must have felt that happiness within you. My son, surely you cannot deny that feeling.
SUPERMAN:	No, I cannot. Any more than I can deny the other, which is stronger in me, father, so much stronger. Is there no way, then, father? Must I finally be denied the one thing in life which I truly desire?[12]

This conflict may seem pretty stark: the deepest desire of Superman's heart pitted against his father's vision of his life's mission. Notice, though, that Jor-El is *not* saying that Superman must set aside his happiness for the sake of his duty. Instead, he claims that the life of service to others brings a higher kind of happiness, reminiscent of British philosopher John Stuart Mill (1806–1873) and his distinction between higher and lower pleasures. Mill argues that pleasures differ not only in quantity, but also in quality. Famously, Mill says that "it is better to be a human being dissatisfied than a pig satisfied; better to be Socrates dissatisfied than a fool satisfied."[13] Perhaps we may read Jor-El as saying that it is better to be Superman dissatisfied, but the savior of the world, than to be Clark Kent satisfied as "merely" a husband to Lois. For Clark to set aside his powers is selfish, but only in the sense that he would be following lesser pleasures and ignoring higher ones. In Jor-El's opinion, complying with the S-Principle by remaining true to his Kryptonian heritage is the path to the highest happiness for his son.

Clark's adoptive father Jonathan Kent seems to have roughly the same notion in mind in the following speech from *Superman: Earth One*:

> But there are things you can do that nobody else can. Important things. Things that can mean the difference between life and death for a whole lot of people. I came up believing that sometimes we all have to serve something bigger than ourselves. We don't want to do it, we'd give anything not to have to do it … but we do it anyway. We square our shoulders and we get it done … You've been hiding your whole life, Clark. But if you do anything other than what I think you were meant to do, you'll still be hiding, because you'll never be able to show people who you really are, and what you can do. Life was meant to be lived full measure, flat out, pedal to the metal. Don't live the rest of your life like a Porsche that never leaves the garage because somebody's afraid to scratch it. Live, Clark. Follow your passion. Show the whole world what you can do. Fly, Clark …[14]

Neither Jor-El nor Jonathan Kent believes that their son must sacrifice his true happiness so that he may be the hero the world needs. Rather, they argue that it is only by becoming that hero that he will find out who he is and what truly makes him happy. It helps, of course, that calamity strikes any time Superman does lose or surrender his powers, whether it's an alien invasion or a nasty bully in a far northern diner.

Can we, too, find our highest happiness in some kind of noble calling? Certainly helping others can provide us with great happiness, although we have to go about it the right way. Philosopher Henry Sidgwick (1838–1900) wrote of the *paradox of hedonism*, which maintains that the worst way to make yourself happy is to *try* to be happy.[15] Instead of thinking about your own happiness, even through trying to help others, you should just do things that make you happy as a result. Jor-El and Jonathan are urging Clark to accept that he has a *vocation* to serve humanity because of who he is and what he can do, and by following that vocation, Clark will achieve a deep, lasting happiness.[16] But few of us can realistically have that vocation. How often does one of us have the chance and the wherewithal to save the planet? Nonetheless, it's easy to imagine Peter Singer pointing out that you don't need special gifts or a vocation to pull a drowning child out of a pond or to sign a check to your favorite charity.

Lex Luthor, Villain or Hero?

The most extreme response to the S-Principle's demand that we help is simply to deny that the bad things that are happening can be prevented in the first place. The *Neo-Malthusian* view, named in honor of the economist Thomas Malthus (1766–1834), states that any attempt to help those in impoverished conditions is not only likely to fail, but in the end will likely do more harm than good. One representative of this school of thought, the ecologist Garrett Hardin (1915–2003), compared this situation to being in a crowded lifeboat: if we try to save too many who are drowning, then everybody will go down with the ship.[17] In general, those who want to help folks in need may have good intentions, but in the end they will make matters worse. However, while it may be reasonable to argue that on some occasions relief efforts will do more harm than good, it is implausible to think that this is true across the board, or that the lifeboat analogy applies to all attempts to help others.

In his own megalomaniacal way, Lex Luthor often asserts that Superman is doing more harm than good. He often says things like, "You've taught humanity to rely on you and not fight for themselves … They need someone to wake them up. They need someone to show them they can reach for the stars without flying them up there. They need someone human to aspire to."[18] And in the *Justice* miniseries, he lashes out against all superhuman would-be saviors of humanity:

Who decided we needed to be saved? Who decided to roll out the red carpet for the saviors? That's what I want to know. We were the forgers of the planet, the lifters of the flame. We were the dreamers and the myth-makers, we were the inventors, and the industry and the life and the blood. Not them. But it's too late now. We gave it to the aliens and to the robots and to the myths that demanded with their presence that we believe in them. And bow to them. And trust them. We discovered the atom. We created the bomb. It was our responsibility. It didn't have to be, not fully. Not in a world populated by the otherworldly. We should have done all we could despite the rescuers. But we were lazy. Their very being made us lazy. And now it's all going to blow up in our collective face. I hate to say I told you so. But who listens to me? I'm only human.[19]

Superman may save plenty of people, but Luthor believes that he is a menace—in part because of fears he will bring an alien threat to our planet, but more significantly because he threatens to rob us of our self-reliance.[20]

In the Communist "utopia" of *Superman: Red Son*, Kal-El remarks that it troubles him that no one even bothers with life preservers or seat belts any more. In that same world, Batman comments that "we're like his pets. Animals in a cage. He might feed us and shelter everyone. But we're never going to be free while that monster's running the show."[21] Is that where following the S-Principle will lead? This may not be a concern for us, since it is hardly in your power or mine to come anywhere near preventing all bad things from happening. Superman, on the other hand, could pull it off. But maybe he shouldn't. The S-Principle only instructs us to prevent something bad from happening when it doesn't involve sacrificing something of comparable moral importance. But things like freedom and creativity seem very important, not worth trading away for safety and security.

Does that mean we should say goodbye not to Clark but to Superman? Lex thinks so. But this assumes that Superman's various heroic activities will inevitably lead to some nightmarish scenario. And why assume that? The idea that Superman can never help without co-opting our freedom is as implausible as the idea that we can never help without doing harm.

Man and Superman

Clark Kent and Superman: We've had glimpses of worlds in which one exists without the other. But they're both normally there, and occasionally at odds. Jor-El wants Superman to embrace his destiny as Earth's savior, Martha wants Clark to find a life for himself, and Lex wants Superman to leave and let humanity find its own path. As is his wont, Superman somehow discovers a way to find the best in each of these roles. At the end of *Superman: Secret Origin*, Superman sets himself against both Luthor and Jor-El, telling the citizens of Metropolis that

> I want you to stop looking for a great savior. Lex Luthor isn't it. I'm not it. You are. All of you are. I do what I do because I was given a gift, but all of you were given gifts, too. Use them to make each other's lives better. Show the world that Metropolis has a heart.[22]

Superman also makes a life for himself with Lois, which is a good thing both for him and for us all. It is through his relationships with his parents, his friends, and ultimately his wife that he is made human and made to care about a people who are not his own. The speculative future foretold in *Kingdom Come* shows a Superman who abandons the world because he is no longer "tethered to human concerns through the love of an earthly woman."[23] In our time, however, Superman somehow manages to have a life and to save the world.

We, too, need to find a way to help others without pressuring or controlling them, in order to keep our charitable efforts in balance with our efforts to craft a meaningful life for ourselves. These are not easy things to do. But our predicament is somewhat easier to cope with than Superman's is. After all, we share this problem together as human beings, whereas Superman is all on his own—or is he?

Notes

1. *Superman for All Seasons* #1 (September 1998), reprinted in *Superman for All Seasons* (1999).

2. *Batman/Superman/Wonder Woman: Trinity* #1 (August 2003), reprinted in *Batman/Superman/Wonder Woman: Trinity* (2004).

3. Peter Singer, "Famine, Affluence, and Morality," *Philosophy and Public Affairs* 1(1972): 229–243 (and reprinted in countless anthologies). See also the more recent "The Singer Solution to Global Poverty," *The New York Times Magazine*, September 5, 1999, 60–63, and chapter 9 by Gadon in this volume (in which Singer's principle is contrasted with Nietzsche).

4. For more on the topic of how much we can reasonably demand from Superman, see chapter 14 by Anton in this volume.

5. Tom De Haven, *It's Superman!* (New York: Ballantine Books, 2006).

6. This is sometimes known as the principle of "ought implies can"; on this, see chapter 2 by Feltham and chapter 14 by Anton in this volume.

7. In fact, he did suffer from clinical depression after the loss of New Krypton; see *Superman: Grounded Vol. 1* and *2* (2011), discussed in chapter 1 by White in this volume.

8. *Superman: Red Son* #2 (July 2003), reprinted in *Superman: Red Son* (2004).

9. *Superman: Red Son* #3 (August 2003). For more on this story, see chapter 4 by Sharp in this volume.

10. *Superman: Earth One.*

11. On agent-relative and agent-neutral perspectives and "the aim of living our own lives," see Thomas Nagel, "Autonomy and Deontology," in *Consequentialism and Its Critics*, ed. Samuel Scheffler (Oxford: Oxford University Press, 1988), 142–172.

12. *Superman II: The Richard Donner Cut* (2006).

13. John Stuart Mill, *Utilitarianism* (1863), available at http://www.utili tarianism.com/mill1.htm. (The pig/Socrates quote is from chapter 2.)

14. *Superman: Earth One.*

15. Henry Sidgwick, *The Methods of Ethics* (Indianapolis: Hackett, 1884/1981), 48.

16. The ancient philosophers, such as Aristotle (384–322 BCE) called this type of happiness or fulfillment *eudaimonia*.

17. Garrett Hardin, "Lifeboat Ethics: The Case Against Helping the Poor," *Psychology Today* 8 (1974): 38–43.

18. *Action Comics Annual* #11 (July 2008), reprinted in *Superman: Last Son* (2008).

19. *Justice* #1 (October 2005), reprinted in *Justice* (2012).

20. For more on Luthor's fears, see chapter 11 by Donovan and Richardson in this volume.

21. *Superman: Red Son* #2.

22. *Superman: Secret Origin* #3 (January 2010), reprinted in *Superman: Secret Origin* (2010).

23. *Kingdom Come* #2 (June 1996), reprinted in *Kingdom Come* (1996). For more on *Kingdom Come*, see chapter 12 by Hatfield in this volume.

Chapter 14

The Weight of the World
How Much Is Superman Morally Responsible For?

Audrey L. Anton

While it might have been Peter Parker's Uncle Ben who first coined the comic-book adage "with great power comes great responsibility," Superman had already been living it for decades. In fact, Superman's endless list of responsibilities left him little time for the kind of philosophical reflection it would take to come up with such a catchy phrase. Whether it's a natural disaster, a commonplace traffic accident, or the threats of destruction intentionally created by one of Superman's many enemies, the Man of Steel is always busy saving someone—and, occasionally, everyone. Nobody knows better than Superman the kind of responsibilities imposed upon the powerful. That is why he is a perfect case study for a philosophical investigation of the question of whether enough is enough. Is it possible that even Superman has too much on his plate? Is it fair to expect him to save the day every day all day long?

Know Your Role!

If it is true that great responsibilities come with great power, we must first get clear on which type of responsibility we mean. *Prospective responsibilities* are prospective or forward-looking in that they tell us how to behave in the present and in the future. With prospective responsibility, one is responsible if and only if one has a duty or obligation to perform or abstain from a particular action.

Superman and Philosophy: What Would the Man of Steel Do?, First Edition. Edited by Mark D. White.
© 2013 John Wiley & Sons, Inc. Published 2013 by John Wiley & Sons, Inc.

Prospective responsibilities can either be special, applying to only certain people with whom you have some sort of a relationship, or universal, which apply to everyone. *Special responsibilities* are often based on roles, and for this reason are sometimes called *role responsibilities* as well. For example, Ma and Pa Kent have the prospective responsibility of providing for their child, Clark, while he is young. Their role as parents brings with it the prospective responsibilities of providing Clark with food, shelter, an education, and so forth. It is their relationship to Clark that grounds this responsibility to him.

In addition, a person's capacities also help determine which prospective responsibilities he or she has. For instance, only those with medical training are obligated to stop and assist victims of car accidents (the rest of us rubberneckers are permitted—nay, urged—to continue driving). On the other hand, a person with a broken leg is not obligated to save a child from the second story of a burning building. The reason why is grounded in a doctrine attributed to philosopher Immanuel Kant (1724–1804): *ought implies can*. According to this view, if we say that a person ought to do something, then that person must be able to do that thing. For example, if we say Superman *ought* to prevent a powerless helicopter from falling onto a crowd of people, then we have to assume that Superman *can* do so. If he weren't able to do so—as I can't, and I assume you can't either—it would be unfair to hold him (or us) responsible for catching the falling helicopter.

While special responsibilities can be defined by role and capacity, *universal responsibilities* apply more generally, regardless of any special relationship or ability. For example, we all have a prospective responsibility to avoid causing unnecessary harm to anyone. So, any time that Lex Luthor plans to bomb a city, it is morally wrong not only because he has no right to do so, but also because he has a responsibility *not* to do so—as do we all. According to philosophers such as Kant, we all have this obligation in virtue of being rational beings: everyone is obligated, all things considered, not to harm others *because* it is owed to everyone not to be unnecessarily harmed. Typically, non-universal prospective responsibilities generate *special obligations*, which are only owed to a few people, like the Kent's parental obligations to young Clark. Superman's prospective role responsibility to fight for truth, justice, and the American way can be particularly burdensome because all people qualify as beneficiaries (Americans or not).

Superhindsight

Responsibility can also be *retrospective* in that responsibility is often assessed after some action or effect has taken place, and then the person is praised or blamed for it. Depending on the consequences and the motives or intentions of the person, we might also consider the agent deserving of reward or punishment. For example, if Lois risks falling to her death from an elevator shaft in the Eiffel Tower to investigate a story, we might praise her work ethic or her love for the truth. She might even be rewarded with the Pulitzer Prize because her bravery and devotion to the truth was *that* impressive.

However, if we learn that her true motive was to win the Pulitzer, we would likely not consider her praiseworthy, and we might even blame her for putting herself in danger out of vanity. But would we punish her? Typically, we only punish people when the consequences of their behavior are harmful and wrongful. For example, had Lois's behavior resulted in some freak accident where others plummeted to their deaths, we might hold her responsible for those deaths and punish her. Similarly, if it were reasonable for her to anticipate such disaster, even if no disaster occurred, we might find her guilty of negligence or the reckless endangerment of others.

Retrospective responsibility is a *causal* notion: we are responsible for things that happen (or were very likely to happen) only if we played an important role in the chain of events that led to them. So, if Lois's behavior had resulted in death and destruction, she would be retrospectively responsible and held accountable for her actions. But since nothing bad resulted, Lois gets a pass. It is important to distinguish this result from a different one involving *inaction* or *omissions*: while we can't blame someone for causing nothing, we can sometimes blame them for standing by and doing nothing to prevent bad consequences from happening—especially when it's in their power to do so. In the 1983 movie *Superman III*, Superman postpones saving a truck driver from an accident on a bridge in order to further woo (or harass) Lana Lang. As a result of his dawdling, he arrives at the scene a few seconds too late to save the man. Superman is blameworthy because he could have arrived in time to save the man but he chose not to. So, judgments about retrospective responsibility can be about actions as well as omissions, since both are assessed in terms of what actually occurs and the part a person played in causing it.

Furthermore, prospective and retrospective responsibilities sometimes work together to make someone even more blameworthy for something they caused. For instance, Superman is doubly to blame for the truck driver's death when he decided to flirt with Lana first. He could have helped and didn't, which makes him responsible retrospectively, but he also had a prospective responsibility to help because it's his job—he's Superman! And even Superman knows that he, more than anyone else, should save people. He says as much when Henry Johnson heroically saves his colleague, Pete, from falling from the top of the skyscraper they were helping to build. In one motion, Johnson leaps from the structure, grabbing Pete by his belt with one hand and a nearby cable with the other. While Johnson is able to swing Pete to safety, the cable gives way and he begins to plummet to his death ... until Superman grabs him. When Johnson expresses gratitude to Superman, Superman replies: "You know, I saw how you helped that other man. I'd say that your efforts were more impressive than mine. You certainly took a much bigger risk than I just did."[1] The problem for Superman is that *any* courageous or selfless act will be harder for anyone else to perform. That is the burden of being the best among men. As Lex Luthor remarked when speaking to Superman through a frequency only he and dogs could hear, "Nobody's perfect ... well, almost nobody."

In the same way that we are appalled when police officers or prosecutors commit crimes, we are enraged when Superman neglects saving someone. It's their job to do the exact opposite of what they have done! They, most of all, are capable of fulfilling that role well! In Superman's case, he is both the most—if not uniquely—capable, as well as the most trustworthy candidate for the roles and responsibilities we give him. And we do give him a lot.

There's Demanding and Then There's Demanding

Moral philosophy or *ethics* is demanding by nature, telling us what we should or should not do. But one ethical theory in particular, *utilitarianism*, is more demanding than most, and is often criticized as requiring too much of us. Utilitarians hold that actions are morally good in proportion to the overall utility and happiness that they produce, and bad in proportion to the overall pain and suffering that they produce. When determining how to act in a certain situation, the utilitarian must consider how each action will affect everybody—since every person's well-being counts equally under utilitarianism—not just now but into the future, including unintended consequences. Since much of this is difficult to know, the utilitarian must foresee all the possible effects of each action, weighed by their respective probabilities. (Calculators ready?)

Not surprisingly, utilitarianism is often subject to the "demands too much" objection, accused of imposing too much pressure on a person and thereby compromising a person's ability to secure her own happiness. For example, consider your next purchase of a Superman graphic novel. While the comic is sure to bring you great personal happiness and utility, this good thing comes at a cost. It not only costs you a certain amount of money—let's say $15—but there are many other things that you could do with $15. You could give it to a soup kitchen, or the United Way, or a homeless person. This is also true of how we spend our time. Every moment we are watching television or reading comics, minutes are lost that you could be, well, pretending to be Superman! How can you possibly justify the purchase (and reading) of this graphic novel (or the book in your hands, even) when there are so many other ways to spend the money that yield *more significant* consequences for many other people? Contemporary utilitarian, Peter Singer, willingly bites this bullet in his famous paper "Famine, Affluence, and Morality."[2] Singer happily acknowledges this consequence of utilitarianism and implores us to give almost *all* of our wealth to the poor. Few people have jumped on Singer's bandwagon, however; and this consequence of utilitarianism has created many converts for other ethical theories.

It Ain't Right, I Tell Ya, It Ain't Right

Utilitarianism is widely regarded as too demanding, but there are alternative ethical systems that allow more leeway for people to give special consideration to their own good. One such theory is *deontology*, which judges acts to be right or wrong based on the moral quality of the acts themselves, normally using basic rules or duties. Since deontologists don't assess the morality of acts based on their consequences, the "right" action isn't necessarily going to be the one that maximizes an outcome such as total utility, happiness, or well-being.

Many deontologists distinguish between negative and positive obligations. *Negative obligations* tell us what we should never do: do not lie, do not kill, do not steal, and so forth. *Positive obligations*, on the other hand, tell us what we should do: most important, help others. Utilitarians don't care about this distinction—both negative and positive obligations are important insofar as they increase total utility—but deontologists usually consider positive obligations to be less, well, obligating, even optional. They argue that people have *agent-centered prerogatives* which explicitly allow people to act in ways that fail to maximize utility or well-being—such as buying yourself a Superman graphic novel once in a while instead of giving all your money to help feed the poor. Agent-centered prerogatives allow people to give themselves special preference on occasion, rather than having to sacrifice their own well-being for the common good at every turn. This isn't an excuse to be completely selfish, but rather a justification to treat yourself once in a while after doing much good for others.

The distinction between negative and positive obligations even extends to matters of life and death. In 1940, out of concern for young comics readers (and threats of impending censorship), editor Whitney Ellsworth banned Superman (and other DC heroes) from killing.[3] So Superman is required not to kill (a negative obligation), but does he have the positive obligation to prevent *all* untimely deaths? Intuitively, we aren't; we are expected not to kill each other, but we are not required to make it our life's mission to prevent all untimely deaths (though this would be admirable).

Not everyone agrees that killing someone is worse than letting that person die. Philosopher James Rachels (1941–2003) argues that whatever difference there is between killing and letting die is not morally relevant. For example, is it worse to force a child's head underwater and drown her, or to stand inches away from her, watching her drown after falling in? For Rachels, this is a trick question: they are equally horrible things to do.[4] If you pass a small child drowning in a wading pool, you should pull her out. If Superman passes by a busload of people dangling from the edge of a bridge, isn't he just as obligated to pull it up? We expect Superman to fulfill both types of obligation: he cannot kill and *he'd better* save.[5] After all, saving lives is his job!

Why do we expect more from Superman? Obviously, because Superman is capable of saving many more lives than any of us ever could, and most of the time he doesn't even have to break a sweat. Even if he slips up and someone dies, like Lois does at the end of 1978's *Superman: The Movie*, Superman can simply turn back time by flying a few quick laps around the Earth. If Superman is capable of preventing all unnatural deaths, could it be argued that he should?

According to most deontologists, the answer to this question is an emphatic "no." We are only required to fulfill the basic negative duties all of the time, and we can casually or even arbitrarily fulfill positive obligations. This aspect of deontology has a totally different problem from that of utilitarianism—deontology might *demand too little*. Can you imagine Superman lounging by an above-ground pool while the public screams for him to extinguish a nearby fire? What would they think if he were to shout back, "No, thank you. I saved a lot of folks yesterday and boy am I tired!" If he were to respond like this, we would be aggravated for at least two reasons. First, it is intuitive to say that Superman simply *must* save the day. Second, his nonchalant attitude indicates that he just doesn't care about the right things. Both utilitarianism and deontology are satisfied when we do the right thing even if we do it kicking and screaming. But that is not the way of a great superhero—that's the attitude of a big baby!

The Big Blue Boy Scout

While people use the name "big blue boy scout" in a derogatory way with Superman, it is a nice way to capture an ethical theory that might grant Superman's responsibilities while allowing him a chance to live his own life: *virtue ethics*.

Virtue ethics first appears in the works of the ancient Greek philosophers, such as Aristotle (384–322 BCE), and has enjoyed a renaissance among contemporary philosophers since the second half of the twentieth century. According to virtue ethics, we shouldn't try to determine which actions to perform or to avoid consistently. There can be no hard and fast rules. A virtuous person knows when to take a break and when to keep on working. According to virtue ethics, we should try to *be* a certain kind of person, and the right actions will follow. In other words, a person with the right kind of character will likely do the right thing—even if one situation calls for fulfilling an obligation and another calls for maximizing utility.

According to Aristotle's virtue ethics, a human being should aim at his or her own *eudaimonia*, which can be loosely translated as happiness. Aristotle's notion of happiness is more than simple pleasure or a good mood, however; it involves the total flourishing of the human being throughout his or her life. We flourish when we are the best versions of ourselves that we can be, or when we are *excellent* rational animals. This involves a balance between pursuing our own personal development and behaving responsibly as citizens. It requires care for oneself in the manner of maintaining health, resources, and intellectual stimulation, and also concern for your fellow people (or, more generally, creatures). Finally, you should exercise virtues for the sake of being virtuous; such actions must flow naturally from your habits, dispositions, and character traits, rather than from opportunistic or selfish purposes.[6]

Virtue ethics can help us to see how Superman can be a hero without bearing all the weight of the world upon his shoulders. Given his powers, he has many abilities and talents *to* develop, so it makes sense that he would spend time learning, exercising, and experiencing the world. However, he should not focus entirely on making himself excellent in a self-centered way; if he is truly excellent, he should use his abilities to help the world as well. And because he is a good person, he also *wants* to care for the world; helping flows naturally from his character.

But this does not mean that he cannot care for himself too. In fact, he should care for himself in order to stay excellent. Superman does this from time to time, whether it's recovering from injuries or spending time alone or with Lois, both for himself and to be a better hero for the world. But virtue ethics does not permit him to focus solely on himself, for to do so would also compromise his flourishing; selfishness tends to warp our view of the world and drive people away from us. Fortunately for us, selfishness is not in Superman's character, and this is part of what makes him a hero—and a virtuous one at that.

Superman Meets His Match: Supererogatory!

We expect a lot from Superman because he can do a lot. But is it possible for him to do more than we expect or than he "should" do? It would seem that the greater the capabilities and responsibilities people have, the less impressed we are when they fulfill them, and the more upset we are when they don't. On the one hand, this makes sense. If young Lois were expected to clean her room, her father wouldn't praise her when she did. But if she volunteered to mow the lawn and did a great job at it, he would praise her and possibly reward her. She went "above and beyond the call of duty." Philosophers call such actions *supererogatory*. Ironically, however, it might not be possible for Superman to be supererogatory since very little is above or beyond the call of duty for him, given our incredibly high expectations.

Utilitarianism doesn't have much room for supererogatory actions, because it's a *perfectionist* system. As we described, it demands that the absolute best action be performed in any given situation and if you're expected to do the best thing, there is no way to exceed expectations. Deontology would seem to fare better, since many philosophers in that tradition write literally of obligations and duties, beyond which we would find supererogatory actions. But as we have seen, deontology cannot explain why Superman should choose *this* opportunity to fulfill positive duties and forego different ones, and some versions have positive obligations that extend to just about everything.[7] In addition, neither utilitarianism nor deontology requires Superman to *care* about truth, justice, or the American way. It's good enough that we do what we're supposed to—reluctantly or not. But Superman's virtue is that he does care about these (and many other) things. He cares about the *right* things. That's just the kind of person he is—and we wouldn't want it any other way.

Virtue ethics has the best chance to explain how Superman can perform supererogatory acts, since it doesn't focus on good action as such, but rather good character. The virtuous person, by definition, does virtuous things, but these are not defined in a perfectionist way like utilitarians and (some) deontologists would. As a result, the virtuous person can do things that are above and beyond what we expect a virtuous person to do. If someone sees a fire in the top floor of an apartment building, we expect him or her, as a good person, to call 911. If that same person runs into the building to get people out, that is more than we expect, so that is supererogatory. It would not be supererogatory, however, for Superman to fly into the burning building to save the residents, because we expect that of him—that's part of being a virtuous superhero. But we don't expect him to save people 24 hours a day, seven days a week. That would exceed what we have a right to expect. So if Superman does spend an entire week saving people, he would definitely be going above and beyond the call!

The Weight of the World

In the 1980 film *Superman II*, Superman is told by a hologram of his birth mother that if he wishes to be with Lois Lane, he must forfeit all of his powers. Presumably, Superman must do this because marrying Lois would obligate him to care for her in a partial way; she would have to come first and the *rest* of the world second. While he ultimately chooses to remain a superhero, it does not follow that he be doomed to eternal servitude, like the mythological figure Atlas, bearing the world upon his shoulders. As Sir Robert Baden-Powell, the original (though not terribly big or blue) boy scout famously put it: "Leave this world a little better than you found it."

Superman has obligations, but he also has rights. He cares about the future of humanity and the world, which involves considering various possible consequences. But what grounds all of this is the fact that Superman is virtuous; he is a *responsible* person. He takes care to make himself the best version of himself that he possibly can all the while improving humanity writ large. He has left the world a better place already. He is not obligated to make the world perfect single-handedly. He might not even be able to do that. But one thing's for certain: when the chips are down we can count on him, and he deserves more than just a little credit for that.

Notes

1. Roger Stern, *The Death and Life of Superman* (New York: Bantam Books, 1993), 5–7.
2. Peter Singer, "Famine, Affluence, and Morality," *Philosophy and Public Affairs* 1 (1972): 229–243. For more on Singer, see chapter 9 by Gadon in this volume.
3. Will Murray, "'The Driving Force That Really Made DC Great': Whitney Ellsworth and the Rise of National/DC Comics," *Alter Ego* no. 98 (December 2010): 9.

4. James Rachels, "Active and Passive Euthanasia," *The New England Journal of Medicine* 292 (1975): 78–80, and reprinted in roughly 300 anthologies.

5. For a rare case of Superman killing someone, see chapter 1 by White in this volume.

6. For more on virtue ethics, see Rosalind Hursthouse's entry at the *Stanford Encyclopedia of Philosophy*: http://plato.stanford.edu/entries/ethics-virtue/.

7. This is particular problem for Immanuel Kant's deontology and supererogation; see Marcia Baron, *Kantian Ethics (Almost) without Apology* (Ithaca, NY: Cornell University Press, 1995), part I.

Part Five

SUPERMAN AND HUMANITY
A MATCH MADE ON KRYPTON?

Chapter 15

Superman and Man
What a Kryptonian Can Teach Us About Humanity

Leonard Finkelman

History has given us some great rivalries: Joe Frazier and Muhammad Ali, Albert Einstein and Niels Bohr, Batman and the Joker. But few rivalries run as deep as the one between Superman and Lex Luthor. I would argue that the rivalry between Superman and Luthor is greater than any of those already mentioned because it's a *philosophical* one. More than a contest of brute force or a debate over facts, it is a conflict over how to look at the world.

As it happens, the dispute between Superman and Luthor corresponds well with an ongoing debate between philosophers over what it means to be human. Are humans by nature kind and compassionate, like Superman, or mean-spirited and selfish, like Luthor? There is a mystery at the heart of the debate over human nature, and resolution of this mystery may help to finally decide the never-ending battle between Superman and Luthor. You're going to dive into this mystery, but keep your wits sharp: in a battle like this, the only way to keep the opposition from victory is, in Luthor's words, "to be right."[1]

Mystery of the Bizarro World!

In the multiverse of philosophical theories, we find two Earths, which we'll call Earth-P and Earth-O. Earth-P is home to the *human nature pessimist*, who believes that humankind is essentially selfish and

Superman and Philosophy: What Would the Man of Steel Do?, First Edition. Edited by Mark D. White.

quarrelsome. On this world we find, in the words of philosopher Thomas Hobbes (1588–1679), "continual fear, and danger of violent death," and "the life of man [is] solitary, poor, nasty, brutish, and short."[2] Earth-O, by contrast, hosts the *human nature optimist*, who believes that the essence of humanity is selflessness. On this world, to quote philosopher Jean-Jacques Rousseau (1712–1778), "men, being wild rather than wicked, and more intent to guard themselves against the mischief that might be done them, than to do mischief to others, were by no means subject to very perilous dissensions."[3]

These Earths are so diametrically opposed that one simply has to be a Bizarro version of the other. The philosophical debate over human nature comes down to this mystery: do we come from Earth-P or Earth-O? Using Superman as a guide, we're going to visit these two worlds to try to figure out which is ours and which is the Bizarro World. Before we can solve the mystery, however, we're going to need to know what clues we're looking for and how to find them.

First, we need to know what we mean by "human nature." Does Kal-El, the alien we know as Superman, qualify as "human"? In one sense, the answer is obviously no: a *biological human* is any organism in the reproductive chain that includes members of the species *Homo sapiens*, and aliens need not apply. Philosophically, the question may be less about whether Kal-El is part of our biological community and more about whether he's part of our *moral* community. Indeed, a constant theme in the last several decades of Superman comics has been his quest to be a part of humanity, morally if not biologically. Since this book is not titled *Superman and Biology*, we're going to focus on the moral sense of "human" from here on out.[4]

So much for the word "human"—what about "nature"? To a philosopher, nature means *essence*, an object's defining characteristic. It's a tool we use to identify and keep track of objects as they change across time and space. We use this very tool when we read about the Supermen of the multiverse, recognizing Superman in alternate realities wherein he's an Amish farmer (*Justice League: The Nail*, 1999), the champion of the Soviet Union (*Superman: Red Son*, 2004), or a vigilante calling himself Batman (*Superman: Speeding Bullets*, 1993). We don't even need to drag alternate universes into it: we can identify Superman across different artistic interpretations thanks to his essence.[5] So *human nature* is the core characteristic(s) we use to recognize humans as humans.

Now that we know what we mean by human nature, we're going to need a method for finding it, and this often involves finding the most important characteristics of something across various examples of it. Take Grant Morrison's version of Lex Luthor that he created for the *All-Star Superman* series (2006–2008), which is considered by many to embody the true essence of the villain. To escape the many variations and changes made to the character throughout decades of convoluted storylines, Morrison took all the previous interpretations of the character and got rid of everything that varied from one portrayal to another. Things like flowing red hair, ownership of a Fortune 500 company, and the American presidency were cast aside, leaving only the character's "timeless, essential elements"—that is, the nature of Lex Luthor. In much the same way, we can derive humanity's essence by getting rid of everything that we don't really need to be considered human.

Strange Visitor to Earth-P!

Whether or not we accept Superman as one of us says a lot about what we take to be part of human nature. For two and a half thousand years, philosophers have searched for humanity's essence by looking within. Maybe now it's time to look somewhere else—perhaps up in the sky.

One of the elements common to nearly all portrayals of Luthor—part of the character's nature, really—is that he regards Superman as an alien, clearly separated from humankind. Luthor's opposition to the Man of Steel comes from his perception that the alien's presence diminishes humanity by setting a standard that no human can possibly reach. If humanity is going to be in charge of itself, then someone—Luthor, presumably—is going to have to eliminate Superman, or else we run the risk of being dominated by a clearly superior being. These concerns make a great deal of sense when you consider human nature pessimism, and in particular the philosophy of Thomas Hobbes.

There are three main components of Hobbes's philosophy that form the basis of his pessimism. First, he was a *materialist*: he believed that there's nothing more to reality than physical objects and their observable properties. Related to this, he was also an *empiricist*: he believed that experience is the only sure guide to knowledge. Finally, as a consequence of these views, he was a *moral anti-realist*, rejecting the idea that ethical claims—for example, "murdering Superman is morally wrong"—can be objectively and universally judged as true or false. When Luthor sneers at the concept of truth because it has no color, and then sets "the Gospel According to Lex Luthor" in opposition to "all the things you can't weigh or carry" in Superman's moral code, he's really preaching the gospel according to Hobbes.[6]

It might seem surprising, then, that Hobbes would have much to say about human nature. After all, essence is just as weightless and intangible as truth or justice. But even if you can't directly observe human nature, Hobbes thought that you could still discover something about it through things that you *can* observe. Having lived through the bloody English Civil War of 1642–1651, Hobbes had the opportunity to discover the essence of humankind firsthand. Preoccupied with its internal conflicts, the English government was basically shut down, leaving the English people with only the "timeless, essential elements" of human existence. They were returned to what Hobbes called the *state of nature*, before the development of governments, and here he believed he could observe essential human nature.

What Hobbes saw was a nation of people behaving like inmates at Stryker's Island Prison being given their first taste of freedom. In his book *Leviathan*, Hobbes noted four conditions of living in the state of nature: limited resources, similarity of ability, similarity of need, and limited altruism. A criminal would face similar conditions, since living outside the law is just an attempt to live outside government rule. To set yourself up as a criminal in Metropolis, you're going to need a big chunk of kryptonite (to say nothing of a lead-lined hideout and a rocket pack). Unfortunately for you, kryptonite is in short supply and high demand among your competitors. If you find a piece, it's in your rational self-interest to do everything in your power to get it and keep it, but so too should every other criminal in Metropolis. Since your abilities are roughly similar (let's assume that none of you has superpowers) and you're certainly not going to help one another, the only logical result can be your own never-ending battle over the radioactive rock.

Now replace "kryptonite" with "food" or "shelter," and the result will be the rather dismal state of affairs on Earth-P. No wonder Luthor described the community of jailbirds in Stryker's prison as "a world in miniature": without the stability of civil society, we're all prisoners of our needs, restless and ready to riot at the slightest provocation. Earth-P seems to be our state of nature.[7]

Civilizing Earth-P

But why should we believe we come from Earth-P if our world seems to be in such better shape than what Luthor (or Hobbes) describes? According to the pessimist, the reason is that we've created a *social contract* to improve our lot. "Might makes right" on Earth-P—which it must, because a moral anti-realist has no other standard for judging what's right—but no one wants to be ruled by the mighty. A well-run government can play the role of a prison warden: it keeps tougher inmates in line and makes sure everyone is treated fairly and equitably. Rational self-interest—or, less politely, selfishness—therefore demands an exchange of freedom for peace and security from a higher authority. Work for Luthor, give him some of that kryptonite, and he'll protect you from the big blue boy scout. Better safe than sorry, right? Our world may not look like Earth-P now, but it may be just one government shutdown away.

The real problem with Superman, according to Luthor, is that his powers and abilities, far beyond those of mortal men, make him the fittest of all. It's a fear that's been played out in numerous stories: what would happen if a normal human being had to stand against Superman?[8] Good luck getting very far without that kryptonite. If might makes right, as the pessimists suggest, then Superman will *always* be right—and no human can ever be truly free. We can preserve some level of freedom by having a say in who should govern us and how, but no one has a say in who gets to be Superman.

The only reason that Superman doesn't completely dominate humanity is that he uses his powers for the good of humankind rather than to dominate it. Many writers regard this as one of the primary reasons that Luthor cannot help but view Superman as an alien: as Hobbes argued, humans are essentially limited in their willingness to help others.[9] We've all asked the question: what would *you* do if you had Superman's powers? According to Luthor—and any other human nature pessimist—if your answer doesn't include some variation on the term "global domination," then you simply can't be human. On Earth-P, then, Superman's unfailing helpfulness excludes him from being included amongst humankind. It's just too alien a characteristic![10]

The Super-Men of Earth-O!

Does Superman's presence help mankind or hurt it? In his classic story, "Must There Be a Superman?", writer Elliot S! Maggin has Superman confront the idea that his attempts to help humanity have ultimately hindered our "social growth."[11] Perhaps there really is something to the idea that Superman limits human freedom: after all, if we were to depend on Superman to stop every earthquake, deflect every asteroid, or rescue every kitten caught up a tree, then we would be passing up opportunities to grow and better ourselves. Perhaps Superman ultimately hurts us by helping us.

This is how people think on Earth-P—it's survival of the fittest out there, and relying on others for help will only make us less fit—but the human nature optimists of Earth-O think otherwise. Jean-Jacques Rousseau, the quintessential optimist, would have argued that the Bizarros on Earth-P lacked one essential human trait: *compassion*, the innate feeling of aversion to seeing other living things suffer. Pride and jealousy are unknown on Earth-O because those feelings arise only when we notice inequality; since we all have the capacity to suffer, compassion will give us an egalitarian view of humankind. The Superman of Earth-O would never dominate humanity because he would perceive us as his (moral) equals.

It's admittedly difficult to see how Earth-O could possibly be the real Earth. After all, it seems like we have dozens of Luthors for every Superman.[12] The Luthors of the world seem to win pretty often too: as the greatest criminal mastermind of our time likes to brag, "brain beats brawn, every time."[13] Why should you believe that humans are naturally kind and peaceful if you have so much evidence to the contrary? The defense of human nature optimism turns out to be somewhat paradoxical. According to the optimists, our world doesn't look like the idealistic vision of Earth-O because, while our selflessness makes us social animals, society inevitably corrupts our selfless nature.

As a sign of this paradox, Rousseau wrote that mankind is "born free, and everywhere … is in chains."[14] In the state of nature of

Earth-O, you have compassion for your neighbor; however, your desire for compassion from her will compel you toward *vanity*, or the attempt to elevate yourself and diminish others. Since other people will likewise desire compassion from their neighbors, pride and jealousy will insidiously spread among humankind. The only way to guard against this spread is to develop rules of conduct that set limits on acceptable behavior, leaving us with a choice between vanity and restriction of our natural freedom. To wit: forcing Superman to keep decent while changing from his Clark Kent clothes may satisfy those of us with less super physiques, but how many lives may be lost while he looks for a phone booth? We don't like inequality, but our efforts to force each other into equality may have equally undesirable results.

Tellingly, one of the most well-known images of Superman features him bursting through a set of chains. The corrosive influence of society can't completely obscure our essential compassion. Social interactions set humans down the path to corruption, yes, but they're also necessary for the cultivation of knowledge and social virtues such as generosity and friendliness. Maybe it's the case that only the fittest survive, but none of us can be all that fit without getting a little help from our friends. (And perhaps from our enemies as well: if there's an asteroid hurtling toward Earth, I doubt Luthor will object much to a well-timed Kryptonian intervention.) Even though we may bring each other down, we also have to hold each other up, because no one else will. As Superman himself sees things, "it's all just us in here, together. And we're all we've got."[15] It's this view that serves as the source of Superman's compassion, and that same compassion will inevitably break through whatever metaphorical chains we may place on each other.

You can accept human nature optimism even though plenty of humans don't act like citizens of Earth-O, because everyone depends on someone who does act that way. Charles Darwin (1809–1882), for example, argued that humans may be naturally compassionate because society itself prospers from our helping one another, and all humans must live in some society.[16] Luthor himself may act selfishly, but he must rely on the selflessness of others: brain may beat brawn every time, but yellow-sun-powered brawn is sure going to come in handy when that asteroid comes unexpectedly knocking. Maybe we should conclude that we come from Earth-O simply because we wouldn't be here if we had come from Earth-P; if everyone acts selfishly, there will be no selfless people for the selfish to take advantage of.

This can also help to answer Maggin's challenge to Superman. It may very well be true that mankind would become dependent on Superman and his amazing powers, and individual humans might be held back from achieving their potential as a result. However, Superman's presence can also elevate us all if his character tells us anything about human nature. If that nature is defined by compassion, as the human nature optimist argues, then who could be more human than Superman? Accepting him into the human fold, we can admit no greater similarity between ourselves and the Man of Steel: the essence of humankind would be selflessness, not selfishness. To paraphrase Superman's father, Jor-El, from *Superman: The Movie* (1978), for this reason above all—our capacity for good—did Krypton give us its last son.

Let's summarize the difference between Earth-P and Earth-O. On Earth-P, humans are naturally selfish and later made selfless by their social interactions with one another. On Earth-O, humans are naturally selfless and later allowed to become selfish by society. In both cases, individual people may move away from humanity's natural state, but none of us can ever completely escape our birthright.

Humanity's Greatest Power!

"I know there's good in you." That's what Superman says to Lex Luthor as the Man of Steel faces death.[17] Some might call this optimism misplaced or hopeless, and perhaps rightfully so, but it's also quite possible that Superman is making an entirely rational inference from his knowledge of human nature. In the foregoing discussion, we've seen how the two opposing views of human nature may be considered in light of whether or not one considers Superman to be human. If you take the pessimistic view that humankind is essentially selfish, then you'll have to deny that Kal-El has anything in common with us and so exclude him from humanity. If you include Superman as a human being, then you'll have to commit yourself to the view—shared with the optimists—that humankind is essentially compassionate. Superman believes that his upbringing on Earth makes him human, despite his Kryptonian heritage; therefore, he would have to believe that all humans, including his worst enemy, are by nature good.[18]

Opponents of human nature optimism have a rather obvious reply to make here. We can discuss the humanity of Superman in good fun, but it's ultimately a moot point: unfortunately for adventurous female reporters, tree-climbing cats, and human nature optimists alike, Superman doesn't really exist. But consider the experiment Superman runs in *All-Star Superman* #10, wherein he creates an Earth without a Superman in the infant universe of Q. Earth-Q is clearly meant to portray the world in which we actually live, including such historical events as the creation of Australian aboriginal Dreamtime art, the construction of Hindu shrines to Krishna, Giovanni Pico della Mirandola's delivery of the *Oration on the Dignity of Man*, Friedrich Nietzsche's publication of *Thus Spoke Zarathustra*, and the creation of a comic book character by Jerry Siegel and Joe Shuster—all events wherein humans came up with the idea of a superman. Throughout history, the nature of man has been to create Superman to represent a standard of excellence, and that's neither a dream nor a hoax nor an imaginary story. Is it grounds for optimism? That's for you to decide.

Notes

1. *All-Star Superman* #10 (May 2008); reprinted in *All-Star Superman, Volume 2* (2009).
2. Thomas Hobbes, *Leviathan* (New York: Barnes and Noble Books, 1651/2004), 92.
3. Jean-Jacques Rousseau, *Discourse on the Origins of Inequality* (1755), trans. G.D.H. Cole and reprinted in *Political Philosophy: The Essential Texts*, 2nd ed., ed. Steven M. Cahn (New York: Oxford University Press, 2010), 356.
4. On an unrelated note, watch your local bookstore for *Superman and Biology*, coming soon!
5. The essence of Superman is apparently his spit-curl, which explains why some depictions of Supes in DC Comics' "New 52" relaunch are so off-putting. (For more on the essence of Superman, see chapter 18 by Michaud and chapter 19 by Knepp in this volume.)
6. *All-Star Superman* #5 (September 2006), reprinted in *All-Star Superman, Volume 1* (2007).
7. For more on Hobbes, see chapter 17 by Nielsen in this volume.
8. Some recent example are *The Dark Knight Returns* #4 (June 1986), reprinted in *Batman: The Dark Knight Returns* (1997); *Action Comics,*

vol. 1, #584 (January 1987), reprinted in *Superman: The Man of Steel,
Volume 2* (2003); the "Sacrifice" storyline, reprinted in *Superman:
Sacrifice* (2006); and *All-Star Superman* #4 (July 2006), reprinted in
All-Star Superman, Volume 1.

9. In particular, John Byrne, Mark Waid, and Geoff Johns have all
portrayed Luthor this way in their retellings of Superman's origins in
Superman: The Man of Steel (1991), *Superman: Birthright* (2005), and
Superman: Secret Origin (2010), respectively.

10. For more on this theme, see Adam Barkman's chapter "The Ring of
Gyges, the Ring of the Green Lantern, and the Temptation of Power," in
Green Lantern and Philosophy: No Evil Shall Escape This Book, ed.
Jane Dryden and Mark D. White, (Hoboken, NJ: John Wiley and Sons,
2011), 187–198.

11. *Superman*, vol. 1, #247 (January 1972), reprinted in *The Greatest
Superman Stories Ever Told* (1987). Maggin also explored the idea in
his novel *Superman: Last Son of Krypton* (New York: Warner Books,
1978).

12. I admit that this may be a parochial view: I'm writing this chapter in
a library two miles north of Wall Street.

13. *All-Star Superman* #5.

14. Jean-Jacques Rousseau, *Of the Social Contract* (1761), trans. by Charles
M. Sherover and reprinted in Cahn, *Political Philosophy: The Essential
Texts*, 370.

15. *All-Star Superman* #12 (October 2008), reprinted in *All-Star Superman,
Volume 2*.

16. Charles Darwin, *The Descent of Man* (1871), available at http://www.
gutenberg.org/ebooks/2300.

17. *All-Star Superman* #10.

18. See, for example, *Man of Steel* #6 (December 1986), reprinted in
Superman: The Man of Steel (1991).

Chapter 16

Can the Man of Steel Feel Our Pain?
Sympathy and Superman

Andrew Terjesen

In a recent comic book story, Lex Luthor acquired the power of a god and used it to confront his archenemy, Superman. During that confrontation, Luthor revealed the source of his enmity toward Superman. As Luthor sees it, Superman is a superior being who is merely pretending to be like the humans he protects. Lex tells Superman, "You shed the odd dainty tear when you think it's appropriate for a hero to do so. You smile like us. Frown like us—but let me show you now what human beings have to go through every day. I'll show you human pain!"[1] Lex knows that Kryptonians are physiologically different than humans, so he doesn't assume that Superman's expressions reflect the same underlying emotions that similar human expressions do.

It may seem strange for Lex to refuse to acknowledge that Superman experiences emotions like we do. But consider that we don't always assume that animals are thinking the same things we are when they act in a way that seems "human." Likewise, just because the people of Krypton resemble the people of Earth, we can't assume that their brains are wired the same way. Lex suspects that Superman is merely pretending to be human in order to infiltrate human society and that Superman doesn't know what it is like to be human. As Lex tells him, "You simulate such knowledge. You aren't human. You only look like us."[2] That raises an intriguing question: as much as Superman strives to be human, can he ever truly understand us? Can he experience sympathy for human beings?

Superman and Philosophy: What Would the Man of Steel Do?, First Edition. Edited by Mark D. White.
© 2013 John Wiley & Sons, Inc. Published 2013 by John Wiley & Sons, Inc.

Growing Up a Super Boy

In the first Superman story from 1938, the baby Kal-El is taken to an orphanage where he raises a chair above his tiny head.[3] That image of Superbaby is referenced in 1978's *Superman: The Movie* when a Supertoddler raises the pickup truck that has collapsed on top of Pa Kent. For most of Superman's history, he was shown to be "super" the moment he set foot on Earth. But if Clark Kent always had the ability to lift trucks and outrun speeding bullets, then in what sense could he know what it is like to be a not-so-super human being?

Let's assume that Kal-El was unable to feel normal pain once he landed under a yellow sun (until he encountered kryptonite much later). That leaves two distinct possibilities when it comes to understanding pain: he infers what pain feels like from how human beings react to injury, or else his memory of a pain experience (from Krypton, for instance) gives him some basis for understanding the human experience of pain.

The explanation from inference is the understanding of "sympathy" found in the work of philosopher David Hume (1711–1776).[4] Hume would say that when Superman sees Jimmy Olsen rushing toward a disaster with a camera and a smile, he associates those behaviors with the idea of desire. Superman can tell that "Mr. Action" wants to be at the heart of what's going on. Superman does not need to enjoy photographing newsworthy events in order to appreciate Jimmy's excitement. Instead, he simply observes that Jimmy's behavior is connected with desire.

The memory explanation, on the other hand, is found in the work of French philosophers who were contemporaries of David Hume. Philosopher Sophie de Grouchy (1764–1822) argued that the sympathetic understanding of Jimmy's desire has to be rooted in something more concrete than a mere definition of desire.[5] Hume admitted that sympathy occurs when we convert the idea of desire into an impression of desire, but the process by which this happens is a "black box" in Hume's work; he never explains what makes it work. He simply says that we move from idea to feeling through the "force of imagination."[6] But de Grouchy offers a clearer explanation. Superman gets the idea of desire from Jimmy's actions, and then that idea is connected to a memory that Superman has—maybe the first time he flew on his own power—a memory that still contains some residual feeling that gives him an idea of what is going on in Jimmy's mind.

Although the memory explanation does explain how our ideas of emotional states might yield a truly visceral understanding of what someone else is feeling, it does not explain how we associate those initial experiences with the ideas we get from observing others. In the 1980 movie *Superman II*, Clark gives up his powers in order to be with Lois Lane. In his de-powered state, Clark's attempt to defend Lois's honor in a diner goes disastrously wrong. Admittedly, the beating he receives would be enough to cause most of us a lot of pain, but Clark seems to be in shock after he sees his blood for the first time.

We see the same reaction in a recent retelling of Superman's first exposure to kryptonite (thanks to Brainiac). As he experiences the effects of the radioactive fragment of his home planet, he asks himself, "Is this pain?"[7] Hurting Superman does not imply that he knows he is experiencing pain. If he is not sure that what he is feeling is what humans call "pain," then he can't be sure that his memory of being beaten in an Alaskan diner, or being exposed to kryptonite on Brainiac's ship, is the right thing to recall when he sees a human being grimacing or doubling over.

The memory explanation provides a plausible explanation for how Superman's sympathy works, but it doesn't address the underlying conceptual question: how does one being know that their experiences are similar to another if they cannot get inside that person's head? It was easy for de Grouchy to overlook this issue because she was concerned with human beings understanding each other, and it's not a large leap to assume that when two similar beings are put in similar situations they will experience similar emotions and feelings. But Kal-El is of a different species and we can't assume that he experiences the world the same way that the rest of us do.

The inference explanation might seem to do a better job of addressing this conceptual question because inferences do not appear to be limited to a specific physiology. We can understand abstract concepts, like infinity, without being able to experience them directly. If we can understand concepts like those, we should have a good chance of understanding what another person is feeling when he or she has a familiar reaction, even if that person is from another sex, race, ethnicity—or planet.[8]

Men Are from Earth, Supermen Are from Krypton

Both the memory explanation and the inference explanation are examples of what philosophers call *theory theory*. (Really really.) Theory theorists argue that we can understand someone else's thoughts by using an information-rich theory of how human minds function. For example, Superman sees someone walking on a narrow ledge and hugging the wall—behaviors that are suggestive of a desire not to fall—and swoops down to save that person from falling. But, if the person on the ledge tells Superman not to come any closer, this would be more indicative of a suicide attempt and Superman would need to act differently.

The difference between the memory explanation and the inference explanation can be understood in terms of how Superman accesses his theory of human minds. The inference explanation says there is a set of rules that Superman applies to every situation: for instance, when a person on a ledge refuses help, that means she wants to be left on the ledge. The memory explanation says that Superman relies on his ability to match a situation to something he remembers happening to him, such as an occasion when he wanted to do something self-destructive and other people tried to stop him.

Not every philosopher holds that our understanding of others relies upon a worked-out theory of human behavior. *Simulation theory* is based on the idea that our ability to understand what someone else is thinking is based on using our imagination to guess what we would be thinking in the same situation.[9] According to the simulation theorist, when Superman sees that person walking on a narrow ledge, he imagines what he would think if he was unable to fly and standing on a ledge high above the ground. Whereas simulation theory does seem to accurately describe what we do when we try to understand people who are in situations that we have never experienced, it does not address the conceptual question. How does Superman know that he is correctly imagining what a person who cannot fly feels when they are walking on a ledge when he isn't that person? Even if he were human, this would still be a problem.

Contemporary philosophers Stephen Stich and Shaun Nichols have proposed a hybrid theory that combines elements of theory theory and simulation theory.[10] From theory theory, they borrow the idea that "mind-reading" (as they call the task of understanding what other people are thinking) is an information-rich process that involves inferences from beliefs and desires, which themselves are the result of a form of simulation. In order to understand what someone else is thinking, we begin by creating a model of that person's mind using our own beliefs and desires as a starting point. This process creates a basic model for understanding others based on the assumption that everyone else is like us. But as we notice that the person has different beliefs and desires, we update our basic model, gradually forming a more accurate idea of how the other person thinks.

The appeal of the simulation theory, as well as Stich and Nichols's hybrid theory, is that they operate much like our everyday descriptions of feelings like pain. It is difficult for any ordinary human to articulate what pain is. When we try to describe pain, we say things like "it feels like someone is sticking a fork in the back of my eye." We describe pain by describing its cause, not how it feels. It seems unthinkable to us that anyone can describe or understand pain without experiencing it.

While simulation theory and hybrid theory are attractive, they imply that it would be impossible to accurately understand something that you have not experienced. If Superman has never been frail and mortal, then it would be hard for him to really understand how other sentient beings on Earth feel. There are certain subjective facts about what it means to be human that Superman is not privy to. He doesn't know what it's like to walk around worried that something might hurt you. Sure, he knows that people get hurt more easily than he does, but that objective fact is not the same as being acquainted with the subjective feel of what it is like to be vulnerable.

Just Another Kid from Smallville

The intuitive appeal of simulation theory and hybrid theory can be seen in the reboot of Superman that writer/artist John Byrne started in 1986.[11] This version of Superman started as a baby who appeared to be no different than any other human baby. Little Clark had no superpowers and could be hurt just as easily as any human child. As he grew up under a yellow sun, he grew stronger and his powers developed. Byrne eased Superman into his powers and even made sure that he was not the omnipotent planet-pusher he had been in the 1970s comics and *Superfriends* cartoon. Since this version of Superman starts out no different than us, he has the kind of experiences that enable him to simulate what it is like for humans to feel vulnerable. The television show *Smallville* continued in this vein, showing the world a Clark Kent who was only beginning to notice how different he was.

The "humanization" of Kal-El was also intended to make Superman more relatable to his readers. To be honest, I have never been a fan of these attempts to make Superman more relatable. We try to make Superman like us because we suffer from the sympathy problem as well. We don't try very hard to understand what it is like to be a powerful being among mortals. Instead, we make Superman into either a big blue boy scout (as portrayed by George Reeves or Christopher Reeve) or someone who is just as deeply morally flawed as the rest of us, such as when Superman became a deadbeat dad in the 2006 film *Superman Returns*.[12]

After years of attempting to make Superman just like us, the recent 2011 reboot of Superman tries to have it both ways. Clark Kent was always different from the humans around him, but his more extraordinary powers were slow to develop. This recognizes the fact that no matter how long he spent as a "mere" mortal, his time as Superman will distinguish him from other people and make it difficult for him to bridge the gap between his experiences and ours: "Just knowing I'm different makes me feel different."[13] Clark has to hide his abilities in a way that most people can't relate to. One aspect of being Superman that many people overlook is how careful he needs to be. Superman knocks out ordinary people with light taps. He has to constantly pull his punches and handle things delicately. Living like you're always the bull in a china shop probably takes its toll.

There's Pain and Then There's Pain

Even if Superman began his life on Earth just as vulnerable as the rest of us humans, all of his "human" pain is located deep in the past and in a stage of his life he has left behind. It is easy for those experiences to become forgotten or overshadowed with time. If Superman is going to be able to call upon those experiences in order to understand the humans around him, he needs to have them reinforced from time to time.

One way that could happen is that he could experience pain when he is temporarily vulnerable, such as when he is exposed to kryptonite. The problem, though, is that these moments of temporary vulnerability have a lot of additional baggage. When Superman is made vulnerable to cuts and bruising through kryptonite, there is additional—and different—pain caused by exposure to the kryptonite itself. When kryptonite was originally introduced in the 1940s radio series, it merely weakened Superman. But more recently he describes exposure as extremely painful: "As if my blood had been replaced by battery acid … Like all the gravity I'd ignored over the years had suddenly decided to yank my muscles from my bones."[14] So for Superman, the experience of pain from being cut is far more severe than it is for humans. As the theory theorists and hybrid theorists recognize, our ideas of pain are information-rich. Humans can understand a number of different kinds of pain, from throbbing to stabbing, but Superman's understanding of pain would be both limited (since he's known so little of it) and unique (because of the threat of dying involved with every instance of pain).

Admittedly, there are less fatal ways that Superman could be made susceptible to pain, but they involve the same psychological complexities as the pain from kryptonite. Exposing Superman to the rays of a red sun takes away the source of his powers, and gold kryptonite (as opposed to the more familiar green variety) can rob him of his powers permanently without causing him pain. But again, it seems that Superman would not develop exactly the same idea of pain that humans do. Humans have *always* been vulnerable, whereas Superman has very little experience with pain and vulnerability. That feeling of loss—not to mention his very identity, his purpose, and the desire to get his powers back—would all be lumped in with his feelings of pain. Being cut would seem much worse than it would to most people.

I Am Curious (Superman)

Perhaps it is unfair to focus on an *embodied* concept like pain. Pain receptors are a biological mechanism that differ from species to species and even person to person. Not everyone has the same pain threshold. Just because Superman does not understand pain does not mean he cannot understand a more abstract feeling like suffering, loss, or alienation. He is one of the few survivors of his entire species, has lost one or both of his adoptive parents (depending on the version of events), and recently lived through the death of the 100,000 Kryptonians he freed from the Bottle City of Kandor.[15] Nonetheless, Lex Luthor challenges Superman's ability to comprehend even common human experiences: "you think you can sympathize with refugees and disaster victims on Earth ... But really, this is quite different."[16]

Superman's lack of understanding could be likened to the lack of understanding between the sexes on topics like sexual harassment. On the average, men do not view certain actions as sexual harassment while women do. The reason seems to be that men think of such actions as harmless flirtations, because this is how *they'd* view them if they faced them, while women view the actions as dangerous, because they're often in a more vulnerable position physically or profession- ally—largely due to this difference in perception of sexual harassment. In the law, this has led to calls for a "reasonable woman" standard— to supplement the famous "reasonable man" standard—that would ask men to view the actions differently by imagining what they think a woman would feel in that situation.[17] Sympathizing with our fellow human beings is often difficult enough, so imagine what it must be like for Superman!

This particular problem is illustrated in a well-meaning but problematic story from the 1970s. The story is entitled "I Am Curious (Black)!" and features Lois Lane's attempts to investigate the condi- tions in a predominantly African-American part of Metropolis.[18] No one will talk to her, so Lois convinces Superman to "turn her into" a black woman with one of his Kryptonian devices. Once she "becomes" black, Lois finds that white people treat her differently. For example, the cabbie who gave her a ride earlier ignores black Lois when she tries to flag him down. After several experiences like this, Lois feels that she "finally understands" the life of a black woman in Metropolis. While her appearance has changed, however, she knows she's not a part of the African-American community. At one point, she observes the mistreatment of African-Americans and is amazed at how "these human beings" are treated. The clinical approach she takes to their situation shows that she doesn't really see it as something that is happening to her.

Lois fails to learn the Soul Man lesson. In the 1986 film *Soul Man*, a white law student named Mark Watson passes himself off as black in order to get a scholarship. After he is caught, a professor remarks that Watson now understands what it is like to be black. But Watson realizes what Lois didn't, and quickly replies to his professor that he doesn't, because he could have stopped being black whenever he wanted to. Being mistreated because of the (intentionally altered) color of one's skin is not the same as being unable to avoid such mistreatment.

Since Lois doesn't recognize that she's filtering her experiences as a black woman through her lifelong experiences as a white woman, she doesn't see the condescension inherent in thinking, "She lives in misery ... yet asks if she can help me!" From Lois's perspective, the conditions of the neighborhood are miserable compared to what she is used to, but it is not likely that the residents of that neighborhood would describe their existence as miserable. They can find joy in the life that is available to them, but Lois has difficulty because it is so different from her normal existence.[19]

Even abstract experiences depend on a frame of reference that is situated in our experience in order to fully understand them. If Superman is going to understand human suffering and loss, he needs to be aware of how that suffering and loss would feel to someone else who lacks his particular abilities. Otherwise he would be as patronizing as Lois was.

Kneel Before Zod

David Hume wasn't interested in sympathy because it presented an interesting philosophical puzzle. For him, sympathy was the cement of our moral universe. To appreciate why this is, we need only consider what happens when someone with Superman's power lacks his sympathy for human beings.

In *Superman II*, the Kryptonians Zod, Ursa, and Non escape from their imprisonment in the Phantom Zone and find themselves on Earth. Unlike Kal-El, they arrive as adults, born, raised, and immersed in Kryptonian culture. They also find themselves in possession of amazing powers under the yellow sun. They see human beings as a distinct and lesser species as reflected by the following conversation between Zod and Ursa:

> ZOD: I've discovered his weakness … he cares. He actually cares for these Earth people!
> URSA: Like pets?
> ZOD: I suppose.

Zod and Ursa cannot imagine acting as if they were equal to these frail humans. Zod immediately demands that Earth surrender to him, and he has no problem harming humans to achieve his goals.

Sociopaths are often described as lacking empathy—or what Hume would have called sympathy—as a way to explain their horrendous treatment of others. Like Zod, Lex Luthor is puzzled by Superman's behavior, even though he too wants to save the world. He doesn't understand why Superman keeps "pursuing their small needs rather than changing the world."[20] In some recent comics, like 2003–2004's *Superman: Birthright* and 2005's *Lex Luthor: Man of Steel*, Lex is not portrayed as an evil villain. He is someone who does good for people, but he does it as a grand gesture to satisfy his own ego and prove that Superman is a threat to the human race.[21] Lex helps people because they have the misfortune of not being as gifted and talented as himself. But his hubris keeps him from really helping the people, such as when he gave up godlike power simply because he couldn't use it for negative ends—namely, hurting Superman.[22]

What the "S" Really Means

The inability to sympathize with others prevents Lex from being the hero he thinks he is. However, if we don't try to sympathize with Kal-El, we may lose sight of the real example that he is setting. Lex describes Superman as "a hypocrite who told an entirely different species to aspire to his physical type."[23] Many people have turned away from Superman because they think he is unrealistic. He can do the right thing because he doesn't have to worry about the real world consequences. The rest of us "frail" humans have jobs and families, and if we always stood up for the right thing we would risk losing either or both.

If you think about it, however, he does give up a lot to be Superman. The song "Superman's Song" by Crash Test Dummies repeatedly refers to the fact that Superman had a real job—mild-mannered reporter for a large metropolitan newspaper—even though he didn't need one.[24] Superman fights crime and saves people, never seeking our gratitude or praise, even though it interferes with his "day job." He doesn't have to play by the same rules as the rest of us, but he does: as the song points out, he earns money legitimately rather than stealing it, as he could easily do. He doesn't claim any special privileges or rights, *and* he saves the world on a regular basis. He realizes he has amazing powers he could take advantage of, but he doesn't. In a sense, he's trying to live as normal a life as we normal folk do—and helping us "on the side."

I'm not claiming that Superman is someone with whom everyone can easily sympathize, for many of the reasons we discussed in this chapter. The only people with experiences that can even begin to approximate Superman's are the most powerful in society: the fastest, the smartest, the wealthiest, and so on. If you look at it this way, Superman is not a moral exemplar primarily for the masses—it is the elite among mankind who need to understand why Superman does what he does. From his example, the most privileged can appreciate the need to sympathize with those who don't wield as much influence as they can.

This doesn't mean, however, that Superman is morally irrelevant to the rest of us. If we're honest with ourselves, most of us will realize that we are often the ones who are in a better position than others. As low as we feel at times, there is always someone lower. As much as we are in need, there is always someone in greater need. We can miss these facts if we focus too much on our experience and do not try to understand how others view the situation. When we try and imagine how others feel—when we sympathize with others—we may be surprised to learn that there is always somebody who can use our help. Superman certainly knows that.

Sympathy for the Hero

As the band Five for Fighting explained, it's not easy being Superman.[25] It's hard to see that because most of us daydream about all the awesome things we could do if we had superpowers under a yellow sun.

We don't think about what it would be like to be Kal-El with those powers—to be someone who is so grateful toward his adopted world that he wants to use his powers to help others. We don't think about how hard it must be for someone like that to try and understand what it is that we really need. Most of us stumble upon an opportunity to sympathize; we don't seek it out. That's because sympathy, in the sense of understanding what it is like to be someone else, is really hard to achieve—especially for a strange visitor from another planet.

Notes

1. *Action Comics*, vol. 1, #900 (June 2011).
2. Ibid.
3. *Action Comics*, vol. 1, #1 (June 1938). I'm sure you have a copy lying around somewhere.
4. Although "sympathy" nowadays is often synonymous with "pity" or "feeling sorry for," it's original meaning is much more expansive, referring to feeling not only someone's pain, but also their joy and everything in between. Before the word "empathy" was coined in the early twentieth century, sympathy could refer to our ability to understand what someone else was thinking or feeling. Since most of the philosophers discussed in this chapter pre-date the invention of the word "empathy," I will use "sympathy" in this chapter in the same broad sense that they did.
5. Karin Brown, *Sophie de Grouchy Letters on Sympathy: A Critical Edition,* letters translated by James E. McClellan III (Philadelphia: American Philosophical Society, 2008), 9–10.
6. David Hume, *A Treatise of Human Nature*, ed. David Fate Norton and Mary J. Norton (Oxford: Oxford University Press, 2000), 273.
7. *Action Comics*, vol. 2, #8 (June 2012).
8. For discussion of related issues, see chapter 20 by Ananth in this volume.
9. Hume's friend, the economist and moral philosopher Adam Smith (1723–1790), proposed a notion of "sympathy" that is much more suggestive of simulation theory because he describes sympathy as the ability to imagine being the person we're trying to sympathize with. Smith's theory can be found in his *Theory of Moral Sentiments* (Indianapolis, IN: Liberty Fund, 2009).
10. Stephen Stich and Shaun Nichols, *Mindreading: An Integrated Account of Pretence, Self-Awareness, and Understanding Other Minds* (Oxford: Oxford University Press, 2003). This is a slightly different sense of mind-reading than discussed in chapter 20 by Ananth in this volume.

11. See *The Man of Steel* #1–6 (1986–1987), collected in *Superman: The Man of Steel, Vol. 1* (1991).
12. Another view, expressed by esteemed Superman writer Mark Waid, is that Superman is not meant to be relatable. "You know what makes Superman 'relatable'? CLARK KENT" (https://twitter.com/MarkWaid/status/93171997491732480, July 19, 2011).
13. *Superman*, vol. 3, #12 (October 2012).
14. *Superman: Birthright* #8 (May 2004), reprinted in *Superman: Birthright* (2004).
15. See *Superman: War of the Supermen* (2011). Superman's struggle with this loss (and the death of Jonathan Kent just prior) was shown in *Superman: Grounded Vol. 1* and *Vol. 2* (2011), and is discussed in chapter 1 by White in this volume.
16. *Action Comics*, vol. 1, #900.
17. For the history of the reasonable woman standard, see Robert S. Adler and Ellen R. Pierce, "The Legal, Ethical, and Social Implications of the 'Reasonable Woman' Standard in Sexual Harassment Cases," *Fordham Law Review* 61 (1993): 773–827.
18. *Superman's Girl Friend, Lois Lane* #106 (November 1970). (Maybe they should have used the "reasonable woman" standard when deciding on the title of the book!)
19. Oprah Winfrey made a similar gaffe recently while taping a television show in India; during a visit to a lower-income family living in a 10-by-10-feet room, she marveled at what she saw as horribly cramped living space, asking them if they were happy living in such conditions. See Rajyasree Sen, "You Still Eat With Your Hands? Oprah's magical mystery tour on India," *Firstpost. Bollywood*, July 21, 2012, http://www.firstpost.com/bollywood/you-still-eat-with-your-hands-oprahs-magical-mystery-tour-of-india-385494.html.
20. *Action Comics*, vol. 1, #900.
21. For more on this theme, see chapter 11 by Donovan and Richardson in this volume.
22. *Action Comics*, vol. 1, #900.
23. Ibid.
24. From Crash Test Dummies, *The Ghosts That Haunt Me* (BMG/Arista, 1991).
25. "Superman (It's Not Easy)" from Five for Fighting, *America Town* (Aware/Columbia, 2000).

Chapter 17

World's Finest Philosophers
Superman and Batman on Human Nature

Carsten Fogh Nielsen

Superman and Batman are close friends and colleagues in the Justice League. But they are very different, especially when it comes to their views on humanity and their opinions of human nature. Superman (or, rather, Clark Kent) grew up on a small farm in Kansas, with two loving parents who taught him to respect, support, and trust other people. Their influence is probably one of the main reasons why Superman believes the human race to be fundamentally good and capable of continual, perhaps infinite, self-improvement. In fact, Superman's general view of human beings is surprisingly optimistic given the criminals he constantly finds himself confronting, especially his arch nemesis, Lex Luthor.

Batman has a rather more bleak and cynical view of the human race. Batman did *not* have a happy childhood. Indeed Batman's very existence is the direct consequence of human cruelty and greed. The experience of seeing his parents killed was the determining moment in Batman/Bruce Wayne's life, and it has influenced, or perhaps rather tainted, his view of humanity ever since. Batman has witnessed first-hand the horrors human beings are capable of inflicting upon each other, and this has taught him that human beings in general are not to be trusted. True, Batman has a small circle of trusted friends and associates, with whom he cooperates and shares information.[1] But even their love and support has not been enough to erase the memory of his parents' murder.

Superman and Philosophy: What Would the Man of Steel Do?, First Edition. Edited by Mark D. White.
© 2013 John Wiley & Sons, Inc. Published 2013 by John Wiley & Sons, Inc.

Superman believes that human beings are fundamentally good, that the human race possesses a natural capacity for moral self-improvement, and that human society is a force for good. Batman on the other hand believes human beings to be fundamentally corrupt; he trusts no one, and he seems to regard human society as a cesspool of corruption and greed. In this chapter, we look to the philosophy of Thomas Hobbes (1588–1679) and G.W.F. Hegel (1770–1831) to better understand these friends' difference of opinion on humanity and human nature.

Batman, Hobbes, and the War of All Against All

Batman's somewhat depressing view of human nature is shared by the British philosopher Thomas Hobbes. In *Leviathan*, one of the most influential books on political philosophy and moral psychology ever written, Hobbes claimed that human beings neither do nor should trust each other, and described the natural state of human association as a war "of every man against every man."[2] Hobbes recognized that many people might not agree with this somewhat depressing analysis, and that some might claim that human beings are not nearly as bad as Hobbes portrays them. In response to this, Hobbes asked those who disagreed with him to take a closer look at how they themselves actually behave, and then reflect upon what this behavior actually says about their true views of human nature:

> Let him therefore consider with himself, when taking a journey, he arms himself, and seeks to go well accompanied; when going to sleep, he locks his doors; when even in his house he locks his chest … what opinion he has of his fellow subjects, when he rides armed; of his fellow citizens, when he locks his doors; and of his children, and servants, when he locks his chests. Does he not there as much accuse mankind by his actions as I do by my words?[3]

According to Hobbes, all of us in our day-to-day interactions with others implicitly express the same bleak view of human nature that he supports. If this is right, then Batman's worldview is not as paranoid and strange as it might initially appear, but is simply the logical extension of a very basic form of distrust toward other people, which (according to Hobbes) we all share.

Even if we are convinced by Hobbes's argument, people might still object that such a basic distrust toward others doesn't necessarily imply that we actually go around and fight everybody else all the time. And at first glance Hobbes's claim that the natural state of human association is a war of all against all does appear somewhat exaggerated. Clearly most people do not go out and physically fight each other on a daily basis. If we take a closer look, however, it turns out that Hobbes's point about the war of "every man against every man" is a bit more sophisticated than it first appears. Hobbes does not claim that human beings always and constantly fight each other. His point is rather that in the "state of nature," in the absence of a supreme authority, who can settle disputes between persons once and for all, human beings will always be tempted and willing to employ violence in order to achieve their ends and protect their interests. "The nature of War," Hobbes states, "consisteth not in actual fighting; but in the known disposition thereto, during all the time there is no assurance to the contrary."[4]

Once again, this seems like a perfect description of Batman's view of the world. People might not actually be fighting all the time, and in fact they might actually appear to be cooperating and working together for the sake of a common good. But, Batman believes, beneath this thin veneer people always stand ready to defend their own interests and pursue their personal aims by any means necessary, including the use of violence. This is why Batman always has to be on guard—and this is why he feels the need to devise contingency plans for even the most farfetched scenarios, including betrayal by his closest friends.

To most people, the Hobbesian view of human nature and society appear rather harsh and depressing—and with good reason! In *Leviathan* Hobbes himself famously (or infamously) described the "state of nature," in which there is no supreme authority, as a state in which

> every man is Enemy to every man ... there is no place for industry; because the fruit thereof is uncertain: and consequently no Culture of the Earth ... no Arts; no Letters; no society; and worst of all, continual fear, and danger of violent death; and the life of man, solitary, poor, nasty, brutish, and short.[5]

Batman might agree with this analysis, but it is not exactly a heartwarming message.

As Hobbes points out, though, we need to look the unpleasant reality of the world straight in the face in order to change it. And Hobbes does in fact believe that his analysis provides us with the means for leaving the state of nature with its continual war and entering a more peaceful form of human association. Hobbes believes that highlighting the disadvantages of living in a perpetual state of war gives self-interested individuals an incentive to leave it. More precisely Hobbes believes that even the most callous, egocentric person will agree that almost any other form of human society is better than the perpetual state of war that Hobbes describes.

Batman and the Sovereign

How should human society be organized if we are to avoid the war of all against all? Hobbes's answer is simple: To stop the perpetual fear that others might attack us at any moment we must vest a single individual, the Sovereign, with the authority and the means to settle all disputes between persons. In other words, all people should agree to give up their right to govern their own lives and put absolute power into the hands of the Sovereign.

According to Hobbes, the Sovereign should have "the whole power of prescribing the Rules whereby every man may know, what Goods he may enjoy and what Actions he may do, without being molested by any of his fellow Subjects." He also has "the Right of Judicature; that is to say, of hearing and deciding all Controversies which may arise concerning Law." Finally, the Sovereign has the power "of punishing with corporal, or pecuniary punishment, or with ignominy every Subject according to the Law he hath formerly made."[6] So the Sovereign unites the legislative, the judicial, and the executive powers in one person.

The Sovereign's job is to ensure, by any means necessary, that peace is preserved and that the life, freedom, and possessions of each individual are protected.[7] Hobbes believes that only a person vested with such awesome powers and privileges would be able to do this, because only such a person would be able to guarantee that people never (or at least almost never) violate the laws he implements. The Sovereign's extensive powers, and his willingness to employ these powers to preserve the peace, will make the public afraid of him.

And this fear, combined with the advantages of no longer living in a state of perpetual war, will by and large be enough to prevent people from violating the dictates of the sovereign. And in the unlikely case that people *do* violate his dictates, they will be caught and punished.[8]

Batman would probably agree with at least some of these ideas. Although Batman himself embodies several features of the Hobbesian Sovereign, he does not have all the powers of the Sovereign. Batman has the powers and the means to effectively pursue and catch criminals and hoodlums, but he doesn't make the laws he enforces—and he doesn't prosecute and punish the criminals he catches. Batman's explicit aim is to preserve the peace and protect the life, liberty, and possessions of the citizens of Gotham City. He is widely feared, not only by criminals but also by a significant proportion of the general populace. And he deliberately employs this fear as a weapon in his fight against crime, famously saying that criminals are a "superstitious cowardly lot."[9]

According to both Batman and Hobbes, human beings are untrustworthy, egocentric creatures, whose mutual distrust can at every moment potentially erupt into violence. For this reason they both believe that human society is fragile and in constant danger of devolving into a war of all against all. And they both think that only a person vested with powers and privileges beyond those of ordinary citizens and feared by the general populace can bring us out of this terrible state of war.[10]

The Most Perfect Line

Let's turn back to Superman now: as we saw at the beginning of this chapter, Superman's view of human nature is much more optimistic than that of Batman and Hobbes. A very good example of this is *All-Star Superman* #10.[11] The *All-Star Superman* series, written by Grant Morrison with art from his frequent collaborator Frank Quitely, is widely regarded as providing an iconic version of Superman, and this issue in particular shows why many people find Superman to be such an inspiring figure.

As the comic begins, Superman is busy performing the kinds of superheroic feats we all know and love: battling Mechano-Man, saving the Bottle City of Kandor, rescuing Lois, and fighting the radiation poisoning (induced by Lex Luthor) which is slowly killing him. About halfway through the issue, however, something remarkable happens. While talking to Lois during a brief break in his hectic schedule of averting Earth-shaking disasters, Superman suddenly flies off to save a suicidal teenage girl who is about to jump off a skyscraper. As he gently embraces her to prevent her from falling to her death he whispers, "It's never as bad as you think. You're much stronger than you think you are. Trust me."

In my opinion, this particular scene stands out as one of the defining moments in Superman's history. And I'm not the only one who thinks so. In the introduction to volume 2 of the *All-Star Superman* trade paperback, Mark Waid—a comic book writer who knows a thing or two about Superman—claims that this scene contains the "perfect line of dialogue ... the most moving words we have ever read in a Superman story":

> They are perfect because they reveal, in one sentence, the fundamental secret of Superman and why we love him so much. Gods achieve their power by encouraging people to believe in them. Superman achieves his power by believing in us.[12]

Superman trusts and has faith in humanity. In fact he often seems to have greater faith in the human race than we have in ourselves. Superman believes that we are creatures who are capable of much greater goodness than we think. He believes that human beings both need and are worthy of care and respect, and he has dedicated his life to this belief. This, not the powers, not the costume, not even the indefatigable righteousness, is what makes Superman *Superman*.[13]

You Matter–To Me

The German philosopher G.W.F. Hegel provides an alternative perspective to Hobbes. In his two most famous books, *Phenomenology of Spirit* and *Outlines of the Philosophy of Right*, Hegel presents an elaborate and sophisticated account of the moral and cognitive development of human beings and of the human race as a whole that stands in stark contrast to Hobbes's dour and pessimistic view.[14]

An important concept in Hegel's account is the notion of *recognition*. Hegel believes that human beings require external recognition of their status as valuable persons or subjects. Being recognized as a subject by someone or something external to me is, Hegel claims, the only way in which I can acquire assurance that I am not simply an object, not simply a thing to be manipulated. And the only way to get such external recognition is from other people, subjects who, just like me, need and demand recognition. As Hegel somewhat cryptically puts it in the *Phenomenology*, "a self-consciousness exists *for a self-consciousness* ... Self-consciousness exists in and for itself when, and by the fact that, it so exists for another; that is, it exists only in being acknowledged."[15]

We can get some insight into what Hegel means by this if we once again take a look at the scene from *All-Star Superman* discussed above. When Superman rescues the suicidal teen girl, he does not simply prevent her from jumping. He also tries to change her mind by talking to her and showing her that her life is worth living. When Superman tells the girl that she is much stronger than she thinks she is, he is not merely stating a fact. He is actively trying to bring about a fundamental change in her self-understanding. More precisely, Superman attempts to provide the girl with an external validation of her own worth, to tell her that she is special and that her life has more worth than she herself seems to recognize.

Superman shares Hegel's belief that human beings rely on and need recognition and external validation of their own worth from other human beings. If they are deprived of these things, their moral and psychological development is stunted, as is the case with the suicidal teen girl. Superman clearly thinks that preventing her from jumping to her death is not enough to heal her or solve all her problems—she also needs to be assured of her own intrinsic worth, which is precisely what Superman attempts to do.

Securing Recognition

In the *Phenomenology of Spirit* Hegel outlines the first stages in the development of a comprehensive system of mutual recognition. Hegel here imagines a kind of mythological original position without established social structures—much like Hobbes's state of nature—in which human relationships take the form of either brutal life-and-death struggles or unequal social relationships such as those between a master and his slave. The problem with such a pre-social world, Hegel argues, is that neither struggle nor unequal social relations can provide the sort of mutual recognition that human beings require in order to develop and flourish.[16]

How then are we to ensure that everybody receives external validation of their status as subjects? How are we to ensure that equal, mutual recognition is available to all? If we lived in the DC Universe, then superheroes like Superman might be able to provide those in need with support and recognition. But even though Superman is able to save particular individuals, like the suicidal girl from *All-Star Superman*, it seems highly doubtful whether even Superman has the strength and capacity to actively reach out to everybody who needs recognition. And anyway, we do *not* live in the DC Universe (unfortunately) and cannot—and *should* not—rely on superheroes to solve our problems.

Hegel believed that the only way to solve this problem is to establish a society in which the basic social institutions provide everybody with a certain fundamental "recognitional status" and enable people to both recognize others and be recognized by others. In *Outlines of the Philosophy of Right*, Hegel provides a sketch of the basic structures of such a society, which would include an impartial legal system, private property, a market-based system for the production and distribution of goods and services, and a modern, secular state.

Each of these institutions, Hegel explains, embodies a different way of recognizing and acknowledging human beings as subjects. An impartial legal system ensures that everybody is formally recognized as a legal subject and is accorded equal and basic legal standing in society. Private property is an external sign of one's legal and moral status as a subject. Market-based production and distribution of goods and services enables people to express their individuality and participate in and contribute to society's material reproduction. Finally, a secular state ensures that everybody is granted certain basic rights as citizens and provides a common framework within which the other social institutions can function.[17]

Batman or Superman? Hobbes or Hegel?

At the beginning of this chapter I claimed that Superman and Batman have radically different views on human nature, the state, and society. For Batman and Hobbes the state is simply a means of escaping the harrowing war of all against all. Human nature doesn't change just because we enter into a political community with other human beings. We are (and will always remain) self-centered egoistic creatures, who are willing to pursue our individual aims and desires by any means necessary. But Superman and Hegel present a different view, maintaining that the state, and more generally human society, is not merely a means to an end, but an end in itself. Human beings are fundamentally social creatures who need to be recognized as subjects by other human beings. The state provides institutions that mediate and enable the required sort of mutual intersubjective recognition on a social level. Being a member of a state is therefore a necessary condition for, and an integral part of, living a good and fulfilling human life.

So perhaps the difference between Superman and Batman is not simply that the former thinks that people are inherently good, whereas the latter believes they are inherently bad. Perhaps the difference is rather that Batman and Hobbes think that human nature with all its many imperfections is given and fixed, whereas Superman and Hegel believe that people can improve, but only within a society in which they can live together and which allows and enables everybody to recognize and be recognized by others. And in a society based on mutual intersubjective recognition the (initially self-centered and egoistic) nature of human beings can and will be fundamentally transformed. But even if Supes and Hegs are right, we can't be sure since the "experiment" of society is ongoing. Hopefully, Superman is right, and we are much stronger than we think we are. We're gonna need to be!

Notes

1. In fact, even the people Batman chooses to trust are not above suspicion. In the "Tower of Babel" storyline the Justice League learns that Batman has developed contingency plans for stopping the other members, in case they turn (or be turned) evil. See *JLA* #43–46 (July–October 2000), reprinted in *JLA: Tower of Babel* (2001).

2. Thomas Hobbes, *Leviathan*, ed. C.B. Macpherson (London: Penguin Classics, 1985), chapter 13.

3. Ibid.

4. Ibid.

5. Ibid.

6. Ibid., chapter 18.

7. Ibid.

8. Ibid., chapters 27–28.

9. *Detective Comics*, vol. 1, #33 (November 1939), and repeated a batzillion times since. (Holy hyperbole!)

10. For more on Hobbes, see chapter 15 by Finkelman in this volume.

11. From May 2008, reprinted in *All-Star Superman, Volume 2* (2009).

12. Mark Waid, "Introduction," in *All-Star Superman, Volume 2*.

13. For another idea of what makes Superman *Superman*, see chapter 18 by Michaud in this volume.

14. G.W.F. Hegel, *Phenomenology of Spirit*, trans. A.V. Miller (Oxford: Oxford University Press, 1977), and *Outlines of the Philosophy of Right*, trans. T.M. Knox (Oxford: Oxford University Press, 2008).

15. Hegel, *Phenomenology of Spirit*, 110–111.

16. See Hegel, *Phenomenology of Spirit*, part B, chapter IV, section a: "Lordship and Bondage."

17. A concise account of the role of recognition in Hegel's political philosophy is given by Allan Patten in his "Social Contract Theory and the Politics of Recognition in Hegel's Political Philosophy," in *Beyond Liberalism and Communitarianism: Studies in Hegel's Philosophy of Right*, ed. Robert Williams (Albany, NY: SUNY Press, 2011), 167–184. Stephen Houlgate's introduction to Knox's translation of the *Outlines of the Philosophy of Right* provides a clear overview of the aim and structure of Hegel's political philosophy.

Part Six

OF SUPERMAN AND SUPERMINDS

WHO IS SUPERMAN, ANYWAY?

Chapter 18

"It's a Bird, It's a Plane, It's ... Clark Kent?"
Superman and the Problem of Identity

Nicolas Michaud

One of my favorite Superman moments happened during an episode of the 1990's TV show *Lois and Clark*. Lois Lane meets the villain Tempus, who has traveled from the future and explains to her who Superman really is:

TEMPUS: Lois, did you know that, in the future, you're revered at the same level as Superman? Why there are books about you, statues, an interactive game. You're even a breakfast cereal.

LOIS: Really?

TEMPUS: Yes. But, as much as everybody loves you, there is one question that keeps coming up: "How dumb was she?" Here, I'll show you what I mean. [Puts glasses on.] Look, I'm Clark Kent. [Takes glasses off.] No, I'm Superman. [Puts glasses on.] Mild-mannered reporter. [Takes glasses off.] Superhero. Hello! Duh! Clark Kent *is* Superman. Ha, ha, ha. Well, that was worth the whole trip.[1]

Tempus—and, to be honest, I too—enjoy mocking Lois for the fact that a simple pair of glasses somehow prevents her from realizing Clark is Superman. How is it that Clark's identity is so easily obscured by blue tights and a confident attitude?

What seems like Lois's "duh" moment, though, actually raises a fascinating philosophical issue. Lois has trouble with Superman's and

Superman and Philosophy: What Would the Man of Steel Do?, First Edition. Edited by Mark D. White.
© 2013 John Wiley & Sons, Inc. Published 2013 by John Wiley & Sons, Inc.

Clark's "identity." Perhaps Lois is so easily deceived by Clark's glasses and mild-mannered demeanor because identity isn't nearly as clear as we'd like to believe. In fact, maybe there is a strong sense in which Clark Kent and Superman really *are* two different people.

The Question-Begger, the Greatest Villain in Philosophy

Clark and Superman have the same cellular structure, same origin, same memories, same causal connection to the past. Surely, with a list of shared qualities like that, they must be the same person. Clark is Superman ... duh. You could even pull out a really well-respected philosophical rule called *Leibniz's law*, named for philosopher Gottfried Wilhelm Leibniz (1646–1716), which states that two things are identical if, and only if, they have *every* property in common.[2] Don't Clark and Superman have every property in common? Well, yes and no. The properties listed above are actually really problematic for locating identity. And, even worse, there is one small property Clark Kent and Superman don't have in common that is much more important than we would think, which we'll talk about later.

Philosophers have been struggling with the problem of identity for thousands of years. What seems obvious to most people is actually almost impossible to prove—what makes me, *me*. What should seem obvious to you is that you, well ... are *you*! But if I asked, "What makes you *you*?", you would likely reply with an indignant, "What a stupid question!" But obviousness aside, seriously, what does make you *you*? One of your first answers might be something like, "I'm me, because I'm me!" Saying something like "I'm me" doesn't prove anything, though. It's like saying, "Superman is strong because he's *strong*," as if the greater emphasis makes the answer more informative. If we wanted to actually explain it, we would need to say something like, "I know Superman is strong because he can leap a tall building in a single bound, and because he can bend steel bars with his bare hands."

So let's look for other answers. One popular answer is, "What makes me *me* is my soul." To make a long story short, while your soul might be what does, in fact, make you who you are, saying that it is yours doesn't answer our question. We still haven't figured out what the "my" refers to. You might argue that "my" means something like, "what belongs to me." This argument doesn't say much: "What makes me, *me* is my soul" is just a way of saying, "What makes me, *me*, is the fact that my soul belongs to me." What we still don't know, though, is what makes it belong to you and no one else. If you say, "Because it's mine," we are just back at the beginning again!

Philosophers call the problem we just ran into *begging the question*, which means that we are answering a question with something that needs (or begs) questioning itself. If you say that you know Superman is awesome because he is really cool, you have begged the question, since saying he's cool doesn't explain why he's awesome, but rather restates it using a different term. Trying to answer questions about identity often results in begging the question. People believe they know what makes them *them*, but when they try to figure it out they tend to say things like "because I'm me" or "I'm myself," which might be true but just begs the question instead of providing an informative answer.

Is It My Super-Body?

The philosopher John Locke (1632–1704) tried to figure out the question of "What makes me *me*?" One possibility is the body. Superman may be who he is because he has his body and no one else has his body. Remember Leibniz's law, though? For two things to be the same thing, they have to have every property in common. But, if you think about it, even though Superman does not age as fast as we do, his body isn't the same over time. So what makes the Superman of tomorrow the same person as the Superman of today? If it is because they have the same body, we have a problem: they don't have the same body. Younger Superman's body is not identical with older Superman's body. Our bodies are constantly growing new cells and losing old ones. Even if this process is much slower with Superman, there will be a time when future Superman's body will contain a completely different set of cells than it does now.

Cell regeneration is just the beginning of the problems for the body answer. If I lose an arm or a leg, am I no longer the same person? If my body is what fundamentally makes me *me*, then any change in my body would make me someone new and different. This problem with change goes against our intuitions. You may even want to respond, "but things change all the time and retain their identity!" And you would be right, but what this implies is that the things that are changing are not essential to their identities. Trees lose leaves and we shed skin cells, but it is because those losses are not essential to our identities that we continue to be the same person (or tree) even after those changes take place.

Sometimes, though, an object changes so much that it does become something else—its identity does change. Consider Coast City, as an example. Lots of things could change in Coast City without it being destroyed, like buildings, people, and laws. But when Hank Henshaw, the Cyborg-Superman, obliterated the city, Coast City was gone. In other words, if you destroy one building, Coast City still exists, and if you destroy two buildings, Coast City still exists. But there comes a point when Coast City is changed sufficiently so that it is no longer a city—much less Coast City. In the same way that a tree can cease to be a tree and become a piece of paper, Coast City can cease to be Coast City and become a wasteland.

You might argue that I am misunderstanding what you mean by "the body." Okay, so our physical body isn't us because we lose skin cells, hair, and nails, and develop new cells all the time. That doesn't mean that there isn't a way of thinking of the body as essential. What matters is the *structure*, you might argue—what makes me *me* is my DNA. So it's his DNA that makes Superman who he is. But a quick counterexample reveals why the DNA argument doesn't work. Imagine that we cloned Superman so that every single piece of DNA is identical between Supes and his clone. Would the clone and Superman be the same person? No, of course not. Superman and his clone are in two different places at the same time, experiencing and seeing different things, so they can't be the same person. In the same way that you would not be the same person as your identical twin, despite your identical DNA, Superman and even the most perfect clone would not be the same person.

DNA is just a blueprint. The blueprint of a building isn't the building and, similarly, the DNA of the person isn't the person. Remember, we are trying to find out what actually makes people who they are. You might argue that your DNA makes you *you*, but if you had gene therapy that changed your DNA structure slightly, would you be a different person? If you are a different person, then your parents would have to attend your funeral because Old You would be gone, replaced by someone new. The New You could even attend the funeral of Old You! This is a pretty distressing consequence. It makes far more sense to say that your DNA helps make you who you are, but it isn't who you are.

Memories of You, Superman

Locke argued that our minds are far more important to our personal identities than our bodies. The mind, says Locke, is the seat of personal identity, and it is our ability to reflect on ourselves that maintains our identities. In other words, my ability to remember myself in the past, and conjecture about myself in the future, even if my body changes significantly, maintains my identity.

Locke argued that a person is a "thinking, intelligent Being, that has reason and reflection, and can consider itself as itself, the same thinking thing in different times and places."[3] Notice that memory is key to Locke's argument. In essence, it is our memories that make us who we are. Since Superman can reflect on himself – he can remember his family in Kansas, he can remember his first kiss with Lois, and he can recall his many accomplishments – his identity stays static, no matter what else about him changes.

The problem, of course, is that this requires that our memories stay the same. But, of course, they don't. Consider the Eradicator, one of the replacements for Superman (along with Cyborg-Superman) after his death.[4] When the Eradicator first creates a body almost exactly like Superman's, he has no recollection of who he is or how he got there, and genuinely believes himself to be the Last Son of Krypton. During his state of amnesia, does that mean that the Eradicator was dead or someone else? If Locke is right, and our memories make us who we are, then amnesiacs aren't who they once were. I think we can agree, though, that even if Superman lost his memories, Lois would still love him, and so would the rest of his family; they would not treat him as if he were dead or another person.

If he read comic books, Locke might respond to my argument by saying, "the Eradicator gets his memory back, though!" And this is true, but does that mean the Eradicator stopped existing when he forgot and then reappeared as a person when he remembered again, or changed from one person to another as his memories changed? Imagine what would happen if Superman lost his memories and never got them back. You might believe that there is a sense in which Superman ceases to exist if he loses his memories permanently. Certainly, we would mourn the loss of Superman if he lost all sight of who he is. But notice we don't think that because of the memories themselves. We would only mourn the loss of Superman if his memory loss caused him to cease *acting* like Superman.

More to the point, our memories don't create our identities. We are constantly gaining new memories and forgetting old ones. Sometimes, even, the memories that we have are false: we remember something that we never did. So memory isn't the right place to look for identity, unless we want to agree that Superman losing his memory would mean that he was, in effect, dead. In that case Lois could just move on to Jimmy Olsen (or, more likely, Bruce Wayne).

Of course Lois wouldn't leave Superman if he lost his memory! And we are likely to say that she wouldn't leave because he retains the core of who he is. He is still the same sweet, gentle, brave, and loving man, even if he can't remember who he is. So despite his faulty memory, he remains the same person. So maybe our personalities make us who we are? Maybe what makes Superman *Superman* is the fact that he acts like himself. At first this seems like a great answer: memories can be lost, bodies can change dramatically, but our personalities stay the same—right? Well …

Hole-y Personality Superman!

Think about how much your personality has changed since you were a baby. You had different needs and wants. You found different things funny. You might have even have had a different temperament. Head trauma, for example, has been known to cause changes in temperament as well as memory loss. Phineas Gage is a famous example of the head trauma phenomenon: he was nice, kind, and even-tempered before a railroad spike was driven through his skull. Afterwards, he was mean, selfish, and unpredictable. Granted, a blow to the head would make anyone grumpier, but Phineas's story has inspired a huge body of research on how changes in the brain can change personality traits that we thought were permanent.

The TV series *Smallville* provides us with a great example of a Phineas Gage-like problem. In the show, red kryptonite radically changes Clark's way of acting. When he is exposed to it, he becomes impulsive, sexually aggressive, and extremely selfish—the exact opposite of his normal self. When he starts acting this way, do his friends and family treat him as if he is dead? Of course not. The fact that his personality is different doesn't mean that Clark is gone. He is still Clark, but now a "jerk" version of Clark. If Clark's personal identity was lost when his personality changed, then his family and friends would just write him off as gone. But instead, they try to return him to his previous state. They never once think of him as someone other than Clark, but rather a Clark who they need to save.

When you think about it, our personalities change a tremendous amount over time. A sudden change tends to bring attention, but gradual growth and change tends to go unnoticed. After years of gradual change in your personality, though, you may be a radically different person, much as years of cell regeneration leave you with a completely new body. So what connects the present you with the future you who will have different memories, completely different cells, and even a different personality? Given Leibniz's law, how can present you and future you actually be the same when you don't have all properties in common?

Some philosophers, like Locke, try to argue that personal identity is continuous because, even though 20-year-old you is very different from 2-year-old you, 20-year-old you is not so different from 19-year-old you, who is not so different from 18-year-old you, and so forth. So, personal identity would transfer from one to another, preserving the continuity of identity over time. That answer sounds great, but it has a major flaw: we never said that only *big* changes count; *any* changes count. Leibniz's law tells us that to be identical, two objects must have all of the same properties. Well that doesn't mean that two objects are identical if they have mostly, or almost all of the same properties. So 20-year-old you and 19-year-old you—even Monday-you and Tuesday-you, or 3:45 pm-you and 3:46 pm-you—may have *almost* everything in common but not everything, so they can't be identical.

Superman and his younger self Superboy (not the later clone) share many of the same or similar properties—their powers, their DNA, their costume—but we wouldn't call them the same person because they aren't identical. To be identical, they would have to share every property in common, including their location in space and time, what they are seeing at the moment, and what they are thinking at the moment. Two Supermen would not have the same personal identity, as they would not be identical, even if they shared every property in common except location. Imagine these two "identical" Supermen shaking hands. Would we say they were the same person? No.

Would the Real Superman Please Stand Up!

Some philosophers, such as David Hume (1711–1776), argue that it isn't possible to find a singular thing to define a person. To Hume, you are just a "bundle of perceptions," aware of only your present experiences from moment to moment.[5] And when the current moment passes and a new one comes, you are a different bundle of perceptions, and therefore a different person.

Think about Superman for a moment. When Superman was first introduced, he was very different than he is now; for example, he could only leap then, not fly. As the years passed, his powers, demeanor, and looks have all changed, sometimes gradually and sometimes abruptly. As a matter of fact, there have been many different comics, TV shows, and movies, each providing us with a Superman who looks and acts somewhat differently from the rest. So why do we think of all of these different Supermen as Superman? Could it be that because we *call* each of them Superman, we maintain his identity throughout all of those changes?

I'm not arguing that Superman's personal identity *is* his name. For instance, if your parents named you Superman, you shouldn't jump off buildings and try to fly. The name doesn't turn you into the person. But remember, we probably shouldn't expect personal identity to locate some fixed "person" anyway. Maybe names are more powerful than we normally think—not because they create the person, but because the name is what we use to help us locate people or things that are similar "enough" to someone or something else. In other words, we consider the 1930s version of Superman to be so similar to the modern Superman that we just think of them as the same thing— even though they aren't.

What if, after all the trials and tribulations that Lois went through when Superman died and returned, she found out that the "real Superman" she was holding in her arms was actually a perfect copy in every way. Would it be such a stretch for her to accept him as Superman, since there is no perceivable difference in body, memory, and personality? Maybe Superman is more like Coast City than some sort of static object with a mysteriously unchangeable personal identity. Cities change due to growth or decline, governance, and the people who make them up. Their location may even change, either by government order or continental drift. So what makes Istanbul *Istanbul* or Miami *Miami*? To answer those questions, we wouldn't try to find some sort of almost magical "essence" of a city. We would realize that the London of today really isn't the same thing as the London of 50 years ago, but they are so similar that it is easier to just keep calling the new city the same name as the old city. Maybe we can do the same with people—in fact, we could argue that metaphysics aside, that's what we actually do every day.

Maybe you are actually a different person than the reader who started this chapter. As you read the chapter, your brain changed, you lost and made new cells, your thoughts and emotions changed—lots of stuff changed. The person who started the chapter is gone. But the person who is finishing it is so similar to the person who started it that it is just easier to call you by the same name, especially since many of the things you share with the old you are thoughts, feelings, and personality traits.

So Let's Give Lois a Break!

If we look at personal identity as something we just kind of make up about ourselves and others, basically as just using names to avoid confusion and complexity, then we can start to give Lois some slack for never realizing that Superman and Clark aren't the same person. In thinking they are different people, Lois is not missing the "essence" of each person. Lois considers them different people, because, in many ways Clark and Superman are two different people. They may look very similar, but many people look similar—take identical twins, for example. More importantly, though, they act differently; take Christopher Reeve's masterful portrayal of "both" of them, for example. Perhaps most basically, Superman and Clark are labeled in very different ways. When we name things, we give them a common-sense version of identity, and Superman and Clark are given two different identities by society and even themselves. So why should we expect Lois to believe that they are the same person when the one thing we can use to *really* locate someone as a person is very different—one is "Superman" and one is "Clark Kent"? You could argue that Clark and Superman are more different than they are similar, which would go a long way toward vindicating Lois Lane. If a world-famous investigative reporter couldn't tell Clark was Superman, maybe there's something to the claim that they are very different people after all![6]

Notes

1. *Lois & Clark: The New Adventures of Superman*, season 2, episode 18, "Tempus Fugitive."
2. Gottfried Wilhelm Leibniz, *Philosophical Papers and Letters*, trans. Leroy Loemker (Dordrecht: Kluwer, 1967), 308.
3. John Locke, *An Essay Concerning Human Understanding*, ed. Peter H. Nidditch (New York: Oxford University Press, 1690/1975), 335.
4. See *The Return of Superman* (1993).
5. David Hume, *A Treatise of Human Nature* (Oxford: Clarendon Press, 1739–1740/1967), 15–23.
6. I would like thank my dear friend Jacob May for being the most super of my Superfriends.

Chapter 19

Superman Family Resemblance

Dennis Knepp

Superman is the most recognizable hero in the superhero pantheon. The black hair with the spit-curl, the blue eyes, and cleft chin; the blue suit with yellow belt, red boots, and red underwear; the red cape; and the iconic "S" on his chest, all set the standard for superhero costumes. Once, at a party for international students, my kids played with a five-year-old Japanese boy who knew no English but loved our Superman toy spaceship. He ran around the party with it, yelling in Japanese as he acted out Superman beating the bad guys. Superman crosses languages, cultures, and generations. Despite minor changes in appearance—most recently, losing the spit-curl, the yellow belt, and the red trunks—the Superman we recognize today is the same Superman recognizable 75 years ago.

But why is this so? There are so many version of Supes running (or flying) around, if we consider over 75 years of comics—including many versions of him in different realities and timelines—plus numerous movies, television shows, cartoons, and action figures. How can we recognize them all as Superman when they're all so different?

The Eternal Superman

According to the ancient Greek philosopher Plato (429–347 BCE), unchanging characteristics are the mark of the eternal.[1] Plato

Superman and Philosophy: What Would the Man of Steel Do?, First Edition. Edited by Mark D. White.
© 2013 John Wiley & Sons, Inc. Published 2013 by John Wiley & Sons, Inc.

distinguishes between the world of *becoming* and the world of *being*. We live in the world of becoming where things are constantly changing and unstable. Things are born, grow and develop, and die. Plato argues that no knowledge is possible in this world of becoming because knowledge requires stability. He believes, however, that we do have true knowledge, but since it cannot come from unchanging truths, it must come from the unchanging and eternal world of being. Plato's favorite example is mathematics: we can know mathematical truths and we can know that these truths are unchanging. The Pythagorean equation was true in ancient Greece, it is true today, and it will still be true in a thousand years. So, Plato says, we must have knowledge about things that are not of this world of becoming, but rather are from the eternal and unchanging world of being.

Plato argues that this world of being holds not only the realm of mathematical objects, but also the universal patterns or forms of most things. Consider dogs, for instance. There are so many different kinds of dogs in this world of becoming. It is hard to imagine what a Chihuahua and a German Shepherd have in common, and yet we recognize them both as dogs. Plato reasons that we can have knowledge about dogs because we have knowledge of the form or essence of DOG. Our knowledge about dogs is not about any particular dog in this world of becoming, but is rather about the unchanging and eternal essence of DOG in the world of being. All the dogs we know are merely copies of DOG. While dogs come and go, DOG is forever.

If Plato were here today, he would argue that our knowledge of Superman is based on the unchanging and eternal SUPERMAN found in the world of being. A Superman comic can be destroyed by fire because it exists in the world of becoming. In fact, the process of aging can easily destroy the individual manifestations of Superman (which is why Superman comics should be stored in plastic sleeves!). Collectors know that in this world of becoming, even a mighty Superman comic book can be easily destroyed. Destroying a Superman comic, however, does not destroy the form, the essence of SUPERMAN. Nor would destroying all the Superman comics, because, as Plato would argue, SUPERMAN does not exist in this realm of becoming where things are so easily destroyed.

Making slight changes to the appearance, power set, or secret identity of Superman doesn't affect his essence. Even the infamous "Electric Blue Superman" phase, in which our hero became a being of pure energy and needed a special costume to contain his new electricity-based powers, didn't change the fact he was still Superman.[2] Changing facets of his character, like destroying physical versions of him, don't change the ideal nature of Superman. SUPERMAN exists in the realm of being where things are eternal, unchanging, incorruptible, and forever. SUPERMAN can never be destroyed.

According to Plato, this would also explain how knowledge of SUPERMAN can cross cultures and generations. It doesn't matter if the comics are read in English or Japanese because that is just part of SUPERMAN's manifestation in this world of becoming. The actual knowledge of SUPERMAN is independent of what language it's presented in. Our knowledge of SUPERMAN is knowledge of something that is literally out of this world: SUPERMAN resides in the realm of being. That is how Superman can appear in any language and still be the same Superman.

The Challenge of the Supermen

Of course, Superman can't die—or, at least, he can't remain dead. Superman must be brought back, and indeed he was, but loyal fans may have gotten more than they bargained for. After the "Death of Superman" narrative played out, DC Comics introduced four new Supermen. One was a teenaged Superboy, cloned from Superman (and Lex Luthor), which gave him some of Supes' powers and some of his own (such as telekinesis), but none of Superman's memories. Another, the Eradicator, was an energy-based humanoid duplicate of Superman who, unlike Superboy, did have some of the original's memories. The third was Steel, scientist John Henry Irons, who wore armor and wielded a hammer. The last was the Cyborg-Superman, a robot-Superman hybrid with parts of his damaged body replaced with super-robotics and half of his iconic face replaced with a metallic skull and a glowing red eye.

Can any of these four be Superman? Can they *each* be Superman? Or can there be Super*men*? Plato would respond by saying that they can each be Superman, provided they share the form or essence of SUPERMAN. But even if we assume that Superman has an essence, that doesn't tell us what that essence is. What is that universal characteristic that all legitimate versions of Superman share?

Maybe it's something about their appearance, like the costume, the familiar red and blue with hints of yellow. But each of the four new Supermen has a different costume, similar to the original but different enough to identify them as separate. Even the "real" Superman has had different costumes over time, with some drastic changes (like the Electric Blue phase) and some more subtle changes (as in the DC New 52, with the high collar and no trunks). The black hair with the spit-curl and blue eyes have been fairly constant, but the armored Steel shares neither of these, and Superboy has the black hair but not the spit-curl.

What about the iconic "S" logo—certainly that's essential to Superman, right? Whether a teenager, an astral projection, chrome, or a Terminator-robot—or the Electric Blue Superman—all the versions of Superman sport the "S" logo. The colors may differ, and it may be drawn differently at times, but the "S" still means Superman. The "S" logo is a better candidate to represent Superman's essence than other visuals, but it doesn't seem to qualify as the essence of Superman, for two main reasons. First, other superheroes that definitely aren't Superman wear the "S" logo, most obviously Supergirl (and even Krypto the Super-Dog!). Second, there have been versions of Superman who wore different logos, such as the Superman from 2003's *Superman: Red Son* who landed in the Soviet Union instead of the United States and wore the symbol of the sickle and hammer instead of the "S." Nonetheless, however, his other characteristics identify him clearly as Superman (or "a" Superman), so the "S" logo can't be essential to who he is.

Maybe we need to broaden our reach beyond the visual, and consider things more essential to who Superman is rather than what he looks like—such as his superpowers, which set him apart from mere humans as well as most other superheroes. But Superman's powers are a poor indicator of his essence, if only because he is constantly losing them for one reason or another! Even when he loses them, he is still Superman. Since Superman can still be Superman even without his superpowers, they cannot be the essence of Superman.

We could also look at other aspects such as Superman's character, his personality, his memories, and even his soul, all of which may be better candidates for Superman's essence simply because they are more closely related to who he *is*.[3] But the more closely we focus on the traditional Superman who we know and love, the more we risk ruling out other versions who may not qualify. For instance, Superboy was cloned from Superman, but doesn't share his soul, and the Eradicator shares some of Superman's memories, but doesn't share his character. It's much harder to find someone's essence than it seemed; maybe this isn't the game we should be playing after all.

Ludwig Wittgenstein's Family Values

Philosophers struggled with Plato's theory of essences for over 2000 years. Some philosophers, such as Aristotle (384–322 BCE) tried to fix Plato's theory, while other philosophers, such as Friedrich Nietzsche (1844–1900), rejected Plato's concept of essences in favor of maintaining a world of flux and change, death and decay. But both approaches still relied on Plato's basic idea of an essence as something universal, unchanging, and eternal, whether they argued for it or against it. No one really challenged the idea itself until Ludwig Wittgenstein (1889–1951) changed the rules of the game in his enormously influential *Philosophical Investigations*, published after his death in 1953.

Wittgenstein suggests that at least sometimes it does not make sense to look for a thing's essence. He asks us, for example, to imagine finding the essence of a "game." Could competition among players be the essence of games? No, because we consider solitaire to be a game. Could scoring the most points to win be the essence of a game? No, because in golf the winner has the lowest score, and we consider golf to be a game. There are many different kinds of games in the world and it is extremely difficult to find a universal characteristic shared by all of them—yet we have no problem understanding and using the term "game." Wittgenstein argues that we shouldn't worry about finding the one true shared characteristic of things like games. Instead, we should realize that games have a large set of characteristics that are shared by most games, but no one characteristic that is shared by all games.

Wittgenstein called this a "family resemblance" of characteristics, referring to the way blood relatives tend to resemble each other. If all of your relatives got together for a family dinner, a passerby could probably see that you were all related even though there is no one characteristic that you all share. Not all your family members have the same nose, eyes, and hair. You may have your mother's eyes, your father's nose, and your grandmother's hair. Your sister might have your mother's hair and your grandfather's eyes and nose, but only a mild resemblance to your father, and so on.

The same is true of games. Games like solitaire, golf, football, chess, and so on, share many characteristics between them, but they don't all share the same ones, and there is no characteristic that they all share that is the essence of a game. Most games involve two or more players competing against each other. Most games are won by getting the most points. Players take turns in most games. Think of these characteristics as the threads of a rope: there are enough threads through the rope to hold the rope together even though no single thread goes through the entire rope.

The different versions of Superman share a family resemblance much like games do. Most Supermen wear the iconic "S" on their chest; most Supermen wear blue and red; most Supermen have black hair with a spit-curl; most Supermen have superpowers; and most Supermen fight for truth, justice, and the American way. Rather than trying to identify the one true essence of Superman, we can simply say that a candidate for being Superman must have enough of the typical Superman characteristics, though not necessarily all of them or any one in particular.

But Families Also Disagree a Lot

This doesn't mean everybody has to agree on what counts as "enough" or which characteristics are valid. Take Superboy, for instance. He has the "S" logo, some of Superman's powers, black hair (but no spit-curl), and a similarly colored costume. He has many of the Superman characteristics, but does he have enough? Does being a teenager disqualify him from being a Super*man*? Superman's cousin Supergirl has much more in common with him, but most people would say her sex disqualifies her as a Superman (if only in name). Steel has few of the visual characteristics we associate with Superman (other than the "S" symbol and the cape), but his character seems more in line with the Superman ideal than Superboy's (at least in his early days). The "Red Son" Superman lacks the "S" logo but shares most of the other characteristics (aside from a predictably different political outlook). Given that his chest symbol is different, he almost has to have most of the other typical Superman characteristics to assure readers that he is a Superman; otherwise the story itself wouldn't work.

Certainly it helps the artists—comics pencillers, movie costume designers, and more—to take a family resemblance approach to Superman when rendering him on the page or screen. As long as an artist keeps most of Superman's characteristics, he or she can tweak some other characteristics and still have the character recognized as Superman. For example, a penciller can have Superman's hair long enough to touch his collar—like when he "came back from the dead." We will still recognize him as Superman because all of the other characteristics have remained the same. A costume designer for a Superman film can make minor changes to the classic costume, or the actor cast in the role can change, and moviegoers will still know it's Superman.

Electric Blue Superman was a case in which the artist designing him went too far, modifying too much, and leaving the character unrecognizable as Superman. He still had an "S" on his chest, but it was larger and stylized. Practically everything else was changed, including his face, which no longer looked human. His costume was blue with white lightning bolt accents, and he crackled with electric energy. This was just too much change. Faithful fans wrote letters to DC Comics complaining that the Electric Blue Superman was *not* Superman. Even those who took the family resemblance approach to Superman and were relatively flexible when it came to depictions of their favorite superhero did not accept this new Superman.

Having Fun With Big Blue

The great cartoonist Gary Larson once made a Superman joke in *The Far Side*. Larson imagined Superman in his later years growing senile, drawn with one of his trademark "old man" faces and a fedora. As this senile Superman stands in the window ready to jump out, he says, "Dang! Now where was I going?" The joke worked because Larson kept most of the Superman characteristics, and readers could recognize him as Superman even though he had been modified to be an old man drawn in Larson's beloved, distinctive style.

Superman has been around for 75 years and will likely still be around for 75 more and longer. Undoubtedly he will change costumes, powers, and other characteristics as time rolls on. It will be up to future generations to decide how much change is too much and which characteristics are integral to who Superman is—and these may include characteristics that haven't been introduced to the Superman mythos yet. Maybe one day being a philosopher will be considered an important characteristic of Superman. (It'll be about time!)[4]

Notes

1. This aspect of Plato's thought appears throughout his work; for instance, see *The Republic*, part VII, sections 5–7, available at http://classics.mit.edu/Plato/republic.html.
2. This transformation started in *Superman*, vol. 2, #122 (April 1997) and continued throughout all the Superman titles (*Superman*, *Adventures of Superman*, *Action Comics*, and *Superman: Man of Steel*), ending in *Superman*, vol. 2, #135 (May 1998).
3. For more on these things, also aspects of a person's *identity*, see chapter 18 by Michaud in this volume.
4. I wish to give thanks to Eric Van Woert and Jeffrey Byers for their detailed knowledge of alternate forms of Superman, David Soles for the introduction to Plato and Wittgenstein, Mark White and Bill Irwin for their "super" editorial work, and Jennifer McCarthy for the love and encouragement.

Chapter 20

Why Superman Should Not Be Able to Read Minds

Mahesh Ananth

Can you read my mind? Do you know what it is that you do to me?
I don't know who you are. Just a friend from another star.
Here I am, like a kid out of school. Holding hands with a god. I'm a fool.
Will you look at me? Quivering. Like a little girl, shivering.
You can see right through me. Can you read my mind?
Can you picture the things I'm thinking of?
Wondering why you are ... all the wonderful things you are.
You can fly. You belong in the sky. You and I ... could belong to each other.
If you need a friend ... I'm the one to fly to.
If you need to be loved ... here I am. Read my mind.

(Lois Lane, Superman: The Movie, 1978)

Superman's legendary powers include super-strength, super-speed, flight, invulnerability, x-ray vision, heat vision, and super-hearing. You'd think those powers would be enough, but occasionally writers add new ones. In this chapter, we'll consider one of his less common powers—the ability to read minds—and use some basic philosophical thinking about minds to ask why it never caught on as one of Supes's main powers.

The Mind of Superman

So, what about the question Lois asks in the quotation above: *can* Superman read her mind? For those who follow the various incarnations

Superman and Philosophy: What Would the Man of Steel Do?, First Edition. Edited by Mark D. White.
© 2013 John Wiley & Sons, Inc. Published 2013 by John Wiley & Sons, Inc.

of Superman by way of comic books, movies, or TV shows, it may come as a surprise that he has mind-reading and mind-manipulating powers—because he doesn't have them very often. One instance of the powers comes in the 1980 movie *Superman II* when Superman realizes that he cannot have a romantically loving relationship with Lois Lane. After giving up and regaining his superpowers, Superman gives Lois a "super-kiss" that effectively wipes away her memory of their recent romantic adventures and the fact that Superman and Clark Kent are one and the same person. To do this, Superman must be able to determine what set of memories to erase, which in turn means he can interact with and manipulate Lois's mind.

In the TV series *Smallville*, the ability to read minds is given to young Clark by his Kryptonian father Jor-El in the episode "Echo" (season 9, episode 4) to help him better understand himself as distinct from the human race.[1] Jor-El informs his son-of-steel that he gave him the mind-reading and telepathic intuitive abilities and that they are activated when his humanity runs amok. Jor-El is hoping these super-abilities will assist young Superman develop and embrace his Kryptonian heritage and at the same time tone down his human tendencies, which Jor-El fears will cloud his judgment. From a broader view of Superman, what is interesting and humorous about these mental powers is that they not only help him to get a date with young Lois, but they also help make sense of the super-kiss in *Superman II*!

These super mental abilities make sense when we consider Torquasm Vo, an ancient Kryptonian mental training for warriors. In *Action Comics*, vol. 1, #747 (August 1998), one of Superman's most sinister villains, Dominus, takes revenge on our hero for interfering with his plans to commandeer the cosmic powers of his former lover Ahti who had become Kismet, Illuminator of All Realities. (Hey, we've all been there, right?) Dominus takes control of Superman's mind using his reality-altering mental powers and convinces Superman to take control of Earth by creating super-robots. As part of this elaborate reality hoax, Dominus himself transforms into Superman and imprisons Superman (now transformed into Dominus) in his Fortress of Solitude. During this imprisonment, Superman harnesses and hones his own Torquasm Vo abilities, including being able to control one's thoughts, to read the minds of others, and to create mental illusions in others. Using these ancient mental skills, Superman deceives Dominus by controlling his mind and eventually sends him into the Phantom Zone.

If we put these examples from the comics, TV shows, and movies together, they form a coherent picture and history of Superman's mental abilities. In that sense, the answer to Lois's opening question is a resolute *yes*: Superman can not only read other minds, but he can manipulate them as well. However, it's natural to wonder why these powers don't have a more prominent role in Superman's battles for truth, justice, and the American way. From the viewpoint of the creators of Superman's stories, a practical reason for not using these mental powers with regularity is that they would give Superman even more advantages in fighting villainy and protecting humanity. For example, he could avoid opening Lex Luthor's lead container filled with kryptonite simply by reading Luthor's mind beforehand. He wouldn't need to use his other fantastic superpowers to counter dastardly schemes, and as a result most stories would be short and boring!

Great Caesar's Ghost: The Problem of Other Minds!

Setting practical considerations like those aside, are there any philosophical reasons why Superman should not possess mind-reading skills? We'll answer this question by exploring the "problem of other minds," which has vexed philosophers for centuries. And we'll see why, despite mind-reading's occasional usefulness, it would be philosophically prudent to eliminate it from Superman's set of powers.

Let's begin with some assumptions. We'll take it for granted that we have "objects" we call minds; that our minds are not the same thing as our grey matter or the neurons firing in our brains; and that our mental lives can affect our brains. According to this view, mental phenomena such as desires, beliefs, wishes, and so forth emerge from our brains, but are then able to function both independently and together with them.

Even if we accept this theory of mind (known as *emergentism*), there is still the troubling philosophical issue known as the *problem of other minds*. Specifically, just because you behave in a certain way and have a certain set of mental states, that does not mean necessarily that you are justified in believing that other people have similar mental states—or minds at all. Consider the following scenario: Superman presents himself as the son of Jor-El to the Kryptonian criminals General Zod, Ursa, and Non. Since Jor-El played a role in their imprisonment in the Phantom Zone, the three criminals attack Superman. Caught off-guard, Superman attempts a strategic retreat while exhibiting the following behaviors corresponding to certain mental states: (1) quick movements and facial expressions stemming from the mental state of surprise, (2) flying away from his foes based on the mental state of fear of being caught and harmed, and (3) physically relaxing after evading his foes, due to the mental state of relief.

After formulating a plan, Superman returns to face the three Kryptonian villains, and now he has them on the run. Superman notices that Zod, Ursa, and Non respond in the same way that he responded during his initial encounter with them: same facial and body movements, same hasty retreat from the fear of being caught, and, when he stops short of killing them, the same relief. Given his own experiences, could Superman know *with certainty*, based on observing behavior that resembles his own, what Zod, Ursa, and Non are mentally experiencing?

The traditional philosophical reply to the above question is "no," because we are faced with the *epistemological problem*—a problem concerning knowledge. In our example, Superman is so intimately aware of his mental states that he cannot be wrong about them, but he does not have the same access to the mental states of Zod and his cohorts. Indeed, we could accuse Superman of imposing his own mental states onto the behavior of Zod and his little gang, like when he assumes Krypto is happy when he appears to smile. So, not only can Superman not be certain about the Kryptonians' mental states, but he may very well be superimposing his own mental states onto theirs. We cannot know with certainty the mental states of other people based merely on their behavior.

The epistemological problem translates into two distinct knowledge problems:

(1) Can you know with certainty that there is any other mind other than your own?
(2) Can you know with certainty the exact content of another's mind?

Notice that it is possible to answer yes to (1) but no to (2); that is, Superman could know with certainty that there are other minds but not have certain knowledge of their content. But if we answer no to (1), then we must answer no to (2) as well; if he cannot know with certainty that there are other minds, then he surely cannot know with certainty the content of them. I'll explain that the certainty requirement is more than just fancy language; it makes the case that Superman must answer no to both (1) and (2). But take heart, faithful followers of this mild-mannered reporter—his remaining superpowers more than compensate for the loss of mind-reading.

Solving the Kryptonian Knot

One easy solution, were it available, would be to grant Superman mind-reading powers that he could use to determine Zod's actual mental states. In this way, he could support his claims about Zod's mental content without relying solely on his behavior. Unfortunately, even though we now know that Superman can read minds, it is not clear that he can circumvent the epistemological problem, mainly because he would still have to use his mind to access the mind of Zod. Since Superman's mental states will still be present while he is reading Zod's mind, Superman cannot distinguish—with certainty—his own thoughts from Zod's.

The point of the last claim is not that Superman could not distinguish his thoughts from Zod's *at all*. He may very well be able to do this. Rather, the point is that it isn't clear he could do so *with certainty*. There are two ways of looking at this. First, we should remember that the mental life is not to be confused with our "physical" life. For example, when we speak, we are able to distinguish our unique voices from other unique voices. Similarly, when Superman is berating Zod for his evil ways, he can clearly— dare I say certainly—distinguish his voice from Zod's. Even though we seem to "hear" ourselves thinking, we have to be careful not to assume that we would "hear" other people's thoughts in voices that were different from our own. So we can't be sure Superman would be able to distinguish his mind from Zod's in the way he could distinguish between their voices.

Another way of understanding this concern is to think of it in terms of knowledge of what you have said or thought. Even if Zod could perfectly duplicate Superman's "mental voice," he would have thoughts that Superman won't remember thinking. If Superman knows his own thoughts well enough, he would know when a foreign thought is present, and he could know with certainty that other minds exist.

This argument is interesting, but it does not work for two reasons. First, it implausibly assumes that Superman could have a complete catalogue of all of his thoughts. Superman is often shown to have a "super-brain," but having perfect recall of every thought he ever had is unimaginable, even for Superman. Also, even if he could remember all his past thoughts, he can't anticipate all of his future ones, so he wouldn't be able tell Zod's disguised thoughts from his own, unless he judged them out of character or thoughts he would never have. But once again, he can't be *sure*, so the certainty of knowing that he is in the presence of another mind is blocked.

What Are You Thinking?

Even if Superman could distinguish his mind from Zod's, this does not mean that he could precisely know the content of Zod's mind. Again, for instance, Zod could calmly claim that he will spare human lives if Superman concedes to kneel before him. This calm assurance by Zod in no way reveals the true content of Zod's plans or thoughts at that moment; for all we know, he could be making this offer knowing full well he intends the destruction of the human race. What this means is that being able to make certain kinds of distinctions is not enough to get around the epistemological problem. Even if Superman could distinguish his mental voice from Zod's, he still could not know the content of Zod's thoughts with certainty.

Also, even if Superman could distinguish his thoughts from Zod's, this does not imply that he can know, with exact specificity, the content of Zod's thought. Since Superman would be using his mind to read Zod's mind, he would "hear" Zod's thoughts through his own. By necessity, he brings some of his own subjective "coloring" to the mental canvas of Zod's thoughts; the idea of an "empty" Superman-mind interacting with another mind is incoherent. Thus, Superman's intimate awareness of himself is ironically the reason he can't have unadulterated access to the exact content of other minds.

Might Superman's Torquasm Vo ability allow him to have direct access to the minds of others? If it did, he could confirm his beliefs about the content of Zod's mind without his own thoughts interfering.

In other words, his rigorous mental training allows Superman to know exactly what the problem of other minds says he *can't* know. First, one could suppose that Superman's ability to link up with another mind results in a merging of both minds, essentially creating a single consciousness in two bodies. Second, one could imagine that part of what makes Superman's mind super is that it is able to probe another person's mind while shielding itself from being read or interfered with by the other person. If either of these is true, Superman could still employ this super-resource as needed without triggering the epistemological problem of knowing another person's mental states.

Zombie Superman: Even Worse Than Bizarro

While these possibilities are intriguing, they also have their own problems. Consider the creation of a single consciousness during mind-reading as a way to get around the epistemological problem. First, there isn't any evidence that Superman is able "to be one with the mind of the other" or create a "single consciousness" using Torquasm Vo. Second, if there were, Superman would literally become the other person (mentally speaking) such that there would no longer be a Superman distinct from Zod, and he would be in no position to claim that Zod is in a particular mental state since he has basically become Zod himself. Superman must be able to retain his own identity to some degree so that he can ascribe particular mental content to the entities whose minds he is reading.

A better alternative is to find a way that Superman can retain awareness of his own consciousness while simultaneously accessing the minds of others. We can imagine that, as part of his Torquasm Vo training, Superman can shield his own mind when accessing and "merging" with other minds. This would allow him to retain his own identity during the mind-accessing process and solve the epistemological problem. For instance, in a battle with Brainiac, Superman allowed Brainiac to read his anger-filled mind, and the ensuing mental battle resulted in Superman rendering Brainiac unconscious.[2] Clearly, much as in the super-kiss scenario, in order for Superman to be able to respond to Brainiac in this way, he must be able to have a kind of mental power that is able to block a distinct powerful mind like that of Brainiac. But this doesn't imply that Superman also has the ability to interact with another mind while protecting his own.

Even if Superman is able to retain his own identity to some degree, the original problem of other minds remains. Superman is no longer in a position to be able to know *with certainty* whether or not he is "seeing" the content of his own mental state or that of the other person. Again, this is because it is not possible to access another's mind with a content-less mind—even if it is Superman's super Torquasm Vo mind. What this means is that he cannot be certain that it is Brainiac's specific thoughts or his own that are being thwarted. More generally, it's useless to imagine a shield that blocks the content of your mind, because your mind must have some content in order to access another's mind. If not, you would be nothing more than a zombie!

I said earlier that a Superman-mind without any content is incoherent. Now I'm claiming that it's really a zombie-like being: one that behaves and functions like us, but has no consciousness. (Even Bizarro has consciousness, though him no think so.) You might still insist that this underestimates Superman's Torquasm Vo skills, which enable him to access mental states in a way that does not distort the content of the mind that is being examined, and render the zombie criticism irrelevant. It is hard to imagine that Torquasm Vo removes *all* the distortion of Superman's own mind when he accesses others' minds, but that may not matter. He doesn't need his x-ray vision to see through Clark's smudged glasses, so we can assume he can read minds through a little bit of distortion too.

Too Close for Comfort

Our expansion of Superman's mental abilities raises another serious philosophical problem related to the problem of other minds. Even if we could read the mind of another person, and could directly experience what the other person is experiencing, we have no way of knowing *for certain* that the other person is experiencing it too—just that someone is. As contemporary philosopher Alec Hyslop puts it, "Even if they were to be … 'plugged in' to another's mental states, they would need what they do not have, direct knowledge that what they are 'plugged in' to is, indeed, the inner life of another. They would know directly that there is a pain but not that it is someone else's pain."[3]

Even if Superman's mind-accessing ability could allow him to directly access the mental states of Zod by creating a single consciousness, he would still be unable to know with certainty that they are *Zod's* mental states at that particular moment. If we assume that Superman's and Zod's minds were merged into a single consciousness, then Superman can't have direct knowledge that he is reading the mind of a particular person. Whose consciousness is it now? Is it a new and unique consciousness? It's Superman's inability to answer these questions that make it nearly impossible for him to access the inner life of another person *as that person experiences it*. So even if creating a single consciousness is a power stemming from Superman's Torquasm Vo training, he would still not be able to know *with certainty* that the mental states he "sees" belong to the person he assumes has them.

It's a Catch-22: on the one hand, you need to have an intimate relationship with the mental states of others to know anything about those mental states. But on the other hand, if you do have such an intimate relationship, then you can't know whose mental states they are! The lesson that can be gleaned from the epistemological problem is that, in order to know the content of the minds of others with certainty, you must have the ability to access the mental states of others, *as* the mental states of others, without your own mental states or your intimacy with the other person's mental states getting in the way. These conditions are nearly impossible to satisfy—and that's assuming we can read minds at all! In the end, Superman is no better off with respect to knowledge of the content of other minds after we gave him enhanced mind-reading skills than he was before. The epistemological problem stands.

Luthor's Razor

Some philosophers attempting to solve the epistemological problem have tried an indirect route known as the *argument from analogical inference*. This argument uses *inference to best explanation* (IBE) methodology, which is a fancy term for a very common sense way of explaining the world: in the absence of conclusive evidence pointing to one theory or another, it's reasonable to accept the theory that makes the existing evidence least surprising.[4]

For example, the extinction of the dinosaurs could be explained by one of the following theories: (T1) Jimmy Olson killed off the dinosaurs, (T2) Bizarro killed off the dinosaurs, or (T3) a meteor crashed into the Earth, producing dramatic climate changes that killed off the dinosaurs. Given the highly irregular amounts of iridium at a certain level below the Earth's surface, amounts that could only be present as a result of an iridium-based object (or objects) not originally from the Earth, T3 makes the evidence look least surprising. Alternatively, T1 and T2 make the existing data look more surprising than T3 does; we have no evidence of red-headed junior photographers or chalky-faced Superman lookalikes living in the time of dinosaurs, and neither explains the high iridium levels. Thus, the best explanation of the extinction of dinosaurs is that they were killed off as a result of an extraterrestrial object containing iridium striking the Earth's surface. Not exciting, perhaps, but not surprising either. (Science!)[5]

With the help of IBE—and a little evolutionary psychology—we can make a case that even normal people can confidently predict each other's mental states. We can be fairly certain that other people in the same circumstances are in the same mental state that we are because human beings share a similar evolutionary history, which accounts for a basic shared set of behaviors and psychology.[6] For example, Pete Ross's fearful response to being assaulted is likely to be common among all of us because it was an adaptation that enhanced the likelihood of survival and reproduction. If I observe someone retreating from a surprise attack, I can be fairly confident that he or she is in a mental state of fear—the same state I would be in under similar circumstances. At the very least, we can safely assume that there are a number of environmental conditions that lead to fairly predictable and common behaviors and mental states. So I can make an analogy between my mental states and others' by way of inference to best explanation, justified with simple evolutionary logic.

If we expand this line of thinking and grant the influence of evolutionary processes on living beings throughout the universe, perhaps Superman—without using his on-and-off mind-reading abilities—can reasonably infer that other beings are likely to be in the same mental states given similar circumstances. Although Superman cannot know with certainty that this is the case (because of the epistemological problem), he can use IBE to suggest that other alternatives are less plausible. Although Superman's potential use of IBE does not actually solve the problem of other minds, it is possible for him to make plausible inferences about the content of the minds of others.

There are limits to this way of thinking, however. To extend this logic (as we did in the last paragraph) to all beings throughout the universe, we would have to assume that all beings are similar enough in biology, psychology, and natural surroundings to generate the same reactions in terms of behavior and mental states. While most of our comic books and science fictions depict most aliens as looking curiously humanoid, there is no reason to assume this is true. A being with impenetrable skin, for instance, may not have the same reactions to a physical threat as one with very tender skin. Given that Superman was born on Krypton and raised on Earth, there is no reason to think that he should be confident in guessing the mental states of other beings. What's more, it seems that the only minds about which Superman could make reasonable inferences are those of Kryptonians (like Zod), since he shares their evolved psychology, and should be wary about doing so with Earthlings (like Lois) unless he has some reason to believe Kryptonians and Earthlings evolved in similar ways.

Forget It, Supes

What can we conclude about Superman's mind-reading ability? Well, even if he does have "super" mind-reading abilities, it is extremely unlikely that he can read other minds with exact certitude, due to the frustrating implication of the problem of other minds. To make matters worse, even if we assume the normal ability we all have to "read minds," he would lack the common evolutionary history with most beings—including humans—to predict their mental states as well as we can. All of this suggests that Superman's mind is not all that super, regardless of whether creators grant him special mental powers or not. Whether or not they understand the philosophy behind it, it seems the many people who wrote Superman in the last 75 years of comics, movies, and TV shows grasped this, and felt that his "ordinary" powers of super-strength, speed, flight, and all the rest were enough. If only we could read their minds![7]

Notes

1. *Smallville*, season 9, episode 4.
2. The "Brainiac Trilogy," *Action Comics*, vol. 1, #647–649 (November 1989–January 1990).
3. Alec Hyslop, "Other Minds," *Stanford Encyclopedia of Philosophy*, http://plato.stanford.edu/entries/other-minds/.
4. See Andrew Melnyk, "Inference to Best Explanation and Other Minds," *Australasian Journal of Philosophy* 72 (1994), 482–489; Paul Sagal and Gunnar Borg, "The Range Principle and the Problem of Other Minds," *British Journal for the Philosophy of Science* 44 (1993): 477–491; and Robert Pargetter, "The Scientific Inference to Other Minds," *Australasian Journal of Philosophy* 62 (1984): 158–163.
5. It's important to note that, with respect to IBE, a theory is judged best only to the extent that it is better than competing theories. Indeed, it could be the case that T3 is completely wrong, and that T1 or T2 is actually correct, even though the evidence we have now points to T1. Or there may be a T4 we haven't thought of yet, such as the infamous "Wonder Woman did it" hypothesis.
6. See Michael E. Levin, "Why We Believe in Other Minds," *Philosophy and Phenomenological Research* 44 (1984): 343–359, and Elliott Sober, "Evolution and the Problem of Other Minds," *Journal of Philosophy* 97 (2000): 365–387.
7. I would like to thank Ben Dixon and Mike Scheessele for their helpful comments on an earlier version of this chapter. Additionally, I very much appreciate Mark White, Bill Irwin, and David Kyle Johnson for their penetrating criticisms and guidance regarding the appropriate framework in which to discuss these issues. (It's like they read my mind or something.)

Contributors
Trapped in the Philosophy Zone

Mahesh Ananth is an associate professor of philosophy at Indiana University South Bend. His main areas of research include philosophy of biology, bioethics, philosophy of mind, and ancient Greek philosophy. He is the author of *In Defense of an Evolutionary Concept of Health* (Ashgate, 2008) and *Bringing Biology to Life* (Broadview, forthcoming), and has contributed to philosophy and pop culture volumes on Batman and *Star Trek*. Mahesh considers himself to be an eminently moral fellow, but he just does not know what he would do with X-ray vision!

Audrey L. Anton is an assistant professor of philosophy at Western Kentucky University. Her areas of specialization are ancient philosophy, moral psychology, and ethics. She has loved Superman ever since her older brother donned the blue and red costume and "flew" around the house to entertain her. As an adult, she struggled to respect a superhero who thinks that a pair of glasses constitutes a costume, and she has just recently found it in her heart to forgive him for it since, as Luthor says, "Nobody's perfect ... well, almost nobody!"

Adam Barkman is an associate professor of philosophy at Redeemer University College in Ontario, Canada. He is the author of four books, including *C.S. Lewis and Philosophy as a Way of Life*, and is the co-editor of several philosophy and popular culture volumes, including

Superman and Philosophy: What Would the Man of Steel Do?, First Edition. Edited by Mark D. White.
© 2013 John Wiley & Sons, Inc. Published 2013 by John Wiley & Sons, Inc.

ones on manga, Ang Lee, and Ridley Scott. Although he looks nothing like the Man of Steel, Barkman wears so many shirts with the "S" shield on them that his kids call them "Daddy [H]ymbol" shirts. So while Supes is right that "dreams lift us up and transform us into something better," kids do as well.

Arno Bogaerts finished his studies in philosophy and ethics at the Vrije Universiteit Brussel in Belgium, where he wrote several essays focusing on the superhero genre. He is a writer and editor for the Belgian comic book site Brainfreeze and contributed a chapter to *The Avengers and Philosophy*. Currently, he's scanning Brainiac's database and Jor-El's accumulated knowledge of all the known galaxies in order to come up with a snappy ending to this biography.

Sarah K. Donovan is an associate professor in the Department of Philosophy and Religious Studies at Wagner College in New York City. Her teaching and research interests include feminist, social, moral, and continental philosophy. After carefully studying Lex Luthor, she now realizes that not all bald men are attractive.

Brian Feltham teaches political theory at the University of Reading. He is the editor of *Justice, Equality, and Constructivism: Essays on G.A. Cohen's Rescuing Justice and Equality* and co-editor of *Partiality and Impartiality* and *Rational Magic*. He writes mostly on political and moral philosophy, but has also conducted extensive, even obsessive, research on the effects of a yellow sun on Kryptonian physiology.

Leonard Finkelman is fascinated by the idea that birds are actually dinosaurs, and has therefore been driven to study philosophy of biology and evolutionary theory at the Graduate Center of the City University of New York while he teaches at Lehman College/CUNY. Upon seeing a flying object, his enthusiasm sometimes leads him to shout, "It's a bird!", and while the object often turns out to be a plane, it has unfortunately never been Superman.

David Gadon is currently a Ph.D. candidate in the philosophy department of Fordham University in New York City. After spending a hundred years in the Phantom Zone—it's a long story—he discovered an impressive tolerance for absurdity, and therefore decided to pursue academic philosophy. When not teaching courses on human nature, David studies feminism and French existentialism, with a special affinity for Maurice Merleau-Ponty. In his free time he often sits in his underground lair, stroking his Kryptonian cat "Moll-E," and dreaming up ways to make the son of his former captor one day kneel before him.

David Hatfield is associate professor of English at Marshall University in West Virginia. He was fortunate enough to discover the magic of comics during the height of Jack Kirby's "Fourth World," when he and his friend Scott would wait for the delivery truck to drop off the latest issue of *The New Gods* at their local newsstand. His crime fighting career began modestly years earlier, however, with a red towel and blue PJs. He still attempts to use his powers for good.

Randall M. Jensen spends much of his time disguised as a mild-mannered philosophy professor at Northwestern College in Orange City, Iowa. His philosophical interests include ethics, ancient Greek philosophy, and philosophy of religion. He has contributed chapters to volumes in the present series on Batman, *Battlestar Galactica*, *The Hobbit*, *The Office*, *South Park*, and *24*. He often wishes he were able to grade his students' papers faster than a speeding bullet.

Dennis Knepp grew up in Kansas, but the similarities to Superman end there. He now teaches philosophy and religious studies at Big Bend Community College in Washington. He has contributed chapters to philosophy and pop culture volumes on *Twilight*, *Alice in Wonderland*, *The Girl with the Dragon Tattoo*, *The Hobbit*, Black Sabbath, and *Avatar*. As Bizarro might say, Dennis hopes this book is not at all interesting.

Daniel P. Malloy is a lecturer in philosophy at Appalachian State University in North Carolina. His research focuses on issues in ethics, and he has published numerous chapters on philosophy and popular culture, particularly dealing with the illustration of moral questions in movies, comic books, and television shows. When he wears his cape, people just give him funny looks.

Nicolas Michaud teaches philosophy at Jacksonville University, Florida, and Florida State University at Jacksonville. Realizing at an early age that he had a good deal more in common with Lex Luthor than with the Man of Steel, Nick began plotting his global takeover in the third grade. Only three things stand in his way: (1) the realization, which came too late, that his philosophy degree doesn't intimidate the populace all that much, (2) the difficulty of obtaining Kryptonite, and (3) his friend Jacob May, who is much too much like the big blue boy scout for his own good.

Carsten Fogh Nielsen is a mild-mannered Dane whose official job is to teach ethics at the University of Aarhus and research the moral psychology of human beings. When nobody is looking, however, he immediately heads for the broom closet and changes into a colorful costume to help Batman, Iron Man, and Green Lantern solve their moral dilemmas. When he's not busy turning the coal of ideas into diamonds of reason, he likes to cosplay as Krypto the Superdog. Carsten is very proud that "Superman and the Peace Bomb," the first official Superman story produced entirely outside the United States, was written, drawn, and published in Denmark.

Nicholas Richardson is an associate professor in the Department of Physical Sciences at Wagner College in New York City, where he teaches general, advanced inorganic, and medicinal chemistry. He has his fingers crossed that Lex's next scheme will best the big blue boy scout from Kansas.

Christopher Robichaud is a lecturer in ethics and public policy at the Harvard Kennedy School of Government. After watching *Superman II* as a boy, he made it his business to prepare to defeat General Zod (and win the heart of Ursa, though he rarely admits as much). This led to him running around his house while flinging off his fake glasses (alas, they're real now), tearing open his Oxford button-down to reveal his Superman T-shirt underneath, and, to gain superpowers, plunging a spoon into his beloved red, yellow, and blue Superman ice cream. Rumor has it he can still be caught doing this from time to time (although he's managed—so far—to stay off YouTube).

Robert Sharp is an assistant professor of philosophy at Muskingum University in Ohio, where he teaches ethics and the history of philosophy while doing research on ethics and technology issues. His other contributions to philosophy and popular culture volumes focused on the television shows *Heroes, Battlestar Galactica*, and *Family Guy*, which he remains convinced are among Superman's favorites. In order to mimic super-breath, Robert sometimes indulges in excessive garlic and onion recipes. His colleagues assure him that the effect is quite potent!

Jason Southworth is an adjunct professor of philosophy at Fort Hays State University in Kansas. He has written chapters for many philosophy and popular culture volumes, including ones about the Avengers, *Inception*, and *The Walking Dead*. He wishes Superman would put an end to the editorial reign of terror that is the requirement of cute one-liners at the end of philosophy and popular culture bios. [Editor's note: Mwa-ha-ha! You'll never defeat me!]

Ruth Tallman is an assistant professor of philosophy at Barry University in Florida. She has written chapters for other philosophy and popular culture volumes about the Avengers, Sherlock Holmes, and *The Walking Dead*. Being from Smallville, Kansas, herself, she wishes she shared Superman's powers of flight and speed, so popping in for a quick visit to Pa Tallman were as easy as a trip to the Kent farm.

Andrew Terjesen holds a Ph.D. in philosophy from Duke University and is currently a student at the University of Virginia School of Law. He had previously been a visiting assistant professor of philosophy at Rhodes College, Washington and Lee University, and Austin College. His interests are in moral psychology (especially empathy) and eighteenth-century moral philosophy, and he has published both scholarly and popular articles on those topics. His contributions to the current series include chapters on *Avatar*, Green Lantern, the Avengers, and *The Office*. Bizarro-Andrew has no trouble juggling the demands of law school and philosophical moonlighting, and never misses a deadline.

Mark D. White is professor and chair of the Department of Political Science, Economics, and Philosophy at the College of Staten Island/

CUNY, where he teaches courses that combine economics, philosophy, and law. He is the author of *Kantian Ethics and Economics: Autonomy, Dignity, and Character* (Stanford, 2011) and *The Manipulation of Choice: Ethics and Libertarian Paternalism* (Palgrave, 2013), and has edited (or co-edited) books in the current series on Batman, *Watchmen*, Iron Man, Green Lantern, and the Avengers. You will often see him wandering his campus with red trunks over his trousers in protest of Superman's DC New 52 costume. (At least he finally has an excuse.)

Index
From Brainiac's Files

Superman and Philosophy: What Would the Man of Steel Do?, First Edition. Edited by Mark D. White.
© 2013 John Wiley & Sons, Inc. Published 2013 by John Wiley & Sons, Inc.